Studies
in the growth of
nineteenth-century
government

Studies
in the growth of
nineteenth - century
government

edited by
Gillian Sutherland

Routledge & Kegan Paul
London

First published 1972
by Routledge & Kegan Paul Ltd
Broadway House, 68–74 Carter Lane,
London EC4V 5EL
Printed in Great Britain by
Butler & Tanner Ltd
Frome and London
ISBN 0 7100 7170 1

Contents

Acknowledgments

We are obliged to the Controller of Her Majesty's Stationery Office for permission to make use of Crown-copyright material in the Public Record Office. For permission to make use of family papers, we are most grateful to the Earl of Clarendon, the Earl of Halifax, Earl St Aldwyn, Viscount Runciman and the Honourable Sir Steven Runciman, Lord Monk Bretton, Lord Medway, Mr W. R. Collet, Mr R. C. Hutton and Messrs A. and H. Llewellyn Smith. For permission to make use of papers deposited in their care, we are grateful to the British Library of Political and Economic Science, Cambridge University Library, Durham University Library, Manchester University Library, the National Library of Wales, the National Trust, Sheffield University Library and University College, London. We are indebted, too, to the many librarians and archivists in these and other institutions, in the Public Record Office and in the British Museum and the Bodleian Library, who have facilitated our work and given us ready assistance. Finally, we wish to record our thanks to the Past and Present Society for the support they gave to the colloquium in 1969 in which this book originated.

Abbreviations

Hansard	*Hansard's Parliamentary Debates*
P.P.	Parliamentary Papers
P.R.O.	Public Record Office
B.M. Add. MSS.	British Museum Additional Manuscripts

Introduction   *Gillian Sutherland*

In the last decade or so, interest in the development of the machinery of government in England between 1780 and 1914 has been growing, and a great deal of new work has been done.[1] In the summer of 1969 it proved possible to hold a colloquium on the subject under the auspices of *Past & Present*. Fourteen working papers were circulated and some sixty people, including historians, political theorists and practising civil servants, spent a day in discussion of the issues raised by them.[2] All but one of the essays in this collection originated either as working papers or as material introduced into the discussion. In the reflections and speculations that follow, I have drawn heavily on points and issues raised during that discussion, although my comments can in no sense be described as a report or collective statement. They are simply one person's view of the ground so far covered and the questions yet to be answered, after the stimulus of the colloquium; and their principal object is to provoke further discussion.

The one essay which did not originate either as a working paper or as material introduced into the discussion is Professor Finer's 'The transmission of Benthamite ideas 1820–50'. This was first delivered as a paper to the Anglo-American Historical Conference in 1959. It was not then published, as Professor

---

[1] See the full bibliographies contained in the two review articles in *Victorian Studies*: Valerie Cromwell, 'Interpretations of Nineteenth-Century Administration: An Analysis', IX (1966), pp. 245–55 and Gillian Sutherland, 'Recent Trends in Administrative History', XIII (1970), pp. 408–11. I am grateful to *Victorian Studies* for allowing me to repeat here some points I made in that article.

[2] See the notes on the colloquium in *Past & Present*, nos. 42 and 47.

Finer hoped that he would be able to follow up the hypothesis
it presents with more extensive reading and to provide more
extensive documentation. These hopes have been disappointed.
Nevertheless, the typescript has enjoyed a considerable private
circulation—and was invoked and cited a number of times
during our discussion. Its hypotheses focus attention on important aspects of our central concern, the complex relationships between government servants and their world. For these
reasons, Professor Finer agreed to allow his paper, tentative
though his hypotheses remain, to be included in this collection.

The development of the machinery of government in the first
state to industrialize has an obvious interest. The central subjects of debate have been and will remain the sources of growth,
in the sense of the change in direction and the expansion of
government activity, and the development of formal structures
and processes to sustain this. But it has become plain that this
growth cannot be separated in any way from the whole social,
political and intellectual context. The structure of any particular institution cannot be understood without a knowledge
of the motives and circumstances which led to its creation: its
workings do not make a great deal of sense without some knowledge of the policy it was expected to help formulate and implement. Thus our central concern is, as I have said, the complexities of the relationship between the government servant
and his world, the interaction of his work with his social and
personal life; and the very diversity of the essays in this collection is intended to point to these complexities. Some tentative
generalizations, however, are possible; and some questions
demand attention before work can proceed much further.

Some of the generalizations that can be offered are of a semi-
methodological kind. Perhaps the most important concern the
role of ideas in government growth. This has been a preoccupation since Dicey's firm assertion in 1905 that his aim was 'to
exhibit the close dependence of legislation, and even of the
absence of legislation, in England during the nineteenth century,
upon the varying currents of public opinion'.[3] But Dicey dealt
in grand ideas and talked of the triumph of Benthamite ideo-

[3] A. V. Dicey, *Lectures on the Relation between Law and Public Opinion in
England during the Nineteenth Century* (first published 1905, London,
paperback ed. 1963), p. 1.

logy; and it is not too difficult to demonstrate that the views and attitudes of many government servants and, indeed, of many politicians, were neither consistent nor coherent enough to be dignified with the labels 'idea' or 'ideology'. However, it does not seem possible to maintain with Professor Oliver Mac-Donagh, at the other extreme, that the majority of government servants were wholly pragmatic, tidy-minded men, pressing towards solutions inherent in social problems, as they arose.[4] It is very difficult to make sense of Kay-Shuttleworth's career without reference to his Scottish education and his training and early experience as a doctor.[5] Similarly, Sir John Simon's commitment as a doctor surely supplied much of the dynamic of his work in public health; and one suspects that the views and sympathies which made him such a good and devoted friend of Ruskin reinforced this.[6] It might be objected that these two are what Dr Parris has most appositely termed 'zealots',[7] and cannot be considered typical; although it is perhaps worth noting that Simon's biographer offers his career as a demonstration of Professor MacDonagh's 'self-generating bureaucratic growth'. But even if one hunts for 'typical' government servants, simple pragmatism does not explain everything. As Permanent Secretary to the Education Department 1849–69, R. R. W. Lingen encouraged and led a systematic retreat from policy-making of the type Kay-Shuttleworth had favoured.[8] As Permanent Secretary to the Treasury 1870–85 he was the ferocious arch-priest of Treasury control.[9] Pragmatism—or the desire for a quiet life—or meanness—are not much help in explaining these attitudes. More relevant are his long friendship with Jowett, the concept of public service which they shared, and his firm belief that the local community had the primary responsibility

[4] O. O. G. M. MacDonagh, 'The Nineteenth Century Revolution in Government: A Reappraisal', *Historical Journal* I (1958), pp. 52–67.
[5] See Richard Johnson's essay, 'Administrators in education before 1870: patronage, social position and role', below.
[6] R. J. Lambert, *Sir John Simon and English Social Administration 1816–1904* (London, 1963).
[7] Henry Parris, *Constitutional Bureaucracy: The Development of British Central Administration since the Eighteenth Century* (London, 1969), ch. V.
[8] Johnson, *loc. cit.*
[9] See Maurice Wright's essay, 'Treasury control 1854–1914' below.

for providing its own social services, the role of the central government being a limited, supporting one.[10] Even the imperviousness of the ordinary Education Department inspector, in the years after 1870, to the pathos and poverty of the conditions in some of the schools he visited, is made more intelligible by reference to his own social background, education and motives for undertaking the work.[11]

These, it might be said, are not ideas; or, at least, ideas keep merging into social attitudes, assumptions, rationalizations of vested interests, prejudices even. As Newman commented despairingly,[12] the Englishman

gets his opinions anyhow, some from the nursery, some at school, some from the world, and has a zeal for them, because they are his own. Other men, at least, exercise a judgement upon them, and prove them by a rule. He does not care to do so, but he takes them as he finds them, whether they fit together or not, and makes light of the incongruity, and thinks it a proof of common-sense, good sense, strong, shrewd sense, to do so.

But this does not make them less important as impulses to action, or inaction. Instead of expecting every government servant to be his own philosopher, we should be concentrating on unravelling his particular tangle of assumptions and opinions, and their relation to his work. Even with a *real* philosopher, as Alan Ryan shows in his essay on John Stuart Mill, this is a complex task and has to be done virtually afresh with each individual. Finer outlines for us the main ways by which

[10] On the Jowett connection see Johnson, *loc cit.* For one of the fullest statements of Lingen's view of the relationship between central and local government, see the long private Memorandum on the government and finance of education which he prepared for Mr Gladstone and for his successor as permanent secretary, Reginald Welby, on leaving office. The only surviving copy is among the Welby Papers at Lincoln Record Office: Lind. Dep. 24/3/2/3, ff. 214–18: it is reproduced in full as Appendix VII to my unpublished D.Phil. thesis, 'Some Aspects of the Making of Policy in Elementary Education in England and Wales 1870–1895', (Oxford, 1970).
[11] See my essay, 'Administrators in education after 1870: patronage, professionalism and expertise', below.
[12] Quoted in Walter E. Houghton, *The Victorian Frame of Mind, 1830–70* (New Haven, Conn., 1957), p. 105.

disciples of Bentham set out to secure influence between 1820 and 1850—the mechanisms which made the transmission of ideas possible. But although the sheer scale of the assault is highly suggestive, it is impossible to make any firm general statement about the *effective* influence of Bentham's ideas unless we can also discover precisely what was 'transmitted' to whom, and whether he did anything as a result that he might not otherwise have done. Investigations of similar detail and precision are needed into the relationships between what Melvin Richter has termed 'the politics of conscience' and government growth between about 1890 and 1914.[13]

The second generalization which it seems possible to attempt is an insistence on the strongly marked individual characteristics of each department. This was a point made with some emphasis by a present-day civil servant during our discussion. It seems likely that such characteristics were even more marked during the nineteenth century. Since even by 1914 recruiting procedures were still not uniform and each department made its own rules for promotion, some variety is hardly surprising. But without being dogmatically functionalist, it seems possible to suggest also that the organization, the personnel and the particular idiosyncrasies of a department were closely linked to the type of work it did. The Treasury, by definition, was unique. The Foreign Office clearly considered itself unique also—and the comparison with the Colonial Office serves primarily to emphasize how different they were.[14] There seem to be certain similarities between some of the 'new' departments; between the Education Department and the Poor Law and Public Health authorities which finally turned into the Local Government Board, for instance. The sequence which Richard Johnson traces in the Education Department can be roughly discerned

[13] Melvin Richter, *The Politics of Conscience: T. H. Green and his Age* (London, 1964). A beginning has been made in B. B. Gilbert, *The Evolution of National Insurance in Great Britain: The Origins of the Welfare State* (London, 1966), and in Roger Davidson's essay, 'Llewellyn Smith, the Labour Department and government growth 1886–1909', below.

[14] Compare the essay by Valerie Cromwell and Zara S. Steiner, 'The Foreign Office before 1914: a study in resistance' with the essay by R. C. Snelling and T. J. Barron, 'The Colonial Office and its permanent officials 1801–1914', below.

there, too;[15] and it may be that after 1870 this distinction between 'old' and 'new' can be translated into a distinction between departments working directly upon social and economic problems, and departments that essentially serviced or controlled others.

But any attempt to classify departments also draws attention to one of our major areas of ignorance, the absence of much detailed knowledge of the workings of the service departments. W. S. Hamer's important recent book, *The British Army: Civil–Military Relations 1885–1905*,[16] has now provided a picture of the War Office in the last three decades of the century. The value of this study, however, serves to emphasize the need to know more about the War Office in other periods, and to discover something about the Admiralty. These two departments were, after all, far and away the biggest spenders and the ones which had to face the problems of working with experts well before any others.

Differing traditions and differing patterns of development in different departments reflect the impossibility of describing government growth in the nineteenth century as a single phenomenon or process. Rather, there seem a series of impulses towards change and new development. From time to time they interact, but the connections seem coincidental as much as causal. This seems most marked during the period up to about 1870; although—and the importance of this qualification cannot be over-emphasized—this may be primarily a function of the patchiness of our knowledge. But the various impulses seem quite clearly distinguished and, to a puzzling degree, independent of each other. The Select Committee on Miscellaneous Expenditures of 1847–8, which provided a spring-board for Sir Charles Trevelyan's first inquiries, traced its ancestry back to the Economical Reformers of the 1780s.[17] Like them, its primary concern was not so much *good* government as *less*

---

[15] On Poor Law, Public Health and the Local Government Board, see R. J. Lambert, *op. cit.*, S. E. Finer, *The Life and Times of Sir Edwin Chadwick* (London, 1952), and Roy M. MacLeod, *Treasury Control and Social Administration: A Study of Establishment Growth at the Local Government Board, 1871–1905* (London, 1968).

[16] Oxford, 1970.

[17] Henry Roseveare, *The Treasury: The Evolution of a British Institution* (London, 1969), pp. 147, 149, 166–7.

government; although some of them would have contended that
the two were synonymous. The form and content of the
Northcote–Trevelyan Report, however, as Jenifer Hart shows,
derived principally from Trevelyan's—and Gladstone's—preoccupation with internal government efficiency; and although
economy was a factor in this, it was not the dominant one. As
Mrs Hart also shows, the Report itself owed nothing to any
middle-class pressures for improved opportunities for education
and employment; although it seems plausible that the perception of its possibilities in this direction generated support for its
proposals, once published. The trend towards professionalization in other occupations may have operated in the same way.

Most striking, however, is the extent to which Trevelyan's
initiatives seem isolated from other developments within government itself. A. P. Donajgrodzki's essay on the Home Office
throws serious doubt on the relevance of Trevelyan's findings
there and on the coherence in general of his notion of efficiency.
On the evidence we have so far, it seems to be as much a
remarkable coincidence as anything else that the Colonial
Office had, since the 1820s, been watching out for recruits of the
quality which Northcote and Trevelyan advocated; and that
from 1847 the Balliol men had begun to arrive in the Education
Department. Richard Johnson argues persuasively the case for
the Balliol influence on Northcote's and Trevelyan's approach
to the organization of government service, stressing the similarities of approach. But, as he makes plain, the evidence consists
more of associations and analogies than of particular identifiable contributions. Even more important, evidence is so far
lacking to make plain links between the Report and the great
expansion of government activity in the social field; and to
substantiate in full the attractive hypothesis that standardization of recruitment and structures along the lines suggested by
Northcote and Trevelyan was either sought for or welcomed by
some politicians and government servants, as a means of
establishing control over the various *ad hoc* establishments like
the Poor Law Commission, the Education Department and the
General Board of Health, which had been proliferating since
the 1830s.

Nevertheless, the Report did initiate a discussion of government service as a whole, setting the terms for future inquiries

and plans for action. And although, as has been already stressed, departmental individuality remained marked, it does seem easier to discern some regularities, some patterns after 1870. The first and most important thing to be registered is the slowing-down of growth. In the comments above on the earlier period, growth has been used to describe both innovation, the movement of government into new fields, new types of action, and the expansion of numbers and the organization and standardization of procedures. After 1870 there was a further expansion of numbers and elaboration of procedures, but it seems to have been of a rather Parkinsonian kind. There was very much less movement into new fields of action. The general picture is of a bureaucracy gently ossifying, concerning itself primarily with pushing out again the paper that came in. What initiatives there were came from outside, from zealots and from political pressures, programmes and contingencies; and these appear to have increased sharply after about 1890.

It has been argued that there were various exceptions to this general passivity. The sections of the Local Government Board dealing with health continued to take new initiatives, as did some of the larger local authorities. Much of the impetus in both cases came from the medical, scientific and technical experts whom they employed.[18] Roger Davidson, in his essay on the Labour Department of the Board of Trade, suggests that the collection of statistics and the attempt to measure social waste which this brought was also a source of dynamism.

But it is not yet clear how significant these exceptions are. Medical, technical and scientific experts seem to be rather more similar to zealots in their patterns of behaviour than to regular civil servants. As the zealot has his cause, so the doctor or engineer has his expertise; he has criteria for judging problems and situations which do not derive entirely or primarily from within the government service. If the worst comes to the worst, and he falls out with his superiors, either political or administrative, he can always resign and go back to doctoring or engineering.

We simply do not know enough yet to decide whether local authorities can be discussed in the same terms as government

18 See MacLeod, *op. cit.*, and his specialist articles on various aspects of the Board's work, to which he refers.

departments. But their peculiar financial problems and their peculiar vulnerability to local concerns and struggles may well mean that they ought to be treated separately.[19]

The activities of the Labour Department of the Board of Trade are significant and impressive, particularly when contrasted with the marked anti-statistical bias of the Treasury. But it seems arguable that they can best be interpreted in the context of the wave of increased social concern in the 1890s already mentioned. As Davidson shows, the actual creation of the department owed much to the socially conscious group of younger Liberals to whom Morley was playing elder statesman, and was a consolation prize for their failure to secure an independent Ministry of Labour. The fact that it prospered owed much to the brilliant guidance of Llewellyn Smith, who shared many of the preoccupations of the Liberal group. At the same time, Llewellyn Smith's tight control of his own commitments, his scrupulous avoidance of partisanship and controversy, and the sad fate of the Labour Department's imitation, the Department of Special Inquiries in the Education Department,[20] all suggest that the Labour Department may be an exception proving the rule.

There seem to be at least three kinds of interlocking explanations, functional, social and ideological, for the passivity of government servants after 1870. In some departments the sheer scale and complexity of operations demanded some formalization of procedures and structures. And where, as in the Colonial Office, work was liable to mushroom uncontrollably, a rigorous adherence to routine must often have seemed the only way to survive. This is linked, too, to the converse of the point already made about zealots and experts: the development of career structures in government service and the establishment of a profession of 'civil servant' could inhibit and confine initiatives. Disinclination to rock the boat was perhaps also reinforced by the social homogeneity of the service, which, if anything,

[19] On local government finance, see the important pioneer article by E. P. Hennock, 'Finance and Politics in Urban Local Government in England 1835–1900', *Historical Journal* VI (1963), pp. 212–55. For an attempt to consider school boards as innovators, see my unpublished thesis, cited above, n. 10.

[20] See my essay, 'Administrators in education after 1870 . . .', below.

increased during the period. Whatever the formal methods of selection, bright young gentlemen from Oxford and Cambridge predominated: and one of the preoccupations of the MacDonnell Commission in 1912–14 was the social and educational exclusiveness of the service.

Entangled with these factors, too, there seems to be a peculiarly English, negative view of the role of the state. State action—or intervention, as it was usually, significantly, called— was seen in terms of more or less interference. The state acted only when all other attempts at voluntary, local or individual action had failed. The view found fullest reflection in the doctrine of Treasury control, that permanent posture of menace and rejection—'Lingenism', as Sir William Harcourt once called it.[21] Maurice Wright indeed shows us that at most it was a brake, rather than an absolute deterrent: and W. S. Hamer, in his study of relations between the War Office and the Treasury, confirms this. The items of expenditure the War Office really fought for, they got. But Hamer also suggests the deep-seatedness of the negative attitude by his insistence that the real blocks to adequate military expenditure were political, the reluctance of cabinet after cabinet to run the electoral risks of increasing public expenditure. Given these assumptions, efficiency could consist simply of pushing out again the paper that came in. It was a stage further on from 'good government is less government', but only one stage.

The peculiarity of this view was emphasized during our discussion by comparisons with France and, even more, with Germany; where the expectation, at least, was that a permanent bureaucracy would be an independent positive force. It was also stressed during the discussion that bureaucracy and ossification are not synonymous. But it is difficult to see how a bureaucracy developed as the handmaid to a system of representative government could be other than passive, dependent for initiatives on external forces, the onslaughts of the zealots, the preoccupations of the experts, and the periodic goads of the politicians worried about electoral survival.

[21] Gladstone Papers, B. M. Add. MSS. 44,199, ff. 193–4, Harcourt to Gladstone, 15 April 1885. Cf. also the Memorandum referred to above, in n. 10.

The transmission of
Benthamite ideas 1820–50

The profound influence of Bentham's arguments and models on the legislation of the nineteenth century is too well attested for me to elaborate here. There can be no doubt that the fields of colonial and Indian policy, of financial and fiscal policy, of penology and legal procedure, and of social policy and administration, were all fertilized by and to a considerable extent reshaped in accordance with the views of this extraordinary octogenarian. Brougham described him by saying 'the age of law reform and the age of Jeremy Bentham are one and the same'.[1] In 1843 John Hill Burton (the editor of his works) ascribed to him the authorship of twenty-five distinct reforms.[2] In 1905 Dicey characterized by his name the whole legislative era stretching from 1825 to 1870.[3] And while little contemporary research has even attempted let alone succeeded in challenging this purported pre-eminence, a number of specialized monographs have even more amply confirmed it.[4]

Therefore, I do not propose at all to establish the fields wherein Bentham's views prevailed, and the varying degree in which they did so. My question is quite a different one. It may

[1] *Speeches of Henry, Lord Brougham upon Questions relating to Public Rights, Duties and Interests* (Edinburgh, 1838), II, p. 287.
[2] J. H. Burton, *Benthamania* (London, 1843), pp. 381–2.
[3] A. V. Dicey, *Lectures on the Relation between Law and Public Opinion in England during the Nineteenth Century* (paper ed. London, 1963), p. 126.
[4] e.g. Lucy Brown, *The Board of Trade and the Free Trade Movement 1830–1842* (Oxford, 1958) and E. Stokes, *The English Utilitarians and India* (Oxford, 1959).

be put like this: given that the views of this man did indeed
exert a profound effect on a wide range of matters, by what
means did this come about? By what means were Bentham's
thoughts transmitted to those who were not merely willing to
carry them into legislative effect, but able to do so? At one end
of the process we find Bentham scribbling away in Queen's
Square Place. At the other end we find civil servants and judges
busy executing his views. How did this come about?

That this simple, indeed, brutal question has not been put
before is probably due to the muddled thinking of Dicey. He
seemed to be asking this question. 'Why did Benthamism obtain
acceptance?' he wrote.[5] But his answer was: 'It gave to reformers and indeed to educated Englishmen the guidance
of which they were in need; *it fell in with the spirit of the time.*'[6]
Even Dicey recognized that this was no answer: it was, as he
himself admitted, 'very general, not to say indefinite'. So he
tried again, and produced *four* answers. 'Benthamism met the
wants of the day'—by which he meant that Bentham's plans
'corresponded to the best ideas of the English middle class'.
Next—in his words—'Utilitarianism was . . . "in the air".'
Thirdly, 'Benthamism fell in with the habitual conservatism of
Englishmen.' Finally, he concludes, 'Legislative utilitarianism is
nothing but systematized individualism and individualism has
always found its natural home in England.'[7]

The reason that Dicey answered in vague generalities of this
kind is because of his highly idiosyncratic view of what constituted Benthamism. On closer inspection this turns out to be
not the creed of Bentham and his circle but a purported 'com-
monsense Benthamism', which in turn becomes simply 'individualism'. This individualism, again, is alleged to be the
common property of Whigs as much as Philosophic Radicals,
of Conservatives as much as Whigs, and of working-class leaders
as much as Conservatives![8] This is why Dicey alleged that the
acceptance of Benthamism (as *he* called it) was 'all but uni-

---

[5] *Op. cit.*, p. 168.
[6] *Ibid.*, p. 170, my emphasis.
[7] *Ibid.*, pp. 171–5.
[8] *Ibid.*, pp. 177–81. On the idiosyncrasy of Dicey's view, see also
H. Parris, 'The Nineteenth Century Revolution in Government:
A Reappraisal Reappraised', *Historical Journal* III (1960).

versal'. It was a creed held by everybody who was anybody. Hence his problem was to try to explain *why* it proved so overwhelmingly acceptable. And hence the large, vague generalities he offered by way of explanation.

My question is essentially different because it starts with a different view of Benthamism. To me Benthamism means the views of Bentham and his circle of intimates: i.e. the views comprehended by Halévy in his *Philosophic Radicalism.* From this it follows that the number of those who held these opinions was at all times very small. And from this we come back to my original question: how did the influence of this tiny number become so great as to effect the wide changes in law and administration ascribed to them?

Shortly, the answer I propose is this. I maintain that the translation of Bentham's ideas into practical effect took place by a threefold process—or, better, by the interaction of three processes. I call these, respectively: IRRADIATION, SUSCITA-TION, PERMEATION.

IRRADIATION was the process by which small knots of Benthamites attracted into their salons, their committees and their associations a much wider circle of men whom they in-fected with some at least of their enthusiasms and thereby turned into what I might call Second-Degree Benthamites.

SUSCITATION needs a little more explanation. I had origin-ally chosen the word *Publicization*; but on consulting the Shorter Oxford Dictionary, I found that such a word as SUSCITATION did exist. It exactly conveys what I mean: 'To stir up; to excite [a rebellion, a feeling etc.]; to raise out of inactivity; to quicken, vivify, animate.' SUSCITATION was the process of arranging public inquiries or the press or both together in such a way as to create a favourable public opinion, of a temporary kind, amid influential groups in the country.

PERMEATION was the process of securing official employ-ment of oneself and thereafter using this position for further IRRADIATION—on one's supporters and subordinates; and for further SUSCITATION also.

IRRADIATION made friends and influenced people. Through them, SUSCITATION proved possible. SUSCITATION led to official appointment and hence PERMEATION. And permeation led to further irradiation and suscitation; and so on *da capo.*

1 *Irradiation*

Exposure to the thought and attitudes of Benthamism took five main forms. One must not underrate, to begin with, the importance of the salon. In those days the intellectual élite formed a much narrower circle than today. To establish this one has only to compare a copy of *Men of the Time* for this period with a modern *Who's Who*. In such circumstances personal contacts, through a salon, could powerfully affect the whole body of informed opinion. The immediate source of irradiation was of course Bentham's own house. It has been said, by Dicey, that when explaining the hold that Benthamism took one must not forget the fact that he lived a very long time, and that therefore his views had the benefit of prolonged reiteration.[9] Far more important is the fact that through this long life Bentham received a continuous stream of influential visitors. Few of them became wholehearted disciples, most of them—like Brougham for instance—adapting Bentham's views to suit their own; but even fewer went away as confirmed opponents of his views and system. Apart from Queen's Square Place, however, there were other such Benthamite salons. That of James Mill was particularly important. To some extent, his visitors over-lapped Bentham's; but many derived their Benthamism through him alone. A list of the more important of his friends reads like a Benthamite Roll of Honour. It includes Ricardo, Brougham, Joseph Hume, Francis Place, Romilly, Horner, William Allen, Grote, the Austins, Strutt, the Villiers brothers, Coulson, Fonblanque, Bickersteth, McCulloch, Black (of the *Chronicle*), Molesworth and Arnott.[10] Now many of these formed their own 'salons' (if we may call them that). Thus there was a distinct 'Grote clique' to which both Charles Butler and Joseph Parkes belonged. Likewise Francis Place made contacts quite outside the range of James Mill's own circle of friends.

Outsiders could also be irradiated in a second way, if they became part of the team writing for some Benthamite periodical. Contacts between editor and the contributors were very close. Thus Fonblanque refused to take over the editorship of the *Examiner* from Leigh Hunt unless he could bring Chadwick in

[9] Dicey, *op. cit.*, p. 128.
[10] A. Bain, *James Mill* (London, 1882).

as assistant editor; and when he had done so, we find Fonblanque, Chadwick and John Mill writing most of the journal
between them. The teams contributing to a journal or periodical
soon tended—as indeed they do today—to develop a corporate
spirit. Thus the *Westminster* team consisted of Southern, Bowring, James Mill, Perronet Thompson, Charles Barker, W. J.
Fox, Southwood Smith, J. A. Roebuck, William Ellis, James
Hogg, the Austins, Chadwick, and of course John Mill. New
contributors to the journal tended to fall under the spell of
teams such as these. Bentham's correspondence contains repeated references to efforts to found new periodicals—such as
the *Jurist* of which Rosen was the editor. In so far as Bentham's
disciples produced and contributed to such periodicals as *Companion to the Newspaper*, the *Westminster*, the *London Review*,
the *Jurist*, they constituted so many centres into whose orbits
newcomers were attracted and in some cases retained.

Similar in operation and effect were the numerous committees
established by the Benthamites. It was through the Greek
Refugees Committee, on which Joseph Hume sat, that Bowring
and (it appears) Chadwick first swam into the Benthamite
orbit. The 'Diffusion' societies illustrate how Whig noblemen
and merchants could be brought into contact with a nucleus of
Benthamite disciples. The Society for the Diffusion of Useful
Knowledge founded in 1827 not only brought into the Benthamite circle two people who were to become disciples and
propagandists—viz. Joseph Parkes, of Birmingham, and
Charles Knight, the publisher: it associated these two men with
Benthamites like James Mill and Hume on the one side, and
with merchants like Josiah Wedgwood II, and young Whigs like
Althorp and Russell on the other. The Society for the Diffusion
of Practical Knowledge, founded in 1833, had a similar effect.
Its moving figures were three confirmed Benthamites, Place,
Roebuck and Hume; most of its financial backers were well-
known Benthamites too; but it was able to attract others also
such as Warburton, the timber merchant, and Olinthus Gregory,
the mathematician and astronomer.

The irradiation of outsiders is best illustrated, however, by a
fourth channel; the establishment of specialist societies. Of
these the London Statistical Society and the Political Economy
Club are the outstanding examples.

The Political Economy Club, founded in 1821 by James Mill and Thos. Tooke, was not an innocent self-improvement society. It was formed, in the first place, with the deliberate intention of propagating one particular school of political economy: that was the Ricardian system, as against that of Malthus and others, and as understood by James Mill and McCulloch. Professor Checkland, in his article on 'The Propagation of Ricardian Economics in England'[11] has established this particular point definitively. Secondly it had an avowed propagandist intention. 'The Members of the Society', said the Rules, 'will regard their mutual instruction and the diffusion among others of first principles of Political Economy, as a real and important obligation.' Furthermore, the Rules continue thus:[12]

> As the press is the grand instrument for the diffusion of knowledge or of error, all the Members of this Society will regard it as incumbent upon them to watch carefully the proceedings of the Press, and to ascertain if any doctrine hostile to sound views on Political Economy has been propagated; to contribute whatever may be in their power to refute such erroneous doctrines and contravert their influence; and to avail themselves of every favourable opportunity for the publication of seasonable truths within the province of the society . . .

The original founding members numbered twenty-eight. Of the twenty-one identified, seven may be characterized as firm, first-degree Benthamites, e.g. James Mill, Grote, Ricardo, Tooke and the like. Two were miscellaneous intellectuals— Zachary Macaulay and Malthus, both brought in for special reasons. Four were businessmen, merchants and bankers. Two were civil servants. No less than six, however, were miscellaneous professional men: and of these, every one was to be given some government appointment between 1830 and 1840 when the Whigs were in power.

During the period 1821–30, eleven elections were made. Of the nine identified, three were Benthamites—Coulson, McCulloch and (with a certain query) Senior. Three miscellaneous MPs and/or intellectuals were brought in. The most significant

[11] *Economica* XVI n.s. (February 1949), pp. 50–81.
[12] Bain, *op. cit.*, pp. 198–200.

elections, however, were among the businessmen and aristocrats. Among the four businessmen elected were Baring and Poulett Thomson. Both of these were to be at the Board of Trade during the Whig period of office and both were to give their patronage to Benthamite nominees. The sole aristocrat elected was Althorp: and as Whig Chancellor he was to be even more influential in opening the door to the Benthamites. For instance it was through him that Lefevre and Chadwick came into government service.

Between 1831 and 1841, there were twenty-three elections, of which twenty are identifiable. In this decade another six confirmed Benthamites were admitted—Chadwick and John Mill, Romilly and Perronet Thompson, for instance. The number of miscellaneous MPs and intellectuals fell to one. Four businessmen were admitted; among them J. Morrison and S. J. Lloyd (later Lord Overstone). The great difference between this and the earlier period lies, however, among the categories of aristocrats and functionaries. There was now a clear policy of bringing in aristocrats deemed likely to be influential: Villiers, Spring-Rice, Kerry, and above all, Lansdowne, were elected in this decade. Furthermore, one may also infer a novel practice of electing functionaries who appeared worth influencing: thus Deacon Hume, Holt Mackenzie, Sir George Graham and G. R. Porter were brought in.

The composite picture that emerges is of a small group (seven) of Benthamite propagandists who began by associating with themselves a small group of merchants and bankers and a larger group of intelligentsia; who were able, between 1821 and 1830, to influence three important Whigs, viz. Baring, Poulett Thomson and Lord Althorp; and who then had the satisfaction of seeing many of their original number—e.g. Tooke, Torrens, Parnell, Coulson, Senior and McCulloch—in office under the Whigs alongside their intelligentsia friends: and who finally, from this position of strength, brought in important aristocrats and civil servants. Of the sixteen first-degree Benthamites who were members between 1821 and 1841, two had died. Of the fourteen survivors in 1841, one had been a Minister; four were MPs and eight were civil servants or government commissioners. Of the businessmen, Baring and Thomson were of ministerial rank; and of the aristocrats, four were of ministerial rank. In addition, twelve other members were in the government's service. To put this another way: in 1841 there survived sixty-one of the members elected during 1821–41. Of these, fourteen were first-degree Benthamites: seven members had held ministerial rank; eight were MPs and twenty were civil servants.

POLITICAL ECONOMY CLUB

Statistical summary

	Originals	Elected 1821–30	Elected 1831–43	
Hard core	7	3	6	16
Misc. MPs		2	1	3
Misc. Intells	2	1		3
Business	4	4	4	12
Aristocrats		1	4	5
Functionaries	2		4	6 ⎫
Functionaries to be	6		1	7 ⎭ 13
Not identified	7	2	3	12
Total	28	13	23	64

The London Statistical Society was a much more catholic body and it was not a propagandist one. The Benthamites did not hold a dominating position. Nevertheless an analysis of its membership—which was much larger than that of the PEC, of course—shows that they were powerfully represented. Strutt, Molesworth, Hume, Charles Villiers, Bickersteth, Grote, McCulloch, Senior, Tooke and Chadwick, for instance, were all members.

The fifth and final way in which Benthamites tended to irradiate others, and turn them to some extent into second-degree Benthamites, occurred chiefly in the thirties. This was the time when many of them obtained official positions. In such positions it often fell to them to recommend persons for filling vacant positions in their offices. They tended to select persons of their own way of thinking, and these people once appointed were exposed to the force of their Benthamite superior's personality. It is no accident that Edwin Chadwick and Nassau Senior should have picked upon James Kay and E. C. Tufnell to act as Assistant Poor Law Commissioners, and no accident that after close contact with Chadwick both behaved as though impregnated with Benthamite notions. The same is true of a large number of the other assistant commissioners at the Poor Law Office, such as Alfred Day, Edmund Gulson and George Coode.

Perhaps sufficient has been said to make my main point: in an England where the intellectuals formed a very small and confined society, there were various circles containing nuclei of confirmed Benthamites. Clear in their convictions and filled with a missionary zeal, these could and often did strongly influence their non-Benthamite colleagues. The result was to introduce Benthamite precepts and example to a wide circle of influential people: aristocrats who had ministerial patronage, merchants and bankers who were often MPs, and a swarm of humbler persons who were later deployed to fill vacancies in an expanding civil service.

2 Suscitation

I now turn to the second main means by which Benthamism was transmitted—suscitation. This comprehends three main channels: first, the manipulation of public inquiries to return Benthamite answers; second, the manipulation of a select public opinion; and third, both of these used conjointly.

The Benthamites proved adept at manipulating Select Committees of the House and Royal Commissions to their own advantage. One recalls the Select Committees on the Combination Laws in 1824 and 1825, manipulated by Joseph Hume and Francis Place; or the Select Committee on Private Bills, manipulated by Joseph Hume and Edwin Chadwick. The trick was twofold; to get a friendly MP to move the Select Committee, success in which entitled him to nominate the majority of the fifteen members; and thereafter the careful pre-selection of witnesses. The advantages of this technique were that, if successful, the Benthamite view received an *official* status: furthermore, it enabled Benthamite officials to put their views publicly—as part of the minutes of evidence.

An example will illustrate the technique. In 1840 Charles Villiers—a Benthamite—failed once again in his now annual anti-Corn Law motion. It was thrown out by 245 to 129. Deacon Hume, a civil servant at the Board of Trade, who was not an original Benthamite but was a firm free trader, then conceived the idea of getting an inquiry into import duties generally; if properly handled this could be made to indict the Corn Laws in particular. He was abetted by his colleague, McGregor, also a civil servant in the Board of Trade. According to Badham, Deacon Hume's biographer,[13] they thought that

> If those who were, or had been in office at the Board of
> Trade could be transferred for a short time from their
> homes or from their private offices in Whitehall, into a
> committee room of the House of Commons . . . not only
> would their evidence be given publicly but it would be
> ordered to be printed and circulated through the country.

They thereupon approached the good Joseph Hume who, as we have seen, was very partial to this technique. He was successful in his motion and, the lion's share of its membership falling to him to nominate, there were nine Whigs and Radicals out of fifteen members of the Committee. Apart from himself there was Villiers, Ewart, W. J. Blake and W. Williams, Labouchere, of the Board of Trade, Sir Henry Parnell and Henry Tufnell, a Lord of the Treasury. All were free traders. Furthermore, the committee hearings took place during the summer recess: as a result, members began to drift away. The only members who never missed a session were Hume, Villiers, Thornley and Ewart. Only seven members drafted the report, and these four therefore formed the majority and drafted the report to their own liking!

Nor was that all. They also carefully pre-selected their witnesses. They were able to throw into prominence the views of merchants whom they knew to be free traders. Above all, however, they called for the views of the officials of the Board themselves. One by one this group of purportedly anonymous public officials, all dedicated free traders, came forward to say their piece: John Bowring, G. R. Porter, and then the perpetrators of the inquiry, Deacon Hume and McGregor them-

[13] Quoted in Brown, *op. cit.*, p. 71.

selves. All in all their evidence, publicly given, publicly disseminated—and publicly paid for—makes up more than one
half of the minutes of evidence!

This committee provides an excellent illustration of the use
of a Select Committee as an offensive weapon. But sometimes
the tables were turned: an anti-Benthamite Member might
successfully move a Committee in order to expose or combat
a Benthamite department. But a good tactician might turn
even this to advantage. In 1837 three anti-Poor Law Tories
succeeded in a motion to set up a Select Committee into the
New Poor Law. Its terms of reference were to examine and
report on the numerous anti-Poor Law petitions now pouring in
from all over the country. Chadwick—with Russell as Home
Secretary in full support—was more than equal to this. He
resolved not simply to rebut the charges against the New Poor
Law, but to get the Committee, of its own apparent volition, to
recommend the very changes in the law which Chadwick and the
Poor Law Commissioners themselves wished to introduce. To
this end he seems, with Russell's help, to have packed the
Committee. Only four known antagonists of the Law sat on it:
while for the other side there were two of the ministers who had
passed the Law, one former Assistant Commissioner, and no
less than eight Chairmen of Boards of Guardians against whom
some of the complaints were proffered! Furthermore, he persuaded Russell to sit on the Committee and provided him with
a brief on the amendments the Commissioners wished to have
the Committee recommend to them—trusting Russell to
conduct the necessary manœuvres. Not only that. When asked
to index the petitions to be examined, Chadwick so arranged
them that they seemed to favour the Act. He had all the
favourable petitions printed in the *Morning Chronicle*. Finally,
since he had the petitions he knew what charges had to be re-
butted. He accordingly drew up a list of the witnesses to be
called for the rebuttal and arranged for documentary support of
the viewpoints they would be putting forward. Walter had
hoped to investigate charges in more than one hundred unions.
Owing to Chadwick's tactics, it took four months to investigate
only *two*. When the Committee came to report, it rejected every
one of John Walter's resolutions and with one important
exception—due to an accident—passed all the resolutions

Chadwick had suggested! No wonder that a cheap octavo edition of the Committee's proceedings was printed and disseminated throughout the Poor Law Unions![14]

What was done for Select Committees could be done, and was done, even more effectively for Royal Commissions. It was equally easy, perhaps easier, to pre-select the witness; even more important was the facility with which the authors of the Report could pick and choose among the evidence supplied by them, giving prominence to the views they wished to recommend and suppressing views which contradicted them. For the mass of evidence supplied to a Royal Commission was so great that few would take the trouble to read through it, and fewer still would be able to produce, as it were, a counter-report of their own.

Of this technique, the famous *Report of the Municipal Corporations Commission* is a classic example. The Commission consisted of twenty lawyers—mostly 'briefless barristers'—whose task it was to compile reports on the corporation under review in accordance with instructions drawn up by the Secretary. These reports—on 285 towns—fill four bulky volumes of Appendices. With few exceptions they are accurate, lucid and complete. But this is not true of the *General Report*, which alone was the document which the public read and on which the government acted. This report was written by the Chief Commissioner, Blackburne, and Joseph Parkes, the Secretary. Blackburne we know of as 'an excellent Rad. Ballot etc.' He was MP for Huddersfield. Parkes had for some years been in touch with Benthamite circles, e.g. with Place, Hume and Charles Knight.

How did Parkes and Blackburne go about their work? Blackburne began his draft 'before any of the evidence collected by the individual commissioners had been circulated and before many of their reports on the several towns had even been sent in'. The draft report was first circulated on 25 February 1835 (although even at that time one-third of the reports were still in MSS., while a general index to them did not appear until four years later!). The draft report was considered at only three meetings of the Commissioners, although Sir Francis Palgrave

[14] On the Select Committees of 1837, see also my *Life and Times of Sir Edwin Chadwick* (London, 1952, reprinted 1970), pp. 129–35.

protested and offered to disprove its assertions by analysing the evidence. His offer was rejected and the Report was even presented to the government five weeks before it was formally signed. There is no reason to dissent from the Webbs' judgment that 'both as a summary of facts and as an analysis of causes the General Report is inaccurate and misleading. The historical student must dismiss it as a bad case of a violent political pamphlet being, to serve Party ends, issued as a judicial Report.'[15] No more would I dissent from their estimate of its general tenor: 'A plan of local government in which we may detect the pure milk of Benthamism, (and) quite contrary to the ordinary proposals for local reform and to the usual action of Parliament.'

It would be otiose to multiply examples. To illustrate the generality of the practice, however, let me recite briefly two or three other cases, omitting the detail. Elsewhere I have shown how much evidence there is to support the view that Chadwick's *Instructions* to the assistant commissioners in the 1833 Factory Inquiry presupposed the solution he wanted to put forward; and did so. Likewise I have shown how selective is the evidence used in the 1834 Poor Law Report to support rigidly Benthamite conclusions: evidence which can be contradicted only by a careful perusal of the *twelve* bulky volumes of evidence appended to the Report. Or finally how the Health of Towns Commission 1844/5, of which Chadwick was not even a member, was directed and two-thirds written by him to elaborate and sustain hypotheses he had put forward in 1842.[16] Likewise the celebrated *Report of the Royal Commission on the Condition of the Handloom Weavers* (1841) was throughout directed by Nassau Senior and S. J. Lloyd. This deliberately confuted the earlier suggestions, made by a Select Committee of the House, that a minimum wage should be introduced: and instead, it recommended the repeal of the Corn Laws and reaffirmed the importance of free contract. Also, in this last respect, where it

---

[15] S. and B. Webb, *The Manor and The Borough* (London, 1908), II, pp. 721–2.
[16] Finer, *Chadwick*, bks. 2 and 5: on the Poor Law Report see also Mark Blaug, 'The Myth of the Old Poor Law and the Making of the New', *Journal of Economic History* XXIII (1963), and 'The Poor Law Report Re-examrned', *ibid.*, XXIV (1964).

touched the trade unions, Senior introduced into the Report the tract that he had written on this subject for Lord Althorp in 1830.

So much for one aspect of suscitation. Its second aspect was the attempt to manipulate public opinion by the press. The Benthamites set great store by the press. They recognized its importance much earlier than the traditionalist ruling élites—the aristocratic elements of which regarded connection with the press (other than the quarterlies) as socially contemptible. Many Benthamites made their living precisely by the pen, e.g. Coulson and Chadwick, Fonblanque and McCulloch. Their attitude to the press is illustrated by their motives for rejecting the 'taxes on knowledge'—in order to permit what they deemed *sound* opinion to circulate freely and combat the cheap unstamped and demagogic popular press; by the anxiety constantly shown by Bentham and Mill to launch organs of their own, an anxiety which led to the at least partially successful *Westminster Review*; by their concern to keep contact with the editors of the dailies and supply them with material favourable to the causes they were advocating; and by the enthusiasm they brought to all efforts 'to diffuse knowledge' among the working classes.

In this last respect, their efforts, though continuous, can hardly be deemed successful. The Society for the Diffusion of Useful Knowledge's publications proved grotesquely academic. The *Penny Encylopaedia* soon failed, and in any case circulated mostly to middle-class readers. The Society for the Diffusion of Practical Knowledge's *Companion to the Newspaper* expired within four years (in 1837). Large quantities of tracts were circulated such as Harriet Martineau's *Tendency of Strikes and Sticks to Produce Low Wages*, Charles Knight's *Results of Machinery* and *Letters to working People on the New Poor Law*. But neither of these, nor Harriet Martineau's *Political Economy Tales*, nor *Poor Law Tales*, seem to have made any serious impact on the working classes; and if they had any clientèle it appears to have been among the middle orders.[17] The Benthamite grip on dailies was somewhat firmer. It was chiefly centred on the *Morning Chronicle*; but in the thirties and forties this and others were quite overshadowed by *The Times*.

[17] R. K. Webb, *The British Working Class Reader, 1780–1848: Literacy and Social Tension* (London, 1955).

It was in the *Westminster*, but more importantly in the *Edinburgh Review*, that the Benthamites found their most useful instrument. Both periodicals affected the opinion, not of the masses, but of what Dicey called '*legislative* public opinion', i.e. the opinion of those who were MPs or likely to affect the opinion of MPs. But of the two, the *Edinburgh Review* always had the larger circulation, about 10,000 as against the *Westminster* maximum of 3,000, which in any case rapidly declined. Furthermore, the *Westminster* set out with a self-consciously sectarian purpose, and aroused as much animosity as it did enthusiasm. Thirdly, too, the *Westminster* passed into difficulties, and with the quarrel between the Mills and Bowring it lost direction, while the *Edinburgh* continued to enjoy an enormous prestige with the law-makers and law-making opinion. Finally, there was an understanding between the *Edinburgh* and the Whigs which permitted certain of its articles to exert a maximum effect.

Now from the point of view of political economy there is little to choose between the *Westminster* and the *Edinburgh* as vehicles for Benthamite opinion: for until 1837 the *Edinburgh*'s principal and almost sole contributor of economic articles was J. R. McCulloch; and after that date it was Nassau Senior. The prolific output of McCulloch can best be judged by reference to Mr Fetter's check list of 'Economic Articles in the Edinburgh Review' published in the *Journal of Political Economy*, in June 1953. Between 1819 and 1837, he contributed no less than seventy-eight separate articles!

The effect of this output in the propagation of Ricardian economics is clearly immense. More immediate to our purpose, however, is the abundant evidence that articles were often specially written, tailored to the official Whig view and artfully timed, in order to influence the Commons and law-making opinion outside. Thus McCulloch wrote his 1824 article on the Combination Laws to second the efforts of Hume and Place and to such effect that Place wrote: 'Its effect on many members (of Parliament) was remarkable: several of them told me there was no resisting the conclusive arguments it contained, and one of them said he was prepared to speak the substance of the essay in the House.'[18] Miss Lucy Brown has discovered many

18 G. Wallas, *The Life of Francis Place, 1771–1854* (London, 1898), p. 208.

additional occasions on which this technique was used. She shows, for instance, that McCulloch's article on Colonies in November 1831 had been thrashed out with Althorp, Sir Henry Parnell and Poulett Thomson: that the 1832 article on the Bank, also discussed with Thomson and Althorp, was timed to appear 'shortly before the meeting of Parliament and just at the right time': and likewise for his article on taxation in 1833.[19] She also portrays Sir Henry Parnell sending an article on the Import Duties Committee to the *Edinburgh*, in September 1840, with the comment: 'I am anxious that my article should appear in the January number of the *Edinburgh Review* so that it may be in the hands of government and of M.P.s at the beginning of the session.'[20] Nassau Senior contributed his defence of the New Poor Law to the *Edinburgh* in 1841 for the same reason—to stiffen the resolution of Members who were beginning to give way to the anti-Poor Law agitation.

But the most developed—and certainly the most successful—technique of suscitation was the *combining* of a manipulated inquiry with a manipulated publicity. The official blue book was to be disseminated widely amid an orchestrated fanfare of comment; and, by the same token, that which the public was given to read was not (apparently) the private crotchet of an individual but the mature deliberation of an official inquiry. This consummation was accomplished by the simultaneous circulation of very large numbers of the blue book, usually free; by the simultaneous release of tracts and special articles; and by a press campaign. Thus, even before the Poor Law Inquiry had reported, the *Extracts of Information* were published: no less than 15,000 copies were disseminated and there is evidence that they produced a momentary mood of panic. Of the *Final Report* 10,000 copies were sold and another 10,000 were given away. Likewise 10,000 copies of the 1842 *Sanitary Report* were given away. Moreover, these copies went to selected recipients—those who were deemed to be influential. To give a further example, we have the list of recipients of the *Constabulary Report* of 1839. Five thousand copies were sold, but another 3,000 were given away. Half of these went to Lords Lieutenant, Petty Sessions and Watch Committees; 210 went

[19] *Op. cit.*, p. 19.
[20] *Ibid.*, p. 215.

to newspapers. One thousand one hundred went to 'Individuals directed by the Commissioners'.

Tracts and special articles were also prepared. Thus for the Poor Law, Charles Knight prepared a digest of the Report and evidence, of ninety-five pages, price fourpence; the *Companion to the Newspaper* ran one Poor Law Supplement in 1833 and two more in 1834: and Harriet Martineau was induced to write her *Poor Law Tales*. After the Bill was passed both Tidd Pratt and Senior published 'outlines' of its provisions. At the same time every effort was made, by supplying information and articles, to keep the press favourable.

The campaign to secure the passing of the Poor Law used all these artifices, and is well known. Similar campaigns had attended the findings of Hume's Select Committee on the Combination Laws in 1824, and there was a like campaign on the findings of the Select Committee on Rates of Postage (the Penny Post question) in 1837. Miss Lucy Brown, too, describes a campaign of this sort to launch the findings of the Import Duties Committee in 1840. It will be remembered that this Committee was established at the instance of two public servants of free-trading views, in order to give publicity to their views; that it was deliberately packed with supporters of those views; and that by artful manœuvres it was induced to endorse those views. That was not all. Both McGregor and Porter thereupon produced pamphlets on the subject. Sir Henry Parnell, a committeeman, published his special and timely article in the *Edinburgh* on the matter. The *Manchester Times* and the *Manchester Guardian* ran a series of articles on extracts from it. And a special effort was made by Hume to place an article in the *Spectator*. The effect was that the *Edinburgh* or the *Spectator* articles were extensively quoted in the London press; while the *Spectator* article proved to be the medium by which the Committee's findings reached Sir Robert Peel. For this article had much impressed Wellington, and also Graham; and Graham thereupon called Peel's particular attention to it. And it is to the careful propaganda work that Miss Brown ascribes the important tariff changes of 1842.[21]

---

[21] *Ibid.*, p. 229.

3 Permeation

I turn now to the third of the three interconnecting processes by which the notions of the Benthamite circle were diffused to a widening public: to the process of permeation.

The great obstacles to practical Benthamism were the general incapacity of the contemporary public servants to grapple with the new activities which such Benthamism demanded; and next, the administrative indolence, linked with the lust for patronage, of the Whig cousinhood. It is owing to these two factors, *par excellence*, that no Benthamite reform—whether in Poor Law, Education, Public Health, Factory Legislation, local administration or financial reform—ever became anything but a rude approximation to the original plan. But paradoxically these two obstacles to tidy Benthamism were also the very factors which gave the Benthamites their opportunity to advise and to administer. Because of the lack of civil servants with the appropriate skills, the Whig aristocrats felt the need for new appointments; and because, in the unreformed civil service, these appointments were in their gift, those who had been irradiated by Benthamism tended to appoint Benthamites to certain key positions. One finds Chadwick at the Poor Law Office, Coulson at the Home Office, McCulloch and Bowring and Villiers at the Board of Trade, and so forth; leaving aside the judicial, the colonial and the very important Indian appointments. One must not overrate this degree of permeation. A glance at the *Imperial Calendar* for, say, 1839 would show the old-established civil servants still in the vast majority. It was primarily in the new or developing offices such as the Poor Law Commission, the Factory Inspectorate, the Board of Trade, that the Benthamite influence was strongest.

Lucy Brown in her study of the Board of Trade provides almost a paradigm of the way in which the infiltration was effected. Poulett Thomson, the Vice-President of the Board during the critical change of government in 1830, and President after 1834, was the agent. He found J. D. Hume, a man after his own heart, already in the office. He then engaged Bowring and George Villiers for the conduct of trade investigations, and commercial negotiations abroad. To the statistical department he appointed, not Charles Knight to whom he offered the place, but someone recommended by Knight, viz. G. R. Porter. As his private secretary, he took Arthur Symonds, the author of the *Mechanics of Lawmaking*, another Benthamite and protégé of Edwin Chadwick.

Once in a position of authority, a Benthamite naturally tended to recruit junior staff of his own way of thinking. It is no accident that Kay and E. C. Tufnell, Arnott and Southwood Smith should have been appointed to, or used for inquiries in, the Poor Law Office. It is no accident that in his turn Kay should appoint inspectors of the character of Tremenheere, or Joseph Fletcher.

The effect of such penetration was twofold. In the first place, the offices—often as in the case of the Poor Law Commission or Factory Inspectorate the result of Benthamite suscitation—became a springboard for further inquiry and further suscitation. The creation, successively, of the Registrar General's Office, the Education Committee of the Privy Council and the General Board of Health, as a result of the interests and dynamism of the Poor Law Commission, is the most outstanding example of this, certainly. But the Mines Act of 1842 may be said to have developed from the Act of 1833 in a not too dissimilar way; for the Royal Commission set up as a result of Ashley's motion consisted of two of the Factory Inspectors (Saunders and Horner) with two well-tried—almost professional—Benthamite Royal Commissioners; to wit Southwood Smith and Thomas Tooke. Likewise the Board of Trade, as staffed by Poulett Thomson, became a springboard for the free-trade agitation.

The second effect was to associate these new administrators very closely with decision-making in their general offices. Once installed they were positively encouraged to suggest to their minister the further measures that their office seemed to call for. The projected amendments to the Poor Law Act, postponed until 1844, were drafted by the Poor Law Commissioners themselves. Similarly, in the Factory Act Department, in 1837 the Home Secretary informed them that he would be consulting them on the amendments they wished to suggest, and after a conference with them told them to draw up the Heads of the Bill for the cabinet. In 1838 after the redrafting of the Bill, its revised text was sent to all the inspectors for consideration, and the Bill was not printed until they had reached substantial agreement with their minister. They were further consulted throughout the Bill's progress in Parliament. The 1844 Act was, substantially, what the inspectors recommended to the Home Secretary.[22] Likewise in the Education Committee: Lansdowne and Kay-Shuttleworth ran the department largely by conferences, and by 1857 it had become the practice to put decisions to a vote, even if it involved an opinion on policy. It was precisely this practice that Robert Lowe—determined to be master in his own house—objected to and discontinued: thus provoking the great crisis in his office. As a last example one may cite the profound effects on Indian policy attributable to James Mill's relationship with Bentinck, and to the subsequent arrival in India of Indian Civil Servants who had used Bentham's works when studying under Empson at Haileybury.[23]

4   The cycle of transmission

For convenience's sake I have divided the processes by which Benthamism was transmitted into three. But the impact of the Benthamites stemmed from the fact that so often the three processes went on together, in a continuous cycle—a kind of chain reaction. Poulett Thomson is drawn into the Benthamite circle—*irradiation*: he acts with them and for them on the 1828 Finance Committee (with Bowring preparing much of the report)—*suscitation*: he bows himself into office at the Board of Trade. As a result of this, in 1830—*permeation*: he appoints Villiers and Bowring and then McGregor—more *permeation*: these, with Hume, get up the Import Duties Committee of 1840 —*suscitation* again. Althorp is drawn into the Benthamite circle—*irradiation*: he appoints Chadwick to the Poor Law Inquiry—and this is manipulated and publicized by Simon and Chadwick—*suscitation*: Chadwick becomes Secretary—*permeation*: he sparks off the Sanitary Inquiry—*suscitation*: he is then appointed to the General Board of Health—*permeation*: he brings in such men (not Benthamites admittedly) as Rawlinson

[22] M. W. Thomas, *Early Factory Legislation* (Leigh-on-Sea, 1948), pp. 147, 153, 157, 176–86, 187, 245, 249, 284, 285.
[23] Cf. Stokes, *op. cit.*

and Simon—more *permeation*: and Simon continues the process of *suscitation*.

Having said all this, I must conclude by saying what I emphatically do not mean to say!

In the first place, I am not claiming that administrative and social reform in the early nineteenth century is due exclusively or even mainly to Benthamite suscitation and permeation. I recognize that there were other factors. There were the *Saints*—though I think their success can be analysed pretty well by the same processes I have suggested for Bentham's followers. There were the Tory philanthropists like John Walter I, Ashley and Fielding. There was the Manchester School —the Cobdens, Brights, Ashtons, James Wilsons. I would certainly not classify them as Dicey does as 'common-sense Benthamites'. Also there were other motives for action than Benthamite suscitation. Very often there was sheer necessity. The Factory Act of 1833 was a response to the Ten Hours agitation; Free Trade was partly a response to a mood of desperation among the factory owners in the 1837–41 depression; joint stock legislation was partly a response to the railway mania.

Second, I am not claiming that all zealous and tidy administrators were Benthamites. Sir James Stephen was not; Trevelyan was not; and I find it difficult to say that Macaulay was. And at the other end of the scale a great part of the new administration devolved upon new men—doctors, engineers, actuaries and the like—who may, or equally may not, have been irradiated by contact with Bentham's disciples.

Third, I am not claiming that Benthamite reforms ever operated in exact accordance with the plans of their progenitors. The Benthamites were never ministers. At the best, 'irradiated Whigs' were minor folk like Thomson or Althorp or Brougham. The Benthamites were public servants; they were never in a position to lay down the law and were always forced to work against aristocratic indolence and interference.

Fourth, I do not assert that Benthamite reform was more than a part of the social, economic and administrative reconstruction that then went on. After all, even John Hill Burton attributed only twenty-five reforms to Bentham, and of these seven are procedural reforms in the law.

But in respect to India and the Colonies, to penology and to health, education, and the protection of paupers and factory workers, to financial administration, fiscal policy and the machinery of central and local administration; in respect to these, it seems to me, Bentham's thoughts and attitudes played a predominant role.

If that be admitted—if that, only, be admitted—I submit to ask the question with which I opened: how did the thoughts of this man come to operate in so many fields? By what processes were they transmitted? I hope that this essay has been able, if not to satisfy, at least to suggest a way in which the question may be answered.

Utilitarianism and bureaucracy: the views of J. S. Mill

I begin, reluctantly, by begging some interesting—and for my purposes rather important—questions that have recently agitated both historians of ideas and historians of administrative reform. I say 'reluctantly' because these are questions on which I have formed some opinions and would by no means hesitate to expound in the right circumstances. But, in the light of this essay's immediate purpose, I shall do no more than dogmatize briefly, and hope only to carry enough conviction to get on with the exploration of those dilemmas about administration which we can see in the writings of J. S. Mill. The first large doubt raised by historians of ideas is—to put it crudely— whether the ideas of professional thinkers and the ideas of the great and nearly great social and political theorists have *any* definite influence at all.[1] Do we have any justification for calling political changes, be they reformist or revolutionary, *Lockean, Benthamite, Rousseauist* or even, to take the fiercest line, *Marxist*? Mostly, there is no reason to think that politicians and administrators are at all well versed in what the 'great men' said. We can take over Keynes's remark about the hold exercised on practical men by obsolete theorists and add to it the observation that even where the theorists in question are not obsolete, they are likely to be second-hand and second-rate. We can all think of good reasons why the minds of practical men will be open to the second-hand rather than to the new, the

[1] Quentin Skinner, 'The Limits of Historical Explanations', *Philosophy* XLI (1966), pp. 199–215 and 'The History of Ideas', *History and Theory* VIII (1969), pp. 3–53.

original, the highly developed and the finely articulated. Even when we consider men like Lenin or Trotsky, who had read widely and were well-versed in a social and political theory by which they professed to direct their activities, is it not clear that what they actually took up and developed was more closely rooted in the needs of their own situation than in the words of their mentors? We can hardly begin to conceive of the views formed by theorists surviving the transition from thought to action unimpaired; we praise the work of the theorist for its subtlety, elegance, sophistication, but the political actor requires above all to make an impact on a rough and unpredictable world of brute fact. It is no wonder, therefore, if we find the theory bending to meet the facts; it is usually a great deal easier to match the idea to the reality than to bend reality to match the idea. Plainly, we can pile up considerations of this sort so as to carry a good deal of weight, and some of the points made are simply unanswerable. But the case is not conclusive; we might, for instance, retort that ideas circulate by other means than the reading of books and the explicit adoption of creeds.[2] The popular notion of the 'climate of opinion' at any rate points towards a recognizable phenomenon in intellectual life, even if it leaves a lot of interesting questions unasked and unanswered.[3] Again, it can be said that it is an oversimplification to look at the political theorist as if what he provided was an exact timetable, a fully drawn blueprint for social and political amelioration. Not only is there a historical puzzle about what practical conclusions, if any, men have drawn from the social and political thinkers of their day, there is a prior intellectual puzzle, that of determining whether logic compels us to draw one conclusion rather than another. The great diversity of interpretations current in the academic discipline of 'traditional political theory' suggests that it rarely does so. Thus, the denial of a direct prescriptive influence is too easy an intellectual victory; the kind of influence which is shown not to exist is not the kind of influence anyone expected to find in the first place.

[2] Jenifer Hart, 'Nineteenth Century Social Reform: A Tory Interpretation of History', *Past & Present* no. 31 (1965), p. 45.
[3] R. K. Webb, 'Benthamites and Unitarians' (mimeo), p. 3. I am grateful to Professor Webb for permission to cite his paper here.

The notion of 'influence' must be elaborated in some more subtle way than this.

Without undertaking to settle the issue, I should say that I am sure we shall have to refine our ideas about the spread of intellectual influence as our knowledge of how ideas are diffused becomes more adequate in the light of historical research and sociological theory alike. But for my present purpose, this hardly matters. Nothing in what follows commits us to the view that political philosophies operate as direct and immediate causes of social change nor to the view that political philosophers who originate them stand behind the scenes with their hands on ghostly but none the less effective levers. All I take for granted is the banality that men in general act for reasons— usually declared, but often only to be extracted with difficulty from their actions—and hence that a large part of historical explanation is devoted to showing what kind of reasons people had for doing what they did, whether they were frustrated by events or not.[4] The relevance to the historian of the social and political theorists lies in the fact that to a large extent the reasons which men offer for their actions only make sense within some particular *Weltanschauung*, some conceptualization of the world within which the agent is situated.[5] This is not to deny that people with a great variety of practical views may share the same conceptual scheme and it is not to deny that people with radically different conceptual schemes may well agree about what to do in practice. None the less, our descriptions of the facts, and our assessments of what these imply for our actions, rest on our acceptance of what in other contexts has been called a 'paradigm';[6] to elucidate what kinds of problem a given paradigm will make visible and what it will tend to hide is thus a contribution to the historical understanding of what men have and have not achieved.

[4] Cf. P. G. Winch, *The Idea of a Social Science* (London, 1958), ch. II and W. Dray, *Laws and Explanation in History* (Oxford, 1957), ch. V.
[5] A. Schutz, 'The Phenomenology of the Social World' in M. Natanson, ed., *Philosophy of the Social Sciences* (N.Y., 1963), pp. 183 ff.
[6] T. S. Kuhn, *The Structure of Scientific Revolutions* (Chicago, 1962), and cf. S. S. Wolin, 'Political Theory and Paradigms' in P. King and B. C. Parekh, eds, *Politics and Experience* (Cambridge, 1968), pp. 125–52.

To descend from the theory to the instance, I must say a few words about the case of nineteenth-century administrative reform in particular. At this level of specificity, the obvious question is: To what extent can we explain the changes in the organization, recruitment and functions of the English bureaucracy as the result of deliberate planning by ideologically sophisticated reformers? One recently popular answer is, to no extent at all.[7] There are two distinct strands in what, following MacDonagh, we may call the 'anti-ideational' case. The first is a plainly empirical argument to the effect that changes in the range of tasks performed by government and in the machinery by which these tasks were performed took place according to no plan whatever. The process was one of incoherently responding to the felt pressure of events—abuses were discovered, were felt to be 'intolerable', were remedied ineffectively, then tackled more effectively; the social and political effects of all this were cumulative, and none too clearly perceived, although they were such as to move English society in the 'collectivist' direction that Dicey described.[8] But this was essentially a process which no-one foresaw and which no-one involved in it would have supported had he understood it to be in train. On this argument I have only two comments. The first is that it *is* essentially a factual matter how the various areas of bureaucratic regulation came to grow and thus that it is a matter which awaits resolution by empirical investigation. The second is that it follows from this that we cannot *a priori* show MacDonagh's account, when it is generalized to provide a 'model', to be any more plausible than what would be my own guess—that different departments probably had very different histories.[9] The tone, rather than the content, of MacDonagh's 1958 article leads me to suspect that he subscribes to some more general philosophy of history which plays down the role of ideas in the causation of events. But in the absence of any explicit and argued statement of this philosophy and the grounds on which it rests, I cannot judge whether it would rule

[7] O. O. G. M. MacDonagh, 'The Nineteenth Century Revolution in Government: A Reappraisal', in *Historical Journal* I (1958), pp. 52–67.
[8] A. V. Dicey, *Lectures on the Relation between Law and Public Opinion in England during the Nineteenth Century*.
[9] Hart, *loc. cit.*, p. 41.

out influences of the kind I hope to elucidate below or not. The second aspect of the anti-ideational case presents no problem, for it is the claim that, no matter what the actual processes, they were not inspired by utilitarian aims and ideals, and that these latter had no great part in bringing about administrative reform. To regard the series of nineteenth-century reforms as Benthamite is to ignore the facts—they were neither inspired by Bentham and his followers nor did they proceed in accordance with their hopes.[10] On this issue, my conclusions hereafter will be mostly negative. I am inclined to think that there was no such thing as *the* utilitarian view on administrative reform, no such thing as *the* utilitarian view of the proper role of government and the best mode of its fulfilling that role—any more, I suspect, than there was any such thing as *the* non-conformist view or *the* evangelical view. Rather, what was involved in accepting a utilitarian view of social and political life was the acceptance of a theoretical framework within which certain ways of describing and explaining social and political matters got to the heart of them; it did not involve the possession of answers to problems of social and political practice so much as the assurance that certain ways of posing these problems was the right way of posing them. Where there were answers to be had, it involved the belief that certain reasons for thinking them to be answers were, in principle, good reasons.[11] But, it is plain enough that many of the assumptions of utilitarianism were up to a point at home in other ways of perceiving the world—for example, in unitarianism after Priestley[12]—a fact which must then have rendered communication as much easier as it now renders the ascription of influence more difficult. And, a final *caveat*, at the level of biographical adequacy, we must remember that all of us are subject to the influence of more ways than one of looking at the world, so that among the ideas to be found in the minds of secular utilitarians there will be ideas that come from other, quite foreign sources—foreign, that is, to the calculus of pleasure and pain. In this respect, as in others, John Stuart Mill has an obvious claim on our attention.

---

10 MacDonagh, *loc. cit.*, pp. 65 f.
11 Kuhn, *op. cit.*, chs IV, V.
12 Webb, *loc. cit.*, pp. 6–8.

The goal of this essay then is the examination of Mill's views on the civil service, its role, its mode of recruitment and so on, in order to assemble a tolerably clear picture of the kinds of difficulty that confront the utilitarian theorist of politics. Mill's writings are readily accessible, both those which stem from his work as a senior civil servant in the East India Company and those which are represented by the more theoretical works such as *Representative Government*. In addition, when Sir Charles Trevelyan was canvassing support for his proposals, Mill wrote him a letter which Trevelyan described as 'the best we have received'.[13] It is in fact a document in which the twin personae of administrator and theorist are strikingly united. For our present purposes, Mill's views have several aspects of some interest. As all the world knows, he was a man whose mind had supposedly been made for him by a utilitarian education amounting to indoctrination, but who spent his life deliberately exposing himself to influences of which his mentors would often have disapproved.[14] Mill's views thus show us how utilitarian doctrines could be strengthened and weakened by influences from such unlikely sources as Coleridge's romantic conservatism, Saint-Simon's managerial positivism, and the continental liberalism of von Humboldt and de Tocqueville. Again, Mill was a man both of the study and the office, and while this in no way lessens the primacy of his intellectual achievements, it does mean that when he talks about government he speaks from thirty years' experience of earning his living as an administrator. In the *System of Logic*, Mill defended his father against the charge of being an impractical doctrinaire by pointing out how extremely practical his father had been when involved in the world of everyday business.[15] And the same claim could be made on behalf of the son. Indeed, anyone who thinks that a concern for the theoretical foundations of politics is necessarily a disqualification for practical life would do well to think hard about the more than adequate services rendered to the East India Company by James and J. S. Mill.

In drawing on the evidence of Mill's work at East India

[13] *The Mill/Taylor Collection*, (MSS. letters), British Library of Political and Economic Science, vol. I, nos 27 & 28.
[14] J. S. Mill, *Autobiography* (N.Y., 1956), pp. 113 ff.
[15] *A System of Logic* (8th ed. London, 1906, n.i. 1961), VI, viii, 3.

House, we ought to bear in mind the importance of India in the context of the nineteenth-century administrative reformation. Merely at the level of personalities, several notable reformers served the government of India, among them Trevelyan himself. More importantly, the need to govern India brought to light some characteristic dilemmas facing nineteenth-century thinking about politics. It raised the question of democratic versus paternalistic government, the merits of a noisy public opinion as opposed to those of a silent expertise; it raised the problem of whether governments should aim at conserving the existing social fabric or whether they should try to innovate and bend their efforts towards the rationalization of institutions.[16] And a variation on the theme permanently to be heard in nineteenth-century English arguments about education occurs in the debate over Indian education too—how much ought the lower orders (or natives) to be educated, and in what kinds of subject? When Mill gave evidence to Trevelyan he was emphatic that civil-service reform should provide a stimulus to national education—an aim shared with Jowett, Vaughan and others.[17] Professor Hughes long ago dismissed this as 'a quite irrelevant educational emphasis',[18] but nothing could be farther from the truth. For it was about issues of this sort that there clustered many of the most basic political differences separating utilitarians from non-utilitarians—utilitarian arguments of a rationalizing kind concerning the need for accurate information when making decisions confronted non-utilitarian, often anti-rationalistic, arguments about the benefits to be had from a wider, more emotionally supportive 'culture'; and such arguments both at home and in India mingled with arguments about whether to stamp Western 'scientific' learning on an alien culture, or whether to try to fuse it with the rich, but superstition-riddled native product.[19]

The East India Company's government of India originated

[16] E. Stokes, *The English Utilitarians and India* (Oxford, 1959), ch. 1.
[17] P. P. 1854-5, XX, *Report and Papers relating to the Re-organisation of the Civil Service, Papers* pp. 87-98 (Mill and Vaughan) and *Report*, pp. 24-31 (Jowett).
[18] E. Hughes, 'Sir Charles Trevelyan and Civil Service Reform 1853-5', pt. 1, in *English Historical Review* LXIV (1949), p. 62.
[19] Stokes, *op. cit.*, pp. 13-16 and chs 1-3 generally.

not only the name of 'civil servant'—distinguishing those of the Company's servants in its civilian employment from those who served in its armed forces—but also many of the practices of efficient bureaucratic government as well. Thus, to take a minor aspect of the matter, when Mill came to describe the working of the Company[20] he drew attention to its control over its records. The government of India was necessarily and essentially a 'government of record'[21] in the sense that it was clearly impossible to exercise detailed control over the decisions made in India, but that much of the effect of doing so could be achieved if every decision was recorded, its grounds noted, and comments on it sent back. Thus the Company obliged every one of its servants to record his decisions and to send a copy of the record to London where it was duly filed. Naturally, this raised questions about the vast army of clerks and the huge mountains of paper that such a system would seem to require. But Mill's reply was that the material was indexed with great accuracy, so that all files were immediately on hand; present-day enthusiasts for systems of instantaneous data retrieval will understand Mill's pride in his system, though no doubt we all regret the other factor which Mill cited on behalf of it—the cheapness of copying done by native labour. Still, a concern for filing systems, though certainly utilitarian enough, could hardly warrant our interest in the East India Company's dealings with utilitarianism. The more substantial question which the careers of both father and son raise is that of how essential it is to good government that it should also be self-government—obviously a central issue in colonial administration. On the matter of whether good government could be provided other than by the people themselves, the two Mills stood in rather different positions. Indeed, there is a tension in utilitarian thought generally as to whether government *for* the people entails government *by* the people. One of the ways in which Bentham and James Mill stood outside the mainstream of liberalism is that they both believed that so long as government operates for the benefit of the governed, their actual participation in their own government is immaterial. In the case of Britain, they both came to

[20] To House of Lords Select Committee, June 1852 (P.P. 1852-3, XXX, pp. 300-32).
[21] *Loc. cit.*, p. 301.

believe that only a government controlled by the people would govern in the general interest and not in some 'sinister interest'. And in Bentham's case, the conversion to democracy was slow and incomplete.[22] But, so far as India was concerned, there was no place for the arguments relevant to Britain. The ordinary objection to foreign rule over a native population was that the foreigners would exploit and plunder the natives and quite fail to attend to their interests. But the case was vastly different with the East India Company's dealings with the native population of India. Even before James Mill had joined the Company, he had written of it in his famous *History*:[23]

> in the highly important point of the servants or subordinate agents of government, there is nothing in the world to be compared with the East India Company, whose servants as a body, have not only exhibited a portion of talent which forms a contrast with that of the ill-chosen instruments of other governments, but have . . . maintained a virtue which, under the temptations of their situation is worthy of the highest applause.

The virtues of the Company were placed in high relief by contrast with the corruption, ignorance, inefficiency and superstition which permeated native rule in India; and as between efficient government by foreigners and inefficient government by natives, utility could only decide one way. Self-rule—and hence the valuing of democracy or some form of Home Rule above no matter how efficient an administration—was alien to the temperament of the theorist and the logic of the theory alike. For James Mill, who saw in government few questions other than those of cheapness, orderliness and effectiveness, the despotism of Britain over Asia was no temporary staging post on the way to some other form of association.[24] But for J. S. Mill, the stage of despotic government can only be justified if it really is a stage on the way to self-rule and independence.[25] The relationship between despotic rulers and their despotically governed subjects is only morally tolerable on what amounts to

[22] S. R. Letwin, *The Pursuit of Certainty* (Cambridge, 1965), ch. XII.
[23] *History of British India* (London, 1856), VI, p. 13.
[24] Stokes, *op. cit.*, p. 64.
[25] *Liberty* (Everyman Edition, n.d.), pp. 73-4.

an educational basis—that the despot is the teacher and the subjects are genuinely instructed; and for examples of such relationships Mill cites Peter the Great and Queen Elizabeth.[26] In the well-known passage of *Liberty* which discusses this issue, he says: 'Despotism is a legitimate mode of government in dealing with barbarians, provided the end be their improvement, and the means justified by actually effecting that end.'[27] We may recoil somewhat from the readiness with which nineteenth-century Englishmen equated the richness of Indian culture with barbarism as much as from the readiness with which they believed that what England had to offer was unequivocally progress; but the argument is not illiberal. Even though any particular claimant was often in danger of seeing the argument used as a *reductio ad absurdum* against him, it was a commonplace among writers from Aristotle to Locke that despotism was warranted where there was a sufficiently clear superiority of ruler over ruled.[28] And Mill certainly improved on the racialist assumptions of intrinsic superiority which became common after his death in emphasizing that what the English possessed they could pass on to the natives of India. In India, he observed a more acute version of what was to some extent visible in England as well—a population which, while perfectly capable of improvement, did not know its own interests through ignorance, and therefore needed advice, information and leadership.

What was significant about India was that the tension inherent in utilitarian thought, when it came to analyse the relative importance of the politics of self-government versus the honesty of administration, was there resolvable in only one way. In India there was no room for the kind of problem which besets the politician under parliamentary arrangements—no need to gain popular support, no manœuvring for votes, no conciliating public opinion. The only problems were those which faced benevolent and enlightened administrators. This is important for a central but not very much discussed reason. Because utilitarian ethics aim at maximizing the sum total of happiness, there is a strong current in the theory which exalts good management as the greatest of skills. Maximizing happi-

[26] *Logic* VI, viii, 3.   [27] *Liberty*, p. 73.
[28] M. Seliger, *The Liberal Politics of John Locke* (London, 1968), pp. 241 ff., 262 f.

ness is a task which calls for organization and methodical administration; hence there is a tendency to look forward to a time when interests need not be conciliated and the political virtues will be summed up by beneficent legislation and the correct administration of the law. Yet, of course, utilitarianism is equally an ethical system predicated upon a view of human nature which assumes conflicts of aims and a continual competition for benefits, so that the problems of ethics are problems of conciliating and adjudicating these conflicting claims.[29] On this view, the best kind of politics must surely be the politics of free competition where all interests can express themselves, strike bargains and rally support. But in India this dilemma could make no impact since there were none of what would now be called the 'functional pre-requisites' of this kind of politics; thus the government of India could become, both in utilitarian theory and to a large extent in East India Company practice, a question of good management. It is thus no wonder that Mill was so concerned to stress the Company's managerial efficiency, both to the Select Committee in 1852 and in the *Memorandum* of 1858.[30] Such efficiency was to a large extent the Company's *raison d'être*. But this efficiency and the probity claimed for the behaviour of the Company's servants is at odds with what utilitarian theory leads us to expect from unchecked governments; the whole point of the utilitarian advocacy of representative democracy was the underlying assumption that unless some check could be exercised by the ruled upon those who ruled them, there would be no hope of curbing the standing inclination of all governors to rule in their own rather than their subjects' interests.[31] Short of taking the standard way out— ascribing the puzzle to Mill's notorious inconsistency—we should expect a man of Mill's intelligence to have given the matter some thought. And indeed, Mill provides a rather coherent explanation of the unlikely state of affairs—an explanation directly relevant to the efforts made by Trevelyan and others to remove patronage from the English civil service.

Although Mill's most interesting explanation of the merits of

[29] James Mill, *Essay on Government* (Cambridge, 1937), p. 3 f.
[30] P.P. 1857–8, XLIII, *Memorandum . . . of the Improvements in the Administration of India during the last Thirty Years.*
[31] *Essay on Government*, pp. 6–7, 13.

Company government relates to his concern for the antagonism of opinion, and is therefore discussed below, he certainly attached great importance to the way in which the Company's methods of recruitment and training avoided the characteristic evils of patronage. Although appointments in the Company were matters of patronage, what Mill claimed was that the evils of such a system were so far as possible absent.[32] One can hardly do better than quote his own summary of the causes of this happy state: 'Among the first of these seems to me to be, that those who are sent to administer the affairs of India are not sent to any particular appointment; they go out merely as candidates; they go out when young, and go through the necessary course of preparation in subordinate functions before they can arrive at the higher ones.'[33] Mill explained that candidates spent an initial period in India simply learning the routines of the office, before they were called on by senior officials to fill some particular vacancy. It is a practice still recommended. The other great merit that Mill saw in the system was that those who made the appointments in India had no interest in considerations other than having the duties performed efficiently by those who were appointed to them; from a variety of causes, among them the rotation of Directors of the Company, there was little need for them to consider how to satisfy some young man's patron.[34]

> A second great advantage of the present system is, that those who are sent out as candidates to rise by degrees are generally unconnected with the influential classes in the country, and out of the range of Parliamentary influence. The consequence is, that those who have the disposal of offices in India have little or no motive to put unfit persons into important situations, or to permit unjustifiable acts to be done by them.

The Select Committee's questioning suggests that Mill may have been exaggerating the absence of patronage, but his replies to their other questions certainly show his hostility to patronage and to the social assumptions surrounding it. It was, of course, impossible to claim that entry to the Company's service was open, so long as aspirants had to go through Haileybury, and

[32] P.P. 1852–3, XXX, p. 303.   [33] *Ibid.*, p. 303.   [34] *Ibid.*, p. 303.

had to obtain the recommendation of a Director to attend the College. But Mill was more than ready to agree that attendance at the College ought not to be a precondition of service.[35] And when asked how he would dispose of the patronage of the Company, if it were to be removed from the hands of the Directors, he replied: 'I think in that case the only proper system, and one which I should myself consider as intrinsically the best would be to bestow it by public competition, by *concours*, as some offices are given in France; to give it to the best qualified among all persons of requisite age and education who might compete for it.'[36] That this entailed opening the service to persons from any social background Mill freely admitted; the Committee asked: 'When you speak of competition, do you mean a bona fide public competition, open to all the world, or would you require any particular qualifications or previous course of education on the part of the candidates?' Mill's reply was: 'I would admit persons to compete in whatever manner they had been educated, and at whatever place.' (Qu. 3,095) 'And in whatever condition of life they might be? And in whatever condition of life.'[37] That Mill meant exactly what he said emerged during two further exchanges with the Committee, in one of which he put forward his view that the elevation of the native population to self-rule was part of the object of the Company's government: 'in proportion as the natives become trustworthy and qualified for high office, it seems to me not only allowable, but a duty to appoint them to it.' (Qu. 3,119) 'Do you think that in those circumstances, the dependence of India on this country could be maintained? I think it might, by judicious management, be made to continue till the time arises when the natives shall be qualified to carry on the same system of Government without our assistance.'[38] The other occasion was less significant perhaps, but it casts an amusing light on the social implications of Mill's radicalism, and in the light of recent debates about the extent to which middle-class pressure for reform was a movement designed to secure employment for middle-class children, it at any rate shows up some less utilitarian motives on the part of the defenders of the *status quo*. (Qu. 2,948) 'Is it not a curious circumstance that the son of a

[35] *Ibid.*, p. 331.   [36] *Ibid.*, p. 321.
[37] *Ibid.*, p. 322.   [38] *Ibid.*, p. 325.

horse-dealer should be sent to India as a cadet? The son of a
horse-dealer is as likely to qualify himself in the subordinate
positions for succeeding to the higher as the son of anyone
else.' (Qu. 2,949) 'But that is not exactly the class from which
you would select persons to be the companions of gentlemen
who are to fill honourable positions? It is not the class from
which writers or cadets are generally selected; but I see no
reason why such persons should be excluded.'[39] Throughout his
life Mill was unwilling to make any concession at all either to
snobbery or to silly fears about the 'tone of society'. As we shall
see below, his letter to Trevelyan defends precisely the attitude
which his replies to the Select Committee evidenced in 1852.

Before we turn to the final flurry of Mill's career, when he
defended the Company against the government's plans for its
dissolution in 1858, there is one further matter on which the
Company's activities shed some light. This is the problem of
why utilitarians were so ready to defend its administrative
activities, if they were, as Dicey believed, enthusiasts for an
individualist and laissez-faire creed. The problem has been more
or less effectively dissolved by Dr Parris's re-examination of
Dicey's views;[40] but it is worth stressing the difference between
a doctrine which is as a matter of logic both atomistic and
mechanistic and one which supports either a romantic or a
rugged individualism. So far as the *logic* of utilitarianism goes,
the only questions we can ask about private versus public
initiative are questions of relative cost and efficiency. There is
no reason to suppose that the earlier utilitarians recoiled from
the public provision of any particular good for any reason other
than their belief that it would be wasteful; and certainly there
is in Bentham none of that enthusiasm for individual liberty
which is so characteristic a feature of the writings of J. S.
Mill.[41] Much the strongest objection to public enterprise seems
to have stemmed from hostility to the aristocratic incumbents
of governmental positions who could be calculated to turn the
public service into a series of jobs for their friends. The creation

[39] P.P. 1852–3, XXX, p. 305.
[40] H. Parris, 'The Nineteenth Century Revolution in Government:
A Reappraisal Reappraised', *Historical Journal* III (1960), pp. 19 ff.
[41] G. Himmelfarb, *Victorian Minds* (London, 1968), pp. 32–81, 'The
Haunted House of Jeremy Bentham'.

of an honest and patronage-free bureaucracy would in principle have gone a long way towards meeting the objection. And even this leaves out one characteristically nineteenth-century note, the concern for *improvement*; although governments might in general be less efficient than private enterprise in providing goods and services, they could still play a valuable role in initiating improvement by supplying goods and services of the right kind to a society whose state of civilization was too low for them to be provided unaided. Schools and communications are two very obvious examples—especially obvious in the context of India. Moreover the example of India illustrates two of this paper's contentions quite neatly. James Mill had been a firm believer in improvement, and what he wanted to see was improvement on a broad front, for it extended to the intelligence, probity and diligence of the Indian population that he had characterized so unkindly.[42] And, unsurprisingly in view of what we said earlier, much of this improvement coincided with the spiritual regeneration planned by the evangelicals for the superstitious Hindus.[43] But we can also see the areas of similarity and dissimilarity in earlier and later utilitarianism here. For J. S. Mill also shared the belief that among the benefits to be sought were the moral and mental improvement of the subject population; he also called that population by some pretty unflattering names; and sometimes his conception of improvement seems no wider than his father's—as when he claims the transformation of the Thuggees into useful tent-makers as one of the striking achievements of the East India Company's rule.[44] But in that *Memorandum* where there are listed 'some of the most important achievements of a Government of which perpetual striving towards improvement is the vital principle',[45] there is more than an echo of the doctrine of *Representative Government*, that progressiveness is the mark of a good form of government and that progressiveness is a great deal more than efficiency and orderliness. James Mill would have been satisfied when the Indians had learned businesslike habits, J. S. Mill only when they had reached the point at which they would spontaneously have begun to develop their own capacities for themselves.

[42] Stokes, *op. cit.*, pp. 52–8.   [43] *Ibid.*, pp. 47–8.
[44] P.P. 1857–8, XLIII, *Memorandum*, p. 17.   [45] *Ibid.*, p. 35.

Mill's career at East India House was mostly uneventful. W. T. Thornton's brief memoir of his chief[46] is mostly devoted to personal reminiscence, including the appalling story of the— incidentally hideously ugly—inkstand which his assistants vainly tried to present to Mill on his retirement. And Professor Stokes spends more time on justifying his own comparative neglect of Mill's career than on that career itself.[47] He says, rightly enough, that Mill's interests were much wider than those which the job involved and that he was in any case not inclined either intellectually or temperamentally to lay down the law in the way his father had done. It was also true that the internal reorganization of the Company had done much to lessen the influence which had been exercised through the Examiner's office in the heyday of James Mill's tenure there. The Company's commercial functions had been taken away from it in 1833 and it was thereafter exclusively concerned with the task of governing the Indian empire; accordingly, Directors took a much more intense and continuous interest in the details of decision-making, so that it was no longer possible to commit them to policies in the way James Mill had managed to do.[48] None the less, at the very end of Mill's career, there was a brief period when he swung all the weight of an office described as 'equal in importance if not in dignity to that of a Secretary of State'[49] against the proposed Government of India Bill. This defence of the Company produced a number of documents, including four pamphlets published by the Company[50] and the *Petition* with its biting opening antitheses:[51]

[46] *Examiner*, May 1873.
[47] *Loc. cit.*, pp. 49–50.
[48] P.P. 1852–3, XXX, Mill's evidence, p. 316.
[49] *Examiner*, May 1873.
[50] The pamphlets were all published by William Penny, London, during 1858; they are anonymous, but Mill's own bibliography of his published writings lists them as his work. I should like to express my gratitude to Mr Martin Moir of the India Office Records for his help in finding these pamphlets and various other East India Company tracts. The pamphlets are: *A Constitutional View of the India Question; Practical Observations on the First Two of the Proposed Resolutions on the Government of India; A President in Council the Best Government for India; The Moral of the India Debate.*
[51] *Hansard*, 3rd series, CXLVIII Appendix, *Petition of the East India Company* (presented to Earl Grey in the Lords, 11 Feb. 1858), col. 1.

your Petitioners, at their own expense, and by the agency
of their own civil and military servants originally acquired
for this country its magnificent empire in the East . . . the
foundations of this Empire were laid by your Petitioners,
at that time neither aided nor controlled by Parliament, at
the same period when a succession of administrations under
the control of Parliament were losing to the Crown of Great
Britain another great Empire on the opposite side of the
Atlantic.

The interest of all these sources for our present purposes is that
they all reiterate the same argument about the causes of good
government in India, and almost as importantly, the same
doubts about the absence of proper checks to misgovernment
under the new proposals. Mill never tired of expressing his
belief that good government relied on the expression of a variety
of opinions; questions had to be looked at from several angles
rather than one, expert advice had to be sought, public opinion
had to be heard, and obstacles had to be erected in the way of
folly and wickedness. In Britain it was public discussion that
acted as the great check against misgovernment; but in the case
of India 'the only means of ensuring the necessary discussion
and collision of opinions is provided for within the governing
body itself'.[52] This was achieved primarily through the division
of authority between a Board of Control and the Court of
Directors, the former answerable in the end to parliament, the
latter representing the continuing administration of the country
and independent of parliament's good and ill will.[53] The ability
of the Court to initiate policy, subject to being overridden by
the President of the Board of Control, meant that knowledge
and political accountability struck a rarely achieved balance;
this, of course, has wider implications for the role of the civil
servant in relation to his politically appointed ministerial
master, implications which Mill draws both in *Representative
Government* and elsewhere. Thus, the *Petition* comments on the
new proposals: 'To believe that the administration of India
would have been more free from error had it been conducted by

[52] P.P. 1852–3, XXX, p. 313.
[53] *Hansard*, 3rd series, CXLVIII, *Petition*, col. 2.

a Minister of the Crown without the aid of the Court of Directors, would be to believe that the Minister, with full power to govern India as he pleased, has governed ill, because he has had the assistance of experienced and responsible advisers.'[54] Mill's emphatic insistence on the need for the expertise of skilled and experienced administrators was further supported by his distrust of what political accountability was likely to amount to in practice; questions about the welfare of India would become weapons in the party competition for office, with the result that concern for the interests of India or the security of Indian government would 'be secondary to the one important question, whether one man, or another much the same as he, shall sit for a while on the Treasury bench'.[55] The contemporary doubt whether politically appointed ministers with little prior knowledge and short tenure in a department are in any condition to head their offices successfully was certainly shared by Mill.[56] But Mill's real scorn was directed at the proposal that the new President of the Board of Control should govern India through a Council chosen by himself. Mill's objection amounts in essence to the argument that a man who chooses his own advisers thereby chooses the advice he receives, and that advice so chosen is not advice at all, but a prop to some pre-existing prejudice. The absence of independent voices is described as 'the most fatal blow which could be struck against good government in that country',[57] while the power of the President to ignore his Council without giving reasons or allowing for appeal was characterized thus: 'your Petitioners cannot well conceive a worse form of government for India than a minister with a council whom he should be at liberty to consult or not at his pleasure, or whose advice he should be able to disregard without giving his reasons in writing, and in a manner likely to carry conviction . . . any body of persons connected with the minister which is not a check, will be a screen.'[58]

Mill did not claim that the good results which he ascribed to the current arrangements owed much to deliberate con-

---

[54] *Hansard*, 3rd series, CXLVIII, *Petition*. col. 3.
[55] *The Moral of the India Debate*, p. 3.
[56] *Representative Government* (Everyman Edition, n.d.), pp. 333–4.
[57] P.P. 1857–8, XLIII, p. 43.
[58] *Petition*.

trivance; what he argued was that since the system worked as well as it did, it ought only to be replaced by a form of government which contained similar provisions for constitutional checks and for independent advice that could not be ignored or overridden in silence. In *Representative Government* he reiterated his gloomy view of the new arrangements.[59] Now, anyone sceptical of the influence of ideas upon the course of events will be quick to remind me that even the ambivalent and qualified attitudes which I have ascribed to Mill failed to get a hearing in 1858, since Mill and the Company were on the losing side; and we have little or no evidence of what effects Mill's criticisms had on the subsequent activities of the government of India. This is true enough, and I should not wish to make any extravagant claims on Mill's behalf. Rather, I should see his influence as one stream of thought which contributed to the increasingly important view of the civil servant as to a large extent his own master, a view which stressed the qualities which he brought to his work that were largely lacking in his political masters—the men Mill described as 'exciting the mirth of their inferiors by the air with which they announced as a truth hitherto set at nought and brought to light by themselves, something which was probably the first thought of everybody who had ever looked at the subject, given up as soon as he had got on to a second'.[60] This belief in expertise, in the independent opinion, and this faith in the man who can press a view of his own without fear or hope for his own position, are all to be found in writers other than Mill and in other utilitarians too. The really distinctive overtones in Mill's account are those which come from his suggestion that administrators should contribute in their way to the wider culture of their society, and these are to be found in *Representative Government* and his occasional essays. For all that, Mill's service in the East India Company served to strengthen rather than weaken these convictions.

Mill's only public pronouncement on the subject of civil service reform was the letter to Trevelyan alluded to earlier. Assessing its importance is complicated by two factors. The first is that the fact| that Trevelyan was very obviously canvassing support—even if he sometimes failed to get it when he expected

[59] *Representative Government*, pp. 334-5.   [60] *Ibid.*, p. 232.

it[61]—might be thought to make it harder to guess whether Mill had unspoken reservations about the proposed changes. It is doubtful whether he did, both because he was extremely harsh on Jowett's proposals about testimonials[62] and because he was at that time in a particularly uncompromising frame of mind following his marriage to Harriet Taylor.[63] The other doubt is raised by Packe's claim that Mill only roused himself to write the letter for the sake of Harriet.[64] So consistent is the letter with everything Mill said on related topics, however, that there is no reason to suspect it reflects anything other than long and firmly held opinions. Mill was enthusiasm itself so far as the proposal to open the civil service to examination went: 'The proposal to select candidates for the Civil Service of Government appears to me to be one of those great public improvements, the adoption of which would form an era in history. The effects which it is calculated to produce in raising the character both of the public administration and the people can scarcely be over-estimated.'[65] But Mill's support of the measure contains several elements which are not run-of-the-mill arguments for efficiency, and it is on these that we ought to concentrate. Mill was quite happy to accept Stephen's charge that what Trevelyan was doing was creating 'statesmen in disguise'.[66] We have already seen how concerned Mill had been to secure the independence and authority of those who administered India. Here he supported Trevelyan's concern that 'the most experienced officers of a department ought not to be so engrossed in disposing of the current business as to have neither time nor strength to attend to the general objects concerned with their respective duties'.[67] Consequently, Mill supported the distinction that Trevelyan drew between the mechanical tasks of the clerks and the genuinely intellectual administrative work. Indeed, as compared with the proposals advanced, Mill's only

[61] P.P. 1854–5, XX, *Papers*; the evidence of Stephen, Cornewall Lewis and Booth among others.
[62] *Ibid.*, p. 95.
[63] M. St. J. Packe, *The Life of John Stuart Mill* (London, 1954), pp. 349–57.
[64] *Ibid.*, p. 368.
[65] P.P. 1854–5, XX, *Papers*, p. 92.
[66] *Ibid.*, p. 76.
[67] Quoted by Hughes, *loc. cit.*, p. 56.

strictures were on the requirement of testimonials where he attacked the 'terrible principle brought in by the truly inquisitor-like proceedings recommended by Mr Jowett'.[68] Jowett was quick to withdraw the implications Mill had seen: 'I should object as strongly as Mr Mill to the proposals contained in the paper relating to the examinations, if I understood them as he does.'[69] Mill's spikiness may well have owed a lot to the horrors surrounding his recent marriage; but it probably owed something to his usual radicalism and dislike of social distinctions of the kind that the apparatus of testimonials from clergymen or tutors would have tended to preserve. For one thing that was quite clear to Mill was that no consideration of social class ought to stand in the way of recruitment by merit. He dealt with the usual objections to open admission very curtly:[70]

> Another objection is, that if appointments are given to talent, the Public Offices will be filled with low people, without the breeding or the feelings of gentlemen. If, as this objection supposes, the sons of gentlemen cannot be expected to have as much ability and instruction as the sons of low people, it would make a strong case for social changes of a more extensive character . . . If, with advantages and opportunities so vastly superior, the youth of the higher classes have not honour enough, or energy enough, or public spirit enough, to make themselves as well qualified as others for the station which they desire to maintain, they are not fit for that station, and cannot too soon step out of it and give place to better people.

Mill's characteristic contribution was his stress on the measure's educational impact, on the 'extraordinary stimulus which would be given to mental cultivation by the effect of the national recognition of it as the exclusive title to participation in so large and conspicuous a portion of the national affairs'.[71] In this, of course, Mill differed from someone such as Chadwick, whose concern was much more straightforwardly for efficiency

[68] P.P. 1854-5, XX, *Papers*, p. 95.
[69] *Ibid.*, p. 96n.   [70] *Ibid.*, p. 94.
[71] *Ibid.*, p. 92.

and honesty even if it was combined with a traditional animus against the aristocratic connection. Mill hoped for results at two different levels. The first was in the universities where he joined forces with Jowett in supporting the reform of government as a step towards reforming the universities. In Mill's view, the universities were national endowments which had for centuries failed to serve any national purpose, but had rather served to cement the alliance between a particular religion and a particular social class in the interests only of unjust privilege. If the English civil service was to be opened to unrestricted competition, there would be more room in public service for the first-rate man, and the universities would have more incentive to turn out first-rate men. Mill seemed unmoved by Stephen's belief that first-class men would be much too good for the jobs they were called on to perform—that it was a matter of putting a racehorse between the shafts of the brewer's dray. Obviously, there was a clash of principle here, with Stephen thinking of civil servants as little more than clerks, where Mill envisaged a much more independent and demanding role for them. Mill foresaw a process of reinforcement whereby more demanding work would call forth a better class of person to perform it. There is, too, a non-utilitarian streak to be observed in all this. In his early twenties, Mill had begun to absorb Coleridge's ideas about the 'clerisy', the class of enlightened leaders in moral and intellectual matters. Three dissimilar streams converged here. There was the old utilitarian belief in an education which amounted to something near a benevolent indoctrination; there was Mill's more emotional response to Coleridge's emphasis on tradition and culture and the need for a class of persons who could be the repositories of that culture; and there was the historical analysis supplied by the Saint-Simonians, who saw society as being in a 'critical' or what we might now call an anomic condition and who looked to an élite which could use its authority to re-create an organic unity. The universities, were they to perform their true functions, would produce many of the members of this clerisy. We might say that Mill almost reverses the switch of meaning between the medieval and the modern usage of the term 'clerk' when he assigns some of the functions of the clerisy to the higher civil servant. The only immediate moral I wish to draw from the varied sources of

Mill's ideas is that it reinforces the point made at the very outset concerning the complexity of anything which we might want to call the utilitarian view of the social and political world. Later, I shall call on this evidence in saying something about the relationship between Mill's concern for progress and his views on bureaucracy.

The other aspect of Mill's concern for education focused on a lower level of attainment. In our concern with the development of the 'administrative' class in the English civil service, it is all too easy to forget that the Northcote–Trevelyan Report anticipated that examination criteria would be applied to all civil-service posts—presumably in much the way that they are applied to those posts in the civil services of the United States that are termed 'merit' or 'civil-service' posts as distinct from those filled by election or patronage. Mill was not one of those who poured scorn on the idea of examining tidewaiters, watermen, postmen and the like; an educated civil service might very well make more impact at that level, where everyone would be reminded of the paths open to a measure of intelligence and application. Many of Mill's opinions are hinted at when he writes: 'A man may not be a much better postman for being able to draw, or being acquainted with natural history; but he who in that rank possesses these acquirements has given evidence of qualities which it is important for the general cultivation of the mass that the State should take every fair opportunity to stamp with its approbation.'[72] Mill was always concerned with devices for diffusing education among the lower classes, and hence always anxious as here to support a measure which might increase the respect felt for education, and which might tend to raise the image of public service among those usually lacking in public spirit.[73]

One of the interesting things to emerge from the letters written to Trevelyan is how little the debate addressed itself to anything resembling the debate of recent years over the individualist and collectivist strains in government. There is little or no sign of antagonism between individualists and collectivists, and practically no general discussion of the merits and demerits of greater governmental intervention in social and economic life. Trevelyan alluded to the 'great and increasing

[72] *Ibid.*, p. 98.   [73] *Ibid.*, p. 92.

accumulation of public business'[74] very much as if it was a familiar part of the political landscape. The reforms were intended to handle this business more effectively, but there is no suggestion of a new role for government. We may, of course, argue that there were great changes in progress of which the actors were unaware; but if this is so, it does not suggest that we should look for any accompanying doctrinal change. Moreover, I should like to stress that the connection between thought and action is such that the fact that our actions are different provides no evidence that the justifying theory we hold has altered at all. The same physical theory explains why bricks fall just as readily as it explains why balloons do not; the same moral framework may enjoin interventionist policies at one time, and condemn them at another. One reason why utilitarianism is a *general* moral theory is precisely that it is not tied to particular injunctions such as hostility to the Corn Laws or a dislike of the aristocracy. Because it was a general theory, it allowed its adherents to frame arguments appropriate to new situations; but because it was a theory, these form more than a series of *ad hoc* responses. So, I want to conclude this paper by turning to *Representative Government*, not so much to show what are the utilitarian prescriptions for our ills, but more to show how these ills appear when they appear as ills to a utilitarian. To say it again, this is not 'the utilitarian theory of the state' that we are explicating, merely a few utilitarian dilemmas.

Although I have said, and stand by having said, that there was no such debate in progress as the debate between individualists and collectivists, there is one distinction worth introducing at this point that relates to the substance of that argument. Mill was aware of the danger of a benevolent oppression in democracy in a way which was foreign both to Bentham and James Mill, and almost as foreign to enthusiasts for spiritual community like T. H. Green. Mill was afraid of the stifling of individuality, a deadening of initiative, especially in moral and intellectual matters; and it was this fear of social oppression more than the fear of political oppression that dominated

[74] P.P. 1854–5, XX, *Report*, p. 3.

Liberty.[75] When discussing the matter in that essay, Mill drew
two different lines along which we might oppose governmental
interference. One ground for resisting is that the activity in
question is simply not the business of society at large—not, at
any rate, in the sense that society has any right to coerce people
into some particular line of conduct; the other ground is that
although the action does fall into the domain of public business,
the odds are that government, being clumsy and expensive, will
do more harm than good by intervening, at any rate coercively.[76]
These are very different kinds of objection, for the former is an
absolute moral prohibition on control and coercion, while the
latter is technical only. Mill, however, takes great care to leave
room for governments to act non-coercively, in collecting and
circulating information, offering advice and helping private
efforts—in other words, there is no antipathy to collective
action as such—except when it is collective coercion.[77] This
means that Mill's views to some extent cut across the usual line
of debate. For instance, he was emphatic that the state ought
to intervene very strenuously in making parents responsible for
the health, education and welfare of their children, but adamant
that neither government nor society at large was entitled to
enquire into the religious beliefs of teachers, members of parliament and so on. A propos of the usual arguments about collectivism, we ought, on this evidence, to be careful to distinguish
the libertarian argument about the undesirability of government
activity in some areas of a sacrosanct kind from the utilitarian
argument about probable ineffectiveness of government activity.
Mill, on this reading, was both more and less of a collectivist
than his father and Bentham had been—more in wanting
government to take a kind of cultural lead that they never
expected of it, but less in that he attached as they did not a
positive value to doing things for oneself wherever possible.
Strictly speaking, there is not much place in utilitarianism for
this sort of argument for the intrinsic merits of self-rule.[78] It
was a notion imported into utilitarianism from outside—Mill's

---

[75] *Op. cit.*, pp. 68–70, cf. Alan Ryan, *The Philosophy of John Stuart
Mill* (London, 1970), ch. XIII.
[76] *Ibid.*, p. 140.
[77] e.g. *ibid.*, pp. 159–63, so far as education is concerned.
[78] Stokes, *op. cit.*, p. 64.

sources being Coleridge's concern for self-culture and von Humboldt's enthusiasm for untrammelled self-expression.[79]

Now, one argument which bears on the above really does seem to have occupied Mill and Trevelyan alike, and this was the continuous nineteenth-century debate about aristocracy versus democracy. It is obvious enough that much nineteenth-century debate centred on the problems of admitting to governmental positions persons who were gentlemen neither in origin nor manner. Trevelyan's leanings towards aristocratic principles have been misrepresented,[80] but there is undeniably a concern for the aristocratic virtues in what he wrote. There are many issues here rather than one; some of them relate to matters of life-style, and whether the leisured and cultivated lives of the aristocracy were to be sacrificed to the perpetual pushing and scrambling that marked the existence of the urban middle class; others were issues of good management, issues which became particularly prominent when the Crimean War revealed the extent of maladministration in both the civilian and military services.[81] Some issues were raised in a spirit of pure moral indignation against the corruption and jobbery which marked aristocratic control; but some of the indignation could well have been synthetic, masking the fact that the opposition was less to the fact of jobbery than the particular distribution of its spoils.

The tension between democracy and aristocracy appears in utilitarian theory as an ambivalence about the role of expertise *vis-à-vis* public opinion and elected governments. There are good grounds for adopting *a* utilitarian view which resembles that offered in James Mill's *Essay on Government*, in which the expert simply decides on the most efficient way of realizing the will of the legislature. This omni-competent body makes its will known, and the only question is that of how to put its will into effect. With a sleight of hand that no-one has ever regarded as remotely convincing, James Mill equated the will of the electorate with the general interest—thus reducing the role of the expert in securing the general interest to a narrowly

[79] See e.g. the quotation from von Humboldt which stands at the beginning of *Liberty*, while the well-known essay 'Coleridge' does more than justice to the latter's influence.

[80] A. Briggs, *Victorian People* (London, 1954), pp. 117–18.

[81] *Ibid.*, pp. 68–72.

technical role. But when J. S. Mill came to write *Representative Government* he saw democracy in no such simple light. In his view, democracy was liable to stagnation, to dead and oppressive conformity, and thus unlikely to make the kind of progress which he saw as the end of good government. What the people wanted, and what they would have wanted, had they been wiser, could by no means be presumed to be the same thing; and Mill's mind was constantly drawn to ways in which democracy could be saved from itself and made to avail itself of superior talents. This preoccupation was displayed in Mill's addiction to proportional representation and a variety of fancy franchises.[82] But the activities of the civil service *vis-à-vis* the legislature provided another opportunity to serve the same ends. Mill's legislature was to be a debating body, not a legislating body;[83] after debating issues, it was to hand down instructions on matters of legislative importance, but it was not to try to draft legislation itself.[84] Drafting was a matter for expertise, and only a legislative commission could tackle the task properly. The legislature might approve or disapprove, or send back for alterations, but it was not to be allowed to amend. Permanent officials are thus given an elevated role, for they would have to go far beyond mere compliance with instructions if they were to translate necessarily general principles into the detail of legislation. It is, of course, true that concern with legislative ability is a continuing utilitarian trait, and one found even more in Bentham than in J. S. Mill—Bentham's major interest was always in the creation of a legal code and it was only towards the end of his life that he turned from the legal question of *how* legislation was to be framed to the political question of *who* was to frame it. But it is only in J. S. Mill that this concern is harnessed to the desire to use whatever means were available to pursue progress in the face of the dangers of democracy.

Clearly, Mill's approach presupposes a good deal of authority among the civil servants whose task it is to advise ministers in their work. Trevelyan, too, emphasized the need for men 'occupying a position duly subordinate to that of the Ministers who are directly responsible to the Crown and to Parliament, yet possessing sufficient independence, character, ability and

[82] *Representative Government*, pp. 260–7.
[83] *Ibid.*, pp. 235–9. [84] *Ibid.*, p. 237.

experience to be able to advise, assist, and to some extent influence those who are from time to time set over them'.[85] We have already seen Mill's scepticism about the newly arrived minister's capacity for business; and as a corrective he advocated setting up a ministerial cabinet—a thing often suggested since—which would guide and advise the minister. But, true to his standing concern for the antagonism of opinions, this was not to be a cabinet appointed by the minister himself, but a council of permanent independent advisers.[86] We need not recapitulate the arguments he employed in favour of such a device when defending the government of the East India Company, for he himself described the arrangements he had in mind as being very like those formerly obtaining in the government of India, arrangements which seemed 'destined to perish in the general holocaust which the traditions of Indian government seem fated to undergo, since they have been placed at the mercy of public ignorance, and the presumptuous vanity of political men'.[87] Throughout *Representative Government*, variations on this theme constantly recur; so much so that there is less need to dwell on them than on the fact that Mill was concerned to point the infirmities of the *best* form of government, and not to argue that some other would be better. Mill maintained that in spite of everything, representative democracy was the best form of government, even though it is perhaps more interesting for our purposes that the second-best governments were those aristocracies which had virtually been bureaucracies, such as the Venetian Republic. Even these were, taken overall, inferior to a well-constructed democracy; but as a rational being, he thought it folly not to try to obtain the advantages of other modes of government and to lessen the infirmities of the chosen mode.[88]

In all this, Mill's élitism was in tune with that of Trevelyan; but Mill perhaps went further in adhering to the principle that this was to be an élite of merit not one chosen by birth; even in *Representative Government* the old-fashioned radical prejudice crops up in statements to the effect that the characteristic concern of aristocratic regimes is to secure a steady supply of jobs

[85] P.P. 1854–5, XX, *Report*, p. 3.
[86] *Representative Government*, pp. 333–5.
[87] *Ibid.*, p. 335.   [88] *Ibid.*, pp. 244–6.

for the friends of the regime.[89] And it is hard to imagine that Macaulay's commendation of the way the young Charles Trevelyan sat his horse would have struck much of a chord with the utterly unathletic Mill.[90] Such qualities were simply not relevant to government, in much the same way that Stephen's charming pleas for the rights of the intellectually mediocre were out of place in the serious business of government service. The point, I think, is of more than biographical interest, for it shows up a certain weakness in the utilitarian dislike of the aristocracy and in Mill's hopes for its replacement by an aristocracy of talent. There is some cause to suppose that moral, intellectual and spiritual leadership owe rather more to the qualities of leadership as such than Mill ever imagined. In other words, there is what we might call an intellectual cavalry with dash, energy and initiative, which are not qualities simply reducible to intellectual ability. To hope to find many of these men in the civil service, or indeed in any routinized occupation, is perhaps asking too much. Stephen may well have been right in doubting that this was their natural arena.

To sum up, then, what I hope I have argued is this. There is no such thing as *the* utilitarian view of bureaucracy, either in the advocacy of more rather than less government or in pressing the claims of expertise against those of public opinion—and vice versa. It is not even the case that there is a single account to be given of the nature of expertise; utilitarianism is ambiguous between depicting the expert as a man who knows what will maximize the general welfare and who ought therefore to be allowed a free hand to manage our lives and depicting the moral arena as one in which free beings make what claims they can on the right to tell experts (who possess a wholly factual kind of knowledge) what goals to pursue, and what policies to implement—and here of course there is no question of the existence of 'moral expertise'. Behind these ambiguities lie the following considerations: to be a theory of any degree of generality, a moral theory like utilitarianism must be able to capture and explain moral attitudes which were not initially couched in utilitarian terms. So utilitarianism tends—as do religious creeds

[89] *Ibid.*, pp. 248–9.
[90] G. O. Trevelyan, *The Life and Letters of Lord Macaulay* (London, 1906), p. 279.

and any other ethical system—to stretch the notions of pleasure and pain in order to accommodate what began as other values. This, I should emphasize, is not to say that there is nothing distinctive about utilitarian ethics, any more than the observation that Aristotelian and Newtonian physics both explain many of the same phenomena would support the argument that they were indistinguishable. What, indeed, I hope that this essay has shown is how the reformer's problems appear, when they appear in a distinctively utilitarian guise.[91]

[91] I should like to record my thanks for help and comments from the participants in the conference of July 1969, and in particular to thank Mrs Gillian Sutherland and Mrs Jenifer Hart for some helpful preliminary 'briefings'.

The genesis of the Northcote–Trevelyan Report

So much has been written over the last twenty-five years about mid-nineteenth-century civil service reform, that it would be legitimate to ask whether there is anything more that can be usefully said. The answer may well be: not much. But there is one aspect of the matter on which interpretations differ. This is on the question of causation: why did it happen? who, or what, was chiefly responsible for the changes which took place? where did the pressure come from? Some writers answer: chiefly from the middle classes who were anxious to find more outlets for their educated sons. Others focus on Sir Charles Trevelyan and his various associates who wished to produce a more efficient public service. It seems worth trying to decide where the truth lies between these two views, not only as part of the history of the civil service, but also because the difference of approach shown by them is of more general interest. For it illustrates the divergence that exists between the type of explanation that focuses on groups and in particular on social classes, and the type that looks more at individuals and in particular at great men. It also provides to some extent an illustration of the contrast between explanations based primarily on economic motivation, and those which rely more on the influence of ideas or of practical experience.

A good example of the first type of view is J. Donald Kingsley's *Representative Bureaucracy* (Ohio, 1944). Kingsley's thesis may be summarized as follows. In the eighteenth century the interests of the effective political community were more or less harmonious with those of the landed proprietors, and the arrangement worked well. But when a new class arose with different interests requiring different treatment, the traditional system proved inadequate, and governmental machinery had to be adapted to the new power realities in the state. In the early nineteenth century an intellectual climate was created favourable to the consummation of the middle-class bid for power. That class largely destroyed the old system within the next generation: it gained control first of the House of Commons, then of the municipal corporations, and finally of the civil service and army. The middle classes weakened the aristocracy, and satisfied the more urgent demands of the proletariat. This left them undisputed masters of the state. The reform of the civil service must be viewed against this background. It was not an isolated event, but one in a series of moves on the chessboard. The substitution of competition for patronage was one more act in the series which destroyed the aristocratic monopoly and cut away the roots of aristocratic power. At the same time the reorganization of the public service is seen by Kingsley as imperative to cope with the rapid expansion of state activities in not too costly a way and to avoid the danger of revolution. It is against this background almost of terror that the Treasury Minute of 3 November 1848 must be viewed. The governing classes were putting their house in order, and the first step was to cleanse the Augean stable of Downing Street. The aristocracy held on to the House of Commons and the Cabinet even after 1832, but only at the price of enacting the middle-class programme and of throwing open the civil service. The middle classes had in fact already penetrated the civil service to a considerable extent: they had representatives in key posts throughout the service. When the situation was ripe, there were the men and they produced the measures. One of these representatives was Charles Trevelyan, who directed the forces making for reform into definite channels. The middle-class desire for free entry to the public offices was a factor of no little importance in civil service reform; the older professions were overcrowded, and the middle classes were troubled about the future of their sons. Kingsley does, however, add that this factor may have had more to do with the acceptance of the proposals for open competition than with their origin, and says that he does not want to belittle the contributions of Macaulay,

Trevelyan and Northcote. However, it is the middle classes who are seen by him as finally winning. In 1870 the last strongholds of aristocratic power, with a few exceptions, gave way before the irresistible advance of the middle classes—and the *ancien régime* was destroyed on almost every front.

The same sort of impression can be got (though perhaps erroneously) from the following passage in Noel Annan's Essay on 'The Intellectual Aristocracy' in *Studies in Social History. A Tribute to G. M. Trevelyan* (1955), p. 247:

> They [the intellectual aristocracy] worked tirelessly for intellectual freedom within the Universities which, they thought, should admit anyone irrespective of his religious beliefs, and for the creation of a public service open to talent. If they can be said to have had a Bill of Rights it was the Trevelyan–Northcote Report of 1853 on reform of the civil service and their Glorious Revolution was achieved in 1870–1 when entry to public service by privilege, purchase of army commissions and the religious tests were finally abolished. Then it was ordained that men of good intellect should prosper through open competitive examination; and that the examination, as Macaulay had recommended for the Indian Civil Service, should be designed for those who had taken high honours at the University. No formal obstacle then remained to prevent the man of brains from becoming a gentleman.

Support for this kind of interpretation can also be found in an article on 'Middle-class Education and Employment in the Nineteenth Century' by F. Musgrove in the *Economic History Review* of 1960. He wrote:

> The expansion of education for middle-class boys that took place after the 1830s was not matched by the expansion of middle-class employment. The educational expansion took place in spite of the lack of suitable professional openings, not in response to the growth of new fields of employ-ment. The increasing number of educated young men created the need for more positions suited to their talents and expectations. The Public Services were particularly sensitive to this pressure from the schools and their

structure tended to follow rather than to dictate the
changing pattern of middle-class education.

He says the civil service was probably the most sensitive pointer
to the surplus of educational talent in the later nineteenth
century, and cites contemporary evidence that in 1860 it was
being used as a dumping ground for educated youths who could
not otherwise obtain middle-class employment. Later he writes
of the growing middle-class anxiety over employment prospects,
and points out that the term 'over-crowded professions' was
often used in vocational handbooks, though he does not think
that the civil service in fact offered a greater volume of
opportunity, at least not comparable with the expansion in
the number of the educated.[1]

A similar line is to be found in a recent book on the professions, viz. W. J. Reader's *Professional Men: The Rise of the
Professional Classes in Nineteenth Century England* (London,
1966). Writing of the 1840s, Reader says that

> Despite the torrent of reform which had been sweeping
> through the land for twenty years or so, the ancient ruling
> classes were still where they always had been: at the centre
> of affairs, . . . This was not an attitude likely to commend
> itself to the kind of people who were fighting their way up
> the social scale and who were looking for wider oppor-
> tunities of employment for themselves and their sons. If
> the gentry wanted to hang on to political power, that in
> itself the middle classes did not very much object to, but
> what did annoy them was to find themselves shut out of
> the material rewards of power. They wanted some of the
> jobs for some of their boys, and they intended to break
> into the official hold in the same way as they were breaking
> into the world of the professions, which also the gentry had
> been inclined to regard as preserves of their own. . . . (p. 73)
> By the middle years of the century the pressure
> towards change—towards a competitive system—was
> growing too strong to resist. (p. 83)

What evidence do these writers offer to support their thesis?
In the case of Kingsley the answer is nothing much other than

---

[1] *Economic History Review*, 2nd series, XII (1959–60), pp. 99–111.

the things which were said by various commentators *after* the Northcote–Trevelyan Report had been published. Annan refers only to Sir G. O. Trevelyan's *The Competition Wallah* (1864). Reader, like Kingsley, refers to the many men who welcomed the new system when it was proposed; and they both mention Trevelyan's oft-quoted statement of 1875 that 'The revolutionary period of 1848 gave us a shake, and created a disposition to put our house in order, and one of the consequences was a remarkable series of investigations into public offices, which lasted for five years, culminating in the Organisation Report'.[2]

In order to test the validity of this thesis, we must ask what evidence we would regard as convincing: first, I suppose, evidence that the education of middle-class children was running ahead of employment opportunities; secondly, evidence that this was the main, or an important, grievance amongst critics of the existing public service; and thirdly, evidence that this point was in the minds of Trevelyan and his associates who put forward the scheme of reform.

On the first point, I do not wish to question the widely accepted view that there was an increased provision of middle-class education in the nineteenth century. The questions are whether this expansion exceeded the demographic need, and whether it was paralleled or not by expansion of the professions. The only attempt I know of to answer these questions is that made by H. J. Perkin in his article, 'Middle-class Education and Employment in the Nineteenth Century: A critical note', in the *Economic History Review* of 1962.[3] Perkin admits the existence of contemporary complaints about overcrowded professions, but points out that they were almost as old as the professions themselves. His conclusions are that the provision for middle-class education in the first two-thirds of the century was not substantially exceeding the demographic need; and that the professions as a whole, whether or not administration is included, expanded faster than population, and considerably faster than the male occupied population in the years 1851–81. These conclusions seem warranted by the figures and other evidence he adduces, though they are perhaps not wholly

---

[2] P.P. 1875, XXIII, Appendix F, p. 100.
[3] *Economic History Review*, 2nd series, XIV (1961–2), pp. 122–30.

conclusive on the issue being debated here, as they refer partly to a later period.

Secondly, is there evidence that the absence of employment outlets for the middle classes was one of the main grievances of the critics of the existing public service in the 1840s and early 1850s, and that it was this which stimulated their criticism? Here we must turn to what started them complaining, and what they complained about. Criticisms of financial and administrative practices were not of course new: as Professor Hughes pointed out in his article 'Civil Service Reform 1853–5', published in *History*, June 1942, before 1830 a merciless war had been waged on sinecures and extravagant establishments, and some action had been taken in the thirties. During Peel's ministry retrenchment demands were not revived, but after 1846 the agitation was resumed, caused probably by the expanding budgets after that date, and the financial and economic depression which set in late in 1847. In particular opposition was roused by Lord John Russell's announcement on 18 February 1848 that the Income Tax, which was due to expire in April, would be continued for five years, and raised from 7d. to 1/– in the £. Public meetings of protest were held in many towns and petitions poured in to parliament attacking the budget and asking that the burden on industry and trade should be reduced.[4] When ten days later the government dropped the proposed increase in the Income Tax, the moral drawn by the critics was that agitation was not only necessary but could be successful. This stimulated them to further agitation, with the result that many Financial Reform Associations sprang up in towns throughout the country but especially in the industrial north.[5] The archetype of these was the Liverpool Reform Association, though its origin can be traced even farther back to a group of merchants and traders protesting against the tea duty in 1846. The aims of the Liverpool Association were rigid economy in government expenditure and a reform of the taxation system, involving a shift from indirect to direct taxes.

---

[4] *Annual Register*, 1848, p. 43.
[5] I am indebted for some of the information in this section of my essay to the unpublished M.A. thesis of A. D. Gidlow-Jackson: 'Public Opinion and Administrative Reform in Britain between 1848 and 1854', presented to London University in 1958.

The agitation assumed such dimensions that one can say that there was a movement in the country and in the House of Commons in 1848 for what was termed 'financial reform'. Different interpretations were put on this term; but essentially it always meant a reduction in public expenditure and an alteration in the sources and incidence of taxation. The movement was active from 1848 to 1850. Thirty-six associations existed by April 1849. Evidence of its activities can be found in many pamphlets (in particular the Liverpool Tracts), in speeches in and out of parliament, and in the press. What remedies did the reformers suggest? Many advocated parliamentary reform, or greater control of the Executive by the House of Commons, or a better system of public accounts; some advocated changes in defence or colonial policy. But several of the reformers were led by their concern with financial issues to think about the public departments. Here the simplest remedies suggested were to reduce the numbers and/or salaries of public servants, the Radicals being more concerned with numbers and the Tories with salaries. On many occasions between 1848 and 1850, motions were proposed in parliament on these two matters. There was talk of needless places and unnecessary establishments. Outside parliament, too, the same remedies are mentioned, e.g. in the Liverpool Tracts which roam widely over excessive numbers of pensions, sinecures and compensations for abolition of office. These do not look like the proposals of men wishing to get employment for their sons.

These criticisms were also stimulated by the various revelations of abuses in particular departments which occurred in the 1840s and early 1850s. For instance Customs frauds had come to light in 1842. The dockyards provided material for critics from 1846 onwards: new rules were introduced in 1847 to prevent inefficiency, waste and bad account keeping, etc., but these did not prevent a further dockyard scandal in 1853. Similarly there were further inquiries into the Customs which received much publicity between 1851 and 1853. Other departments which attracted particular criticism at this time include Woods and Forests, the Irish Board of Works and the Commissioners of Crown Lands. Scandals of this kind moved criticism on from the targets of excessive numbers and excessive salaries to mismanagement and maladministration. Many of the critics were

businessmen who had witnessed improving standards of management and administration in trade and industry and felt these
were not being applied in the public departments. Admittedly
this led them on to thinking more widely about public departments and asking what sort of people were in them and how they
got appointed. Hence there was much talk in and out of parliament of a place-hunting aristocracy and of idlers and pleasure-
seekers who were appointed to oblige the political adherents of
the government. In its widest form this became a general attack
on the aristocracy who were seen as having a hold on other
institutions as well, e.g. the church and the armed forces. But
even here the system was being attacked because it was
inefficient and financially slack, not because it did not provide
jobs for over-educated offspring. It is important in this connection to notice that the financial reform movement lost
momentum after 1850, presumably because of the improvement
in the economy which started in about 1851. If there had been
pressure to get boys into the professions, it would surely have
continued regardless of short-term ups and downs in the
economy. The fact that the financial reform movement lost
momentum in the years immediately before 1854 suggests what
was behind it.

What precise remedies were suggested to avoid these defects?
A few MPs from time to time suggested that departments
should test nominees' abilities by some sort of qualifying
examination if they did not do so already, or that they should
improve existing tests; but in general MPs, whilst critical of the
management of various particular offices, were not inclined to
consider the problems of the civil service comprehensively. Thus
when Hume on 30 April 1850 suggested that in order to get rid
of useless officials an independent board should examine all
candidates,[6] his suggestion was not taken up. And when in 1853
the government proposed the introduction of competitive
examinations for the Indian civil service, MPs did not discuss
whether the principles involved were generally applicable and
should not be confined to India. The Liverpool Tracts make no
suggestions as to how the patronage system could be improved.
Indeed the gap between criticism and constructive suggestion
over the question of initial selection is well shown by the fact

[6] *Hansard*, 3rd series, CX, cols 1016–17.

that many periodicals at this time idealize America as a cheap and well-governed state. As an exception to this kind of attitude one must cite the *Westminster and Foreign Quarterly Review* which even in 1847 carried an article praising the Prussian arrangements for examining all candidates nominated to office, pointing out that these provided a more valuable check on the abuses of patronage than any which existed in this country.[7]

It is also relevant to ask how the financial reformers reacted to the proposals made in the Northcote–Trevelyan Report. Some were actually critical of them. For instance, the City Committee for Customs Reform, which was a committee of London businessmen formed in April 1851, feared that the Report if implemented would involve additional expense, and that a Board of Examiners would afford yet another opportunity for patronage. They thought the Treasury was the proper office to take over entrance exams for the Customs. The committee was also very critical of the idea that university education was inherently superior as a preparation for public service to other forms of education, and suspected that one of the ideas behind the policy of selecting university graduates was to strengthen the element of gentlemen in the public service.[8] A similar view was expressed in a pamphlet called 'Our Government Offices' by J. Herbert Stack issued in March 1855. The assumption underlying much of what Stack says is that the middle classes got quite a number of jobs for their sons under the existing patronage system. For he considers that they would not think it fair to appoint (as proposed) young scholars who in matters of business might be inferior to a shopkeeper's son without a classical education, and that the middle classes thought that the qualities they eminently possessed (business habits and common sense) should be the only passports to service to the state. In general it seems significant that there was not a greater public demand in circles other than the schools and universities for the implementation of the proposals in the Northcote–Trevelyan Report when these became known early in 1854. This perhaps reveals the difference which existed between the standpoint of the financial reformers

[7] Vol. XLVI, 1847, pp. 222–4. Review of Report on Andover Union, Annual Reports of Poor Law Commissioners, and Report of Railway Termini Commissioners. Entitled 'Patronage of Commissions'.
[8] Final Report of City Committee on Customs Reform, London, 1854.

(the businessmen and their spokesmen) whose views have been sketched here and that of the authors of the report.

My conclusion is therefore that public interest in the administrative system at this time stemmed in origin from a desire to cut down government expenditure and to produce a more efficient financial and administrative machine; and that although this opened the door to some thinking about how appointments were made and what types of people controlled and ran the machine, the impetus behind this was mainly a desire to make it more economical and efficient, rather than to increase employment prospects, or to make them more attractive.

Thirdly, did Trevelyan and Northcote and their close associates think there were insufficient employment outlets for the educated middle classes? and, if they did, was it this which made them so keen to reform the public service? or did they approach the question from a different angle? These are large and complicated questions which cannot be fully answered in an essay of this length. All that can be done here is to sketch out the directions in which the evidence seems to point. Some of the evidence I use is old, some new.

What experiences influenced Trevelyan and help to explain his outlook on civil service reform? Firstly, his time at Haileybury and in the Indian civil service. The I.C.S. was in many ways more efficient than the Home Civil Service. This point was put very strongly by William Farr in his paper on 'Statistics of the Civil Servants of England' read to the Statistical Society of London in December 1848.[9] Farr pointed out that the East India Company had for many years had a good system of superannuation; though it was 'a pure despotism in the East' it was in this as well as in some other respects a model not undeserving of the study of free governments of the west; it had generally selected its civil servants with a good deal of care; it also trained young men from the age of seventeen, gave them a professional education and allowed few or none to enter on official duties until they had gone through trials and a long probation in England and India. Trevelyan shared this view. Thus in his Memorandum of August 1849[10] he pointed out that

[9] See *Journal of the Statistical Society of London*, vol. XII, 1849.
[10] Paper 22 of Papers, originally printed in 1850, on Emoluments in Public Offices, 1856, p. 86.

unsuitable men were regularly weeded out at Haileybury who, if they had been nominated to positions at home, would almost always have been placed on the establishment 'to which they would have remained for a long series of years a burden and a disgrace'. And in his Memorandum of March 1850[11] he mentioned that public servants in India were much better cared for and encouraged than they were at home. What he probably had in mind in saying this was that they were not overworked, though they were given incentives for hard work through promotion by merit.

The second experience determining Trevelyan's views was, as has often been pointed out, his years at the Treasury from 1840 onwards. These showed him that there was much waste and extravagance in the public service and a pressing need for a thorough overhaul of the estimates, accounts and auditing systems of many offices. The best remedy was to make Treasury control over expenditure efficient and comprehensive. He had come to this conclusion before the financial reform movement of 1848–50 occurred, as is clear from many of his letters and from his evidence given between March and May 1848 to the Select Committee on Miscellaneous Expenditure,[12] but the movement no doubt strengthened his resolve. In pursuance of his aim to extend Treasury control over other departments, Trevelyan made the best use he could of the talent available in the Treasury, but he soon found that good men were insufficient to carry out the functions which he regarded as the essential responsibility of his department. In this connection he often pointed out that those in important posts were grossly overworked. It is thus clear that a desire to increase the supply of able men in the Treasury was the starting point of Trevelyan's ideas on civil service reform.

What I have tried to show so far is that Trevelyan was concerned with what was wrong with the civil service, and how this could be remedied. He was not trying to provide outlets for the over-educated sons of the middle classes. He was quite simply appalled by what he found in many public offices, and anxious to provide a more efficient and economical public service. But, it may be asked, must he not have seen that his remedies (especially a proper division of labour on which he was extremely

[11] In *idem*.   [12] P.P. 1847–8, XVIII, pt. I.

keen, and promotion by merit) would have appealed to the
educated middle classes? and did not this encourage him in his
enterprise and provide an added reason for making his proposals? It would seem that these ideas were not in his mind
before 1854, though they operated on him later. It is important
not to predate them. The emphasis has been wrongly placed by
many people because they have thought that Trevelyan was
keener on open competition than he was, and that he saw this
as the remedy for what was wrong. The evidence I submit to
support this statement is a letter from Gladstone to Northcote
dated 3 December 1853 which has not as far as I know been
previously published.[13] This letter shows that in the draft of
the Report sent to Gladstone by Trevelyan in November 1853,
there clearly was much less emphasis on the value of open
competition to reduce the abuses of patronage than in the final
version of the Report; for all appointments in departments subordinate to the Treasury were to remain in the hands of the
Treasury. This was the same proposal as Trevelyan had made in
his 1849 memorandum on patronage. The significance of this
will be appreciated when it is remembered that it would have
meant that about seven-eighths of all appointments would still
have been made under the patronage system. It follows incidentally that the Report as we know it should not be dated
23 November 1853, as it is: Gladstone had intended it to be a
private report to him of their thoughts in the first instance (see
his letter to Russell of 20 January 1854).[14] The letter from
Gladstone to Northcote runs as follows:

Hawarden Dec. 3 '53

My dear Northcote

I have read your and Sir C. Trevelyan's able paper on
the organization of the permanent Civil Service.

I look upon this paper as of great importance, and I am
most anxious that it should be in such a form as if it does
not at once secure the execution of the design shall give it
a good start and advance it some way on its road to a state
of vital activity.

With this view there are several points in which I should
be glad to see it fortified or modified: and if I thus assume

[13] Iddesleigh Papers, vol. II, B.M. Add. MSS. 50,014, ff. 76–81.
[14] See n. 16.

the office of a critic before your paper is fairly launched,
it is because I feel myself so thoroughly and heartily
associated with your feelings and purposes in the matter.
I am keenly anxious to strike a blow at Parliamentary
patronage and one which shall, at least within the spheres
to which your investigation refers, be honestly aimed at its
seat of life.

I think it of essential importance in launching such a
scheme as this, to do all we can to prevent its failing
through the reciprocal jealousy of departments. For if it
fails through the operation of that feeling, it will not only
be intercepted but discredited; as the whole discussion
will assume the character of a selfish squabble, strongly
flavoured with hypocrisy.

Now I think the weakest point of your proposal as it
stands connects itself with this remark: it will I am afraid
be viewed as a device for the aggrandisement of the functionaries of the Treasury at the expense, it may be said by
the plunder of other departments. For what do you do?
First as respects the large mass of patronage administered
by the Treasury, in the Customs, Inland Revenue, and so
forth, you withhold or suspend indefinitely any place for
introducing the principle of effective competition. But in
my opinion it is here that the worst appointments are made
and on by far the largest scale: because it is utterly
impossible that the *Parliamentary* Secretary can exercise any
control over the characters and qualifications of those whom
he appoints. You may be right in saying that too much
ought not to be tried at once. It may be well to put into
execution piecemeal a plan in which the first operations on
a limited scale will so greatly help and guide what remains
to be done. But let us get the principle sanctioned in its
full breadth; and particularly let it be applied to the
Treasury with unsparing vigour. It may be true that this
recommendation imposes more labour upon you, for you
refer (p. 13) to the state of your information: but from that
I am sure that neither of you is the man to shirk; and I do
hope that, at any rate as regards the two monster Revenue
Departments, you will consider and report, after
communication with the proper parties, upon the

application of the system of competition to the entrance into these services.

I feel perfectly persuaded that it may be right to introduce reserves as to the time, or successive times, of giving effect to these recommendations: but our first object is the establishment of a very broad principle: and I am convinced that this is one of the cases in which a large and bold design is more practicable, as well as more just, than one of narrower limits. Dealing equally with the cherished privilege of patronage wherever you can make it amenable to your reforming process, you will plant the scheme on firm and solid ground, will get rid of a multitude of petty objections which would disguise the main issue, and will place that issue closely in the public view, thus commencing, if you do not at once carry through, a conflict which can have but one ending and that a good one.

What I have further to observe turns on the same considerations. You recommend in p. 12 that the clerkships in the higher offices should be disposed of by selection among the successful candidates and that this selection should rest with the First Lord of the Treasury, who would give due weight to the recommendations of his colleagues and also of *his Parliamentary supporters*. Pray let this disappear. To me at least it seems that, having slain Patronage in principle by your admirable opening statement of your first recommendations, you revive it by these words, and give it a standing ground from which it would wriggle itself once more into possession of all the spaces from which it had been ejected. The recommendations of Ministers may be supposed to rest on their knowledge: I would give to them and not to the Treasury, these appointments; probably with the check you recommend of a list annually presented to Parliament. But the recommendations of members of Parliament I think can find no place, if the principles of your report are to be maintained.

My objections to any unnecessary lodgement of power in the hands of the Treasury would of course embrace your proposal to give the appointments to the offices of *account* into the control of that department.

Nearly everything else in the report has my unqualified and warm concurrence: but I hope you will confer further with Sir C. Trevelyan on what I have said respecting the power you *give* the Treasury—the patronage in its hands which you *leave* untouched though it is perhaps the least defensible of all—and the policy of avoiding anything which savours of partiality to that department—which already, whether justly or unjustly, has got a name for favouring its own immediate belongings—as well as of giving that breadth and decisiveness of character to your plan, which, whether the execution is to be undertaken piecemeal or not, as an assertion of a great and salutary principle and one requiring above all things to be made palpable to the public mind, it deserves and demands.

Let me repeat that my reason for thus entering on an examination of parts of your report is my desire thoroughly to identify myself with its animating spirit and its main proposals, and to have it such that I may be enabled to use my own best efforts, such as they are, without stint or reserve, in its support.

> I remain my dear Northcote
> Most sincerely yours
> W. E. Gladstone

Exactly what happened as a result of this letter is not clear—though it appears that Northcote agreed with Gladstone, for Gladstone wrote to him on 6 December 1853 as follows:[15]

My dear Northcote

I am very glad to find from your letter that we are so unequivocally in harmony: I write now only to suggest that I think these proceedings ought to be kept closely to *ourselves* for the present . . .

> Yours most sincerely
> W. E. Gladstone

We cannot say whether Trevelyan really altered his views or whether he merely felt the force of the tactical objection to the course he had proposed.

Another important factor contributing to the sense that there

[15] B.M. Add. MSS. 50,014, f. 82.

was a need for some changes was the existence of severe and growing grievances among civil servants. These had existed since the early 1830s, but were increasing as the years went by, as more and more officials were appointed on the extremely hard post-1829 terms. Moreover, anxiety increased with the external pressure for economy, including suggestions that salaries should be reduced. Trevelyan was very aware that the existing pensions arrangements, which were indefensible, had a baneful effect on the morale of civil servants. He thought of justice to the public, but also of justice to civil servants, and he convinced Gladstone of the relationship between the superannuation question and the larger issue of civil service reform: viz. that changes were necessary in the civil service partly in order to make parliamentary and public opinion willing to grant the necessary pension concessions to officials.

What chiefly motivated Gladstone in his views about civil service reform? Probably the letter he wrote to Russell on 20 January 1854[16] pressing him to support the report gives the flavour of his approach better than anything. The last part of this twenty-two-page letter appears in Morley's life of Gladstone, and some of this was reproduced by Professor Hughes in his article in *History* (1942). In the earlier part of the letter Gladstone said that he had for many years thought the condition of the civil service unsatisfactory. He mentioned the warm public approval for the new Haileybury plan and said he linked it in his mind with the reform of Oxford. He referred to the recent revision of the civil departments now nearly completed and the chronic discontent of civil servants with their condition which resulted in half-hearted service. He regretted the premature discussion of the report in the press, mentioning that Northcote acting in his individual capacity had an article actually in type for the *Quarterly Review*. Improvement in superannuation was vital, but real and substantial improvements in the service must also be made to prevent injustice to the public. He disagreed with Russell about the character of the civil service: many men were placed there because they could not make their way in an independent career. They were deficient in persevering industry. A relaxed and relaxing tone was the consequence of the seniority system. It was wrong that good

[16] Gladstone Papers, B.M. Add. MSS. 44,291, ff. 93–104.

and bad should be paid alike, and the promotion system had a deadening influence on the good. They were underpaid and discontented. Exertion was lacking: it was a healthful rule for men themselves and the public was entitled to it. They were besieged by crowds anxious to get in. Half-a-dozen help a man to get in and each unsuccessful candidate has half-a-dozen supporters. This produced a worse than worthless expectancy among many.

These postulants if they succeed, yet succeeding by causes independent of merit, leave as it were half their manhood behind them: if they fail, and we know that the bulk of them fail, can there be, short of actual profligacy, a more wretched case than this, in which time, hope, energy are so largely spent in a line quite distinct to say the least of it from that of honourable masculine exertion. Unhappily that gambling principle of human nature, as Dr Arnold calls it, in a matter of this kind invariably brings into the field numbers of candidates utterly disproportionate to the number of places to be given away: just as we know that many a little charitable endowment causes people to waste ten times its value in efforts to get hold of it. There is plenty of competition God knows: only without any test of merit, or any attempt at such a test. I for one am grieved to think of the multitudes of persons who in different degrees are by a continual daily process being enervated and even demoralised by this longing, craving, and waiting for something not dependent on their labours or virtues: and it seems to me that the extinction of this class, or its being greatly reduced in numbers, would be one of the greatest moral and social benefits that could be conferred upon the community.

Gladstone then went on to say that he did not like getting able men from outside, as good men feel discouraged and are driven out. In very many cases the system is a mild form of corruption. In parliament bad men get the greater share of it. The good deal with it as little as they can, or shrink altogether from touching it. He referred again to the lack of energy and devotion and high moral tone which result when men get there by favour, and compared this to honest industry as a way to the first step on the ladder. Therefore he was in favour of unrestricted competition, though even nomination and competition would be better than now.

I have been concerned in this essay with the genesis of the Northcote–Trevelyan Report—not with the events between 1854 and 1870 which led up to the introduction of open competition. I do not wish to question that once the Report was issued it was seen by some persons as giving an opportunity to middle-class parents to find employment for their sons even if they were not well connected—see e.g. the evidence submitted by the Rev. Charles Graves, Professor of Mathematics, Trinity College, Dublin, and by the Rev. G. E. L. Cotton, Master of Marlborough College in P.P. 1854–5.[17] Moreover, others thought the proposals in the Report would have a good effect on the educational system at all levels, though they were clearly wildly over-optimistic in their beliefs. But some of these were thinking of boys who were not then much educated, not of a surplus of educated youths. Thus the Rev. E. H. Gifford, Headmaster of King Edward's School, Birmingham, believed the proposed exams would have a beneficial influence upon both his classical and English and commercial departments by lengthening in many cases the period of education. In the latter department he said the boys generally left at fourteen: the exams would set up a higher and more definite standard for the education of the middle classes.[18] Similarly Richard Dawes, Dean of Hereford and previously a schoolmaster, saw open competition as encouraging the education of those not now much educated, not as providing employment for the already educated.[19] The mistake is to see in the pre-1854 period some of the pressures which existed only after the Report had come out. This tends to be done by Dorman B. Eaton in his book *The Civil Service in Great Britain* (New York, 1880). Eaton was the chairman of the American Civil Service Commission who was asked by the President of the U.S.A. in 1877 to investigate the British civil service and especially the effects on it of the action taken in the

[17] Pp. 21 ff. and pp. 58 ff.
[18] P.P. 1854–5, XX, pp. 47–9.
[19] Remarks on the Reorganization of the Civil Service in its bearing on educational progress. In a letter addressed to the Earl of Aberdeen, 20 February 1854.

1850s. Eaton spent more than a year in England, working on the published records and interviewing some of the people involved. He writes of 'the radical movement of 1853' and of 'the demand for reform' which was steadily gaining ground. He sees the government as giving way to pressure from the public and the Northcote–Trevelyan Report as the result of this pressure. He no doubt formed this impression by taking a lot of what was said in the 1854–5 debate as if it was evidence of pressure before 1854. Eaton also cites a letter written to him by Trevelyan on 20 August 1877.[20] In this letter Trevelyan repeated the sort of thing he had said in evidence before the Playfair Commission in 1874: namely, that the early supporters of the change could be counted upon the fingers of one hand; that it was made by persons conversant with public affairs from a practical perception of its necessity; that if there had been a secret vote in Parliament, it would have been rejected; that they won in the end because some of the best classes of the population were left out in the cold—busy professional persons of every kind: lawyers, ministers of religion, schoolmasters, shopkeepers, etc.; they became keen on the new institution; hence MPs received such pressing letters from their constituents as obliged them to vote straight. This refers to the events of the sixties. It may well be true, but I know of no corroboration of it, and it is important to remember that Trevelyan was aged seventy in 1877 and inclined to exaggerate and generalize unduly.

My general conclusion therefore (if one is to put the matter in a nutshell) is that the Northcote–Trevelyan Report was the product primarily of Trevelyan's desire for a more efficient public service, and of Gladstone's desire for a purer and more strenuous ethic in public life. They reached this position mainly as a result of their practical administrative and political experience and not as a result of outside pressure—and in particular not of pressure from the middle classes wanting jobs for their sons, for virtually no such pressure existed, though there was a substantial movement earlier for financial reform. After the Report had been published, however, some persons thought it offered new career outlets and welcomed it on this account, which may have helped secure its ultimate implementation.

[20] In Appendix A of Eaton's book.

New roles for old: the Northcote–Trevelyan Report and the clerks of the Home Office 1822–48

Although the Northcote–Trevelyan Report has often and usefully been analysed in general terms, or with reference to the whole civil service, it has not been evaluated in terms of a particular department. Yet a study of this kind ought to be valuable. Contemporary civil servants were almost unanimously hostile to the Report, a reaction which was viewed with scepticism or cynicism. Even more charitable critics could reasonably suggest that the whole bureaucratic process would predispose civil servants to favour a system which had helped to make them the men they had become. The Report reads well; it looks lucid and incisive, it displays great flair, and is a very satisfying document. It is, in fact, much more complex and confused than it appears at first sight, but its ambiguities are well hidden, and perhaps only demonstrable by relating the Report to the structure of individual departments.

The Commissioners claimed that the efficiency of the unreformed civil service was hindered by factors like patronage, work allocation and promotion by seniority. Patronage was the real villain. Thanks to the Report, the phrase 'the patronage system', in the context of the unreformed civil service, conjures up a whole cluster of ideas like corruption, nepotism and inefficiency. It is arguable, indeed, that the Report was implemented because parliament and the public loathed patronage and loved examinations more than they cared about what happened to the civil service. But the concept of efficiency, as the Commissioners used it, needs clarification. They evaluated the work of the civil service in at least two distinct ways, without declaring that they did so. First, efficiency was defined in terms of the response of civil service departments to their acknowledged work goals, and secondly, in terms of a developing role which the Commissioners glimpsed and advocated for the civil service. The Report oscillates between one definition and another, and it is sometimes difficult to disentangle them. Sometimes they use the first definition, as for example when they discuss the entry system or promotion arrangements. But as the Home Office shows, they also proposed new roles for civil servants where they claimed to be describing their existing ones. In their opening comments, on the place of the civil service in modern society, the Commissioners were proposing a new role for civil servants rather than describing their old one.[1] The same was true, at the Home Office, with regard to their division of work into 'intellectual' and 'mechanical', which was ludicrously irrelevant to the work clerks had to do, and the way in which it was organized. This ambivalence helps to explain the inadequacy of civil servants' replies to the Report, and also something of the bewilderment they felt when presented with it. Even where they could dismiss criticisms made under the first definition, they could not claim to be fulfilling roles which they had never been expected to fill, which the structure of their offices made it impossible for them to fill, and for which there was no apparent need.

The object of this essay is to consider the Northcote–Trevelyan Report in relation to the clerical structure of the Home Office, which was in many ways a model of the type of bureaucracy the Commissioners wanted to destroy. I shall argue that the Report failed to describe this type of bureaucracy accurately, and failed to provide a useful new bureaucratic model. The Home Office was not, corporately, inefficient in

[1] 'It may safely be asserted that, as matters now stand, the Government of the country could not be carried on without the aid of an efficient body of officers, occupying a position duly subordinate to that of the Ministers who are directly responsible to the Crown and Parliament, yet possessing sufficient independence, character, ability and experience to be able to advise, assist, and to some extent influence those who are from time to time set over them.' *Report on the Organization of the Permanent Civil Service*, P.P. 1854, XXVII, p. 3.

relation to its work goals, as the Report implied such ministries were. But the Home Office did have defects which led to an unfair division of the work among the staff. The explanation of these defects lay in the clerks' view of the Office, and their conception of their roles. Their attitudes determined the response of the Office not only to its immediate work goals but also to innovation and reform. I shall argue that if more dynamic roles were desirable for the Home Office clerks it was these, rather than more easily measurable factors like the appointment system or promotion arrangements which needed to be altered.

The Home Office clerks

The Home Office was not examined by the Civil Service Commissioners. Trevelyan had, however, already taken part in a departmental investigation in 1848, as a result of which the work of the Office had been reformed in 1849.[2] The 1848 investigation, which was undertaken largely to forestall criticism about civil service expenditure from the economical reform lobby, reviewed the functions of the clerks very much in terms of the department's immediate objectives. The structure which is discussed here is predominantly that which operated before the 1849 reform, but it is interesting to note that even after the reform the Home Office retained many features which Northcote and Trevelyan deplored. All appointments continued to be made without examination. There was no mention of an 'intellectual/mechanical' work division. Promotion according to strict seniority had not in theory been maintained, but it

[2] The report of the 1848 inquiry, which is mentioned by Mrs Jenifer Hart in 'Sir Charles Trevelyan at the Treasury', *E.H.R.* LXXV (1960), is unfortunately lost, but enough material remains to enable its proceedings to be reconstructed in outline, and Grey's reforming minute is in the Home Office papers. See Sir Charles Trevelyan's letters to Sir George Cornewall Lewis, of 18 September 1848 and 20 September 1848 in the Semi-Official Correspondence of Sir Charles Trevelyan, vol. 22, now in private hands; Lewis to Trevelyan, 3 July 1848 and 8 July 1848 in HO 36/29 P.R.O.; an undated Memorandum of Sir G. C. Lewis, Harpton 3606, Lewis Papers, National Library of Wales. A copy of Grey's reforming minute was sent to the Treasury 22 January 1849, HO 36/29.

tended to remain the practice of the department. There was still to be no question of clerks aspiring to staff posts. These features were retained because they were considered to be useful, and an examination of the clerical structure of the Office in the thirty years before the Northcote–Trevelyan inquiry tends to confirm that most of these factors did not in fact impede the Office's efficiency.

The Home Office approximated fairly closely to the type of office which the Commissioners seem to have had in mind when composing their Report. It was considerably smaller than the Treasury, and slightly smaller than the Foreign Office, but it was an important department whose workload had steadily grown since the beginning of the century. But the growth in Home Office business between 1822 and 1848 was not reflected by an increase in the number of its clerks. The volume of business handled by the clerks increased, but the number of new subjects put in their charge was negligible. This was partly because the office accommodation was cramped and inadequate even in 1822. But the conservatism of the clerks was a factor at the Home Office, as it was at the Treasury, in the way the business of the Office was organized.[3] As new subjects, such as factory inspection, police or Poor Law matters, were added to the Home Secretary's responsibilities, new out-departments, with a separate staff and premises, were established to deal with them, unconnected with the clerical organization of the Home Office proper, and responsible directly to the Home Secretary. As a result, the Home Office was the only branch of the Secretariat of State in which the number of clerks did not increase during this period.

All the 'ordinary' business was, however, conducted by the clerks, whose total strength between 1822 and 1848 was between twenty-one and twenty-four, a number which varied according to the number of supplementary clerks employed at different times. The historical core of the Office and the most privileged were the classified established clerks, who were organized as follows: one chief clerk; four senior clerks; nine clerks. In addition, there were three other established officers, the private secretary, the librarian and the précis writer. The total of

[3] See J. B. Torrance, 'Sir George Harrison and the Growth of Bureaucracy in the Nineteenth Century', *E.H.R.* LXXXIII (1968).

twenty-one to twenty-four was completed by the criminal department. The two chief members of this department, the criminal clerk, who was also Superintendent of the Convict Establishment, and the Keeper of the Criminal Register, occupied an anomalous position. Neither of these officers was established, but they had a permanent standing in the Office which was recognized by an Order in Council of 1822.[4] Their assistants, who in some cases were also permanent officers in the department, were unestablished supplementary clerks.

The clerks: functions and efficiency

The Commissioners' attack on the unreformed civil service was partly justified by their definition of the functions of civil service clerks. Surprisingly, the Report is vaguer about these than might have been expected, but its general sense is to suggest that the work of civil servants—and this presumably included those below the rank of under secretary—could be divided into 'intellectual' and 'mechanical'. They argued that men selected for clerkships spent too much time in their early years on 'mechanical' duties and suggested that 'the public service should be carried on by the admission of a carefully selected body of young men, who should be employed from the first upon work suited to their capacities'. This presupposed that departments employed their clerks on 'intellectual' work. This was the case in some departments, but there was no provision in the structure of the Home Office for any of the clerks to fulfil this kind of role, and, given the work goals of the department, no need for the structure to be altered to permit them to fulfil such a role. The work of the Home Office clerks did not fit neatly into either of the Northcote–Trevelyan categories: the 'intellectual/mechanical' model was, in short, inapplicable. To clarify this it is necessary to examine the nature of the Office's subdivisions and the clerks' functions within them. In 1848 the clerical staff of the Home Office were organized into several departments. The chief clerk's department, which had about four clerks, was occupied almost exclusively with formal work. Most English military commissions, warrants, patents and other formal instruments were prepared in the Home Office, and this

4 P.P. 1822, XVIII, p. 147.

was done in the chief clerk's department. It also paid out the Office salaries and bills, and prepared parliamentary returns.

The other large department was the general domestic department. This conducted most of the correspondence—with Lords Lieutenant, magistrates and local government officers, with the Law Officers, and about parliamentary returns. There were about three clerks doing this work. A fourth dealt with the Irish correspondence. There was a military clerk, who had charge of correspondence relating to the yeomanry and militia, while another clerk dealt with correspondence on the Queen's Addresses. After the abolition of the separate Aliens Department in 1835, an aliens clerk had charge of the correspondence relating to applications for naturalization, and kept a register of aliens in the country. The librarian and précis writer superintended the library, and from 1841, when a daily register was begun, registered the papers. The Keeper of the Criminal Register made entries in two registers, one for metropolitan and one for country felons, and he prepared a large and increasing number of parliamentary criminal returns from returns made to him by the Clerks of the Peace of the boroughs and the counties. The criminal department, manned by about four unestablished clerks, dealt with the rest of the criminal business. It was responsible for the preparation of warrants and pardons, for correspondence with the governors of the government prisons, for correspondence about appeals and on other criminal matters and probably also for correspondence on criminal matters with the police offices.[5]

Sir James Graham, giving evidence to the Select Committee on Official Salaries in 1850, established indirectly the contribution that the clerks made to the business. When asked whether much of the business of the Office was of a routine character, he replied,[6]

A certain proportion is; but the mode of transacting business at the Home Office is this: there are two Under Secretaries and a private secretary; the private secretary attends as soon as the letters arrive, the Under Secretaries

[5] For details of the distribution of the business, see P.P. 1848, XVIII, pt. I, pp. 215, 218, 315; HO 36/29, Grey's minute, sent to Treasury 22 January 1849, HO 36/29.
[6] *Select Committee on Official Salaries*, P.P. 1850, XV, p. 236.

at ten o'clock and the Secretary of State ought to be at his post about eleven, and then everything is brought before him which has arrived, either by his private secretary or by the two Under Secretaries: and the answers to be given to the correspondence of the day are settled by the Secretary of State with those three officers, who distribute the correspondence.

Graham was, as an administrator, inclined to keep as much of the business of the Office in his hands as possible, perhaps to an undue extent, and his is the only evidence which is so complete. But the positive way in which he outlined the procedure as the usual practice suggests that it was in use before he entered the Office. The correspondence of the under secretaries with the Home Secretary, when one or other was away from London, confirms that they attended personally even to business of the slightest importance. In addition, there was no change in the way the correspondence was marked during the period, which suggests that procedures for handling it were altered only slightly, if at all.

At the daily meeting to which Graham refers, instructions to the clerks were minuted on the back of the letters. Although these instructions, with few exceptions, were unsigned and uninitialled, their nature sometimes makes it clear who wrote them, whether the Home Secretary himself, or one of his under secretaries. The instructions naturally varied. They were often marked with a single word, such as 'Acknowledge' or 'Nil', if the reply were formal or obvious. But if there was any question of a more difficult or extensive reply, the instruction usually outlined the form it should take and gave precise instructions as to the language to be used. In 1831, for example, Lord Melbourne received a letter from Lord Lonsdale, about a riot at Whitehaven in Cumberland.[7] It was marked, though not initialled 'Take a copy of this', and

> Write that I shall be most anxious to receive the fullest information upon this subject, as soon as his Lordship can possibly collect it, and I particularly wish to be informed whether there is any foundation for the rumours which attribute to the Magistrates who were there present at the

[7] Lord Lonsdale to Lord Melbourne, 7 June 1831, HO 52/13.

time, that they pursued a conduct likely to excite tumult
or that they made no exertion to repress violence when it
began to take place.

The letters, bearing these instructions, were then passed to the
clerks in the departments who wrote a letter from the instructions, and when it had been inspected by the head of his department and the under secretary, wrote a copy of it into the
appropriate entry book and handed it to the chief clerk for
despatch. The letters were then docketed[8] and filed.

These instructions left little to the discretion of those clerks,
about two-thirds of the total number, who conducted the correspondence. There was little or no intellectual work involved
and even the senior clerks working on the correspondence had
no regular advisory role. In some cases the experience and
intelligence a clerk possessed was useful: an alert clerk was an
extra check against the despatch of an inept letter. He might
know what precedents there were for any course of action and
where to find examples from the Office books. Clerks who had
been in the department for many years might remember letters
being despatched on a previous occasion to some correspondent,
before the Home Secretary and the under secretaries entered the
Office, which might be relevant to the reply to be given on the
present occasion. In ways like these, the clerks possessed a fund
of experience which was very valuable and which was doubtless
often used. But there was no office procedure, such as minuting,
designed to record the opinion and advice of the clerks on any
aspect of the correspondence. Their function in the structure of
the Office was narrowly clerical.

Most of the other clerks, for example, those who prepared
formal instruments in the chief clerk's department, occupied a
similar position, but there were two men in the Office who held
positions which, although not 'intellectual', carried responsibility. The chief clerk's post was not different in kind from that
of first senior clerk, in the same way as it was from that of

---

[8] Docketing involved writing the name of the sender, the date and a
brief note of the contents on the back of the letter. When it was
answered the date of the reply was also marked on the letter and it
was then filed so that the details written on the back were easily
visible.

under secretary above it, but it was, nevertheless, an important post.

Apart from his responsibility for the Office accounts and the payment of salaries, the chief clerk corresponded in his own right with other government departments and with the Home Secretary about staff matters. He occupied a similar position, with respect to the preparation of formal instruments, as the senior clerks of the other departments did with regard to the correspondence, but to a greater degree. The preparation of formal instruments was a tedious, but very detailed business. It demanded great precision, since many instruments were rendered invalid by clerical errors and the omission of a name from a long list of appointees in a commission could invalidate the whole document and make it necessary to recopy it. But in some cases a knowledge of precedents was vital and in such cases the chief clerk was the most competent advisory authority in the Office and perhaps the most competent available. Sir George Grey paid tribute more than once to Thomas Plasket's usefulness. A letter to Clarendon, written in 1848, shows the type of assistance the chief clerk gave the Home Secretary. Clarendon, then Lord Lieutenant of Ireland, proposed to visit England. Grey wrote, 'Plasket, who is my great authority, says there ought always to be an official letter from the Lord Lieutenant requesting Her Majesty's permission to leave Ireland and proposing the names of Lords Justices. He has just brought me one of Lord Heytesbury's to Sir James Graham.'[9] In such cases, the chief clerk had an advisory function, although it was very specific in nature and did not correspond to Northcote and Trevelyan's idea of intellectual labour. It was rather a specialized professional knowledge derived from long experience.

John Capper, the criminal clerk, also held a position which was, in some respects, advisory. He held, in addition to the criminal clerkship, the post of Superintendent of the Convict Establishment[10] and it was probably his combination of the two posts which qualified him to act in an advisory capacity.

[9] Grey to Clarendon, 14 July 1848, Clarendon Papers, Bodleian Library MSS. Clar. dep. Irish A Box 12, bundle 21.
[10] The Convict Establishment was the name given to the collection of hulks in which convicts sentenced to transportation were kept while waiting for transports.

He became something of an expert on prison discipline and on general prison matters. He was called as a witness before more than one Select Committee on criminal matters and he gave evidence to the Prison Discipline Society. His post at the Convict Establishment demanded intelligence and initiative. He had the 'general management of all the business of the establishment'. Capper kept an entry of all orders of removal from the hulks and corresponded with the sheriffs, who had to have the Home Secretary's authorization for the removal of prisoners.[11] He corresponded with the Colonial Office and the Admiralty on transportation matters. He inspected the hulks, as he told the Select Committee on Secondary Punishments in 1831, by law four times a year, 'but I go more frequently than that and not at any stated intervals'.[12] Capper prepared a quarterly report on the state of the Convict Establishment and the accounts, the estimates and any returns called for by parliament. He acted as an intermediary between the Home Secretary and the officers and prisoners on the hulks. Any recommendations from the officers for pardon were examined by him before going to the Home Secretary. Capper's position, however, which probably owed much to the curious way the criminal business was organized, was exceptional and his specific expertise was gained from his position in the Convict Establishment, which marked him off from the other clerks.

Work of this kind, neither 'mechanical' nor 'intellectual', was the most demanding expected of clerks, and the most responsible they could hope to achieve. Northcote and Trevelyan envisaged a situation in which clerks might be promoted to staff appointments, of which the only one in the Home Office was the under secretaryship. This was not possible at the Home Office, since the legal aspects of the business made it necessary to appoint a barrister to the post. There was a rigid barrier between the under secretaryship and the posts beneath it, which was not produced by the inadequacies of the clerks, and which a revision in the system of appointing clerks could not remove.

But what about efficiency? Two types of answer might be given here. A case could be made out that the work goals themselves were inadequate; that the Home Office clerks ought to do

11 *Select Committee on County Rates*, P.P. 1834, XIV, p. 70.
12 *Select Committee on Secondary Punishments*, P.P. 1831, VII, p. 44.

more than prepare commissions and answer letters from the country. It might, for example, be argued that they should have a research function or a policy-making function. Or the efficiency of the clerks might be assessed in narrower terms. Did they answer letters accurately and quickly? Were their patents and commissions accurately drawn up? Should we, in short, discuss the validity of the departmental work goals, or the efficiency with which they were executed? The Commissioners' Report, as I have suggested, tends to treat these two distinct questions as one, and to imply that inefficiency abounded in both areas; that civil servants neither had appropriate duties, nor executed those they had efficiently.

It is difficult to speculate on the first question, which may be a speculative rather than an historical question anyway. Unquestionably, there was a fairly obvious need for innovation in certain areas. The statistics returned by local government and the courts, for example on criminal matters, were not checked and were accepted as they stood. More generally, the Home Office should perhaps have been in a position to give more positive help and advice to applicants who sought it—for example magistrates applying for the Home Secretary's advice on public order questions. But the Commissioners, although they proposed a new role for civil servants which might result in changes of this kind, proposed nothing of immediate use to the Home Office in this respect. The introduction of a number of highly educated clerks might lead the department eventually to reassess its duties but, in the short term, might be expected to prove frustrating for new entrants and existing clerks alike. Such evidence as there is suggests that the Home Office clerks were not, in any case, deficient in intelligence or application. If the attitudes of the clerks in the department needed changing, its defects were not due to educational incapacity, nor to promotion by seniority, nor by and large to idleness. Some of the major problems facing the department are discussed in a subsequent section.

The efficiency of the department in a narrower sense is easier to assess. There is no doubt that despite its bureaucratic shortcomings, the Home Office did, by and large, achieve the work goals it set itself. Business fluctuated very noticeably according to whether the country was peaceful or in a state of unrest. The disturbances of 1830–1 and the Chartist disturbances produced a temporary overloading of the Office, which accommodated the extra work by the clerks working very long hours during some short periods. In addition, there was a steady rise in the volume of correspondence,[13] which was absorbed without any apparently greater delays in replies to correspondence, and without any increase of staff. It is my impression that incoming correspondence was usually answered within a week, which compares favourably with modern practice. Judging from the absence of complaints, it also seems to have been executed reasonably accurately. But the efficiency in terms of productivity did not mean that the work was efficiently distributed within the Office. There were, as I shall suggest, clerical malpractices which led to unfair distribution of work, and the criminal department, for reasons which I shall outline,[14] accumulated arrears of business. But this was the only department in the Office which failed to achieve its work goals.

Appointments: the operation of patronage

Since the roles of Home Office clerks were so radically different from those outlined by the Commissioners, it is not surprising that the Home Secretary used very different criteria when recruiting clerks. The patronage system was not, as it worked at the Home Office, the dubious ministerial perquisite which popular opinion came to believe, nor was it an agent of inefficiency as the report implied. Most Home Office clerks recruited under patronage seem to have been entirely capable of fulfilling their duties within the existing system, and some would appear to have been capable of a more demanding role. In addition, the better type of clerk may have been a potentially more promising employee in a reformed structure than the type of recruit the Commissioners proposed to introduce.

The Home Secretary's right to appoint the clerks in his office

[13] The rise in correspondence is well illustrated by the figures of outgoing correspondence for the general domestic department, especially since the domestic department's entry books (HO 43) covered the same area of business throughout the period. In 1822 about 400 letters were entered; in 1825 about 650; in 1830 about 1,400; in 1840 about 1,500; in 1849 about 1,800.
[14] See below.

was not only a very small part of his total patronage, it was in actual numbers very small.[15] Sir Robert Peel, for example, appointed only six clerks in the seven years he spent at the Office, and this was a greater number than any other Home Secretary of the period. Sir George Grey wrote to Lord Clarendon, in 1848, 'Bessborough wrote to me about his brother and I have told him that I would willingly do what I could for him but vacancies in the Home Office are of rare occurrence. There has been one in the last seven years.'[16] Nor was the Home Office, at least in its clerical ranks, staffed by relatives of the Home Secretary. No clerk appointed after 1822 was related to the Home Secretary, although there were still men in the Office who were relatives of former Home Secretaries.[17] The amount of work expected from clerks, though still not excessive, steadily increased during the period, while salaries decreased, and this made clerkships less attractive gifts for relatives and close friends. Peel, who did not disapprove of the principle of appointment by patronage, told a Select Committee in 1850 that he considered patronage a great responsibility.[18] This may have been one of the reasons why the system was abandoned. Conscientious ministers, like Peel, considered the patronage system placed a great responsibility on them. Appointment to clerkships, infrequent though it was, had probably become a nuisance rather than a privilege to ministers, and was not worth retaining if it was going to lead to public criticism. Anthony Trollope argued that the system was abolished because ministers could not be bothered to appoint their clerks.[19]

[15] S. Redgrave, Murray's *Handbook of Church and State* (1852), pp. 243–4, gives a complete list of the Home Secretary's patronage. It includes, however, offices to which the Home Secretary only appointed nominally. The most useful and financially valuable offices in his gift were the parliamentary under secretaryship (there were only two changes of permanent under secretary between 1822 and 1848), the stipendary magistracies, factory inspectorships, Poor Law places and the office of the Registrar of Births, Marriages and Deaths. None of these was affected by Northcote and Trevelyan's proposals.

[16] Grey to Clarendon, 10 July 1848, Clarendon Papers, Bodleian Library, MSS. Clar. dep. Irish A, Box 12, bundle 21.

[17] Lord Liverpool, when Home Secretary, gave his brother a clerkship. Sidmouth appointed two relatives.

[18] *Select Committee on Official Salaries*, 1850, P.P. 1850, XV, p. 236.

[19] A. Trollope, *Autobiography*, World's Classics ed., pp. 33–4.

It was equally true, however, that patronage did not fulfil the more positive role which theoretically might have been expected of it. Patronage might have served, for example, to enable the head of a department to adapt it to suit his needs and/or the requirements of its business. But because of the principle of permanency (i.e. the incoming minister did not dismiss established staff) and the small number of appointments he could expect to make, patronage did not usually help the Home Secretary to re-model the department. Indeed, the pressure on the Home Secretary to conform to departmental norms and attitudes in his appointments, as in other matters, was probably greater than readiness by the staff to alter to suit his needs.

In addition the ineffectiveness of patronage as an agent of modification at the Home Office was intensified by the fact that while some clerks remained in the Office for many years, the wastage rate among newly recruited clerks was high. Four of the eleven established clerks appointed between 1822 and 1848 retired or died within five years of being appointed. Even more remarkable, however, was the number of clerks who remained in the Office for a great many years. The following figures show this.

APPOINTMENTS OF CLASSIFIED ESTABLISHED CLERKS
IN THE HOME OFFICE 1822 TO 1848

In 1825 13 out of 14 clerks had been appointed before 1822
         9 of these 13 were appointed before 1812
In 1832 9 out of 12 clerks had been appointed before 1822
         7 of these 9 were appointed before 1812
In 1839 7 out of 14 clerks had been appointed before 1822
         4 of these 7 were appointed before 1812
In 1845 6 out of 14 clerks had been appointed before 1822
         3 of these 6 were appointed before 1812

Since there was no official retiring age, and all promotion was awarded strictly according to seniority, all the highest clerical posts in the Office were held by elderly or old men. In the 1840s when this was most noticeable, all the highest clerical posts were held by men appointed in the 1790s. Plasket, the chief clerk from 1822 to 1849 was appointed in 1792. Three senior clerks,

John Hicks, Richard Wood and Richard Noble, were appointed in the 1790s, two of them remaining in the Office until the 1830s, the third until 1849. John Capper, the criminal clerk and Superintendent of the Convict Establishment, appointed in the late 1790s, retired from the Office in the 1840s. The way the business was dealt with, the structure of the Office and the response to innovation, were greatly influenced by the absence of satisfactory retirement arrangements. The older men were guardians of the Office ethos, which, it will be suggested, acted as a very effective brake on innovation or flexibility. If the Home Office experience was typical, provisions for retirement were more important than provisions for appointment in determining an office's response to its business.

What type of men did Home Secretaries look for in filling clerkships? Lord Sidmouth, in a Memorandum to the King in Council of 28 March 1822, gave some idea of the qualities he looked for in recruits. He agreed, he said, with previous Home Secretaries, that owing to the necessarily confidential nature of the business, great caution had to be exercised in selecting staff. He considered it impolitic to keep staff numbers too small, since in an emergency this could prove dangerous to security. In a passage advocating fairly generous salaries, he wrote 'it appears to me politic to fix them at such a rate as to render the clerkships desirable to men fit to be trusted with such confidential information as I have above stated'. He continued, 'These are, according to my experience, most likely to be found amongst Youths, respectable for their Birth, who have had the advantage of a liberal education.'[20] The precise meaning which Sidmouth attached to 'liberal education' is unclear, although he did not mean a university education and presumably included in the phrase two clerks he had appointed who had been educated more or less informally. His evidence suggests, however, that he considered educational attainments necessary as an indication of trustworthiness rather than for the adequate performance of the work.

Sir George Grey said, in 1848, that 'an average degree of intelligence' was sufficient for the highest clerical post in the Office. He said, however, that the post of chief clerk, although it did not demand great intelligence, involved a great knowledge

[20] P.P. 1822, XVIII, p. 146.

of precedents.[21] Sir Denis Le Marchant, who gave evidence to the same Committee, agreed that the Home Office was not a department which required any very superior abilities in its upper clerical ranks. He thought, like Grey, that experience rather than great intelligence was required by the senior clerks. He was doubtful about the wisdom of departing entirely from the system of promotion by seniority because of the importance of experience and the amount of work for which a knowledge of precedents was essential.

> So much of the business of the Secretary of State's department consists of routine and precedent; and there are men there who, perhaps, are not men of great capacity, but at the same time, from having been so many years in the office, they are in possession of information which it would be difficult to find in any other quarter. A great deal of that information is not recorded; it exists only in the minds of those who have been there and are the depositaries of that information.[22]

Trustworthiness, industry and experience were uniformly considered the most essential qualities for clerks to possess; an extensive education, great intelligence, enterprise or initiative were not necessary. The biographical information which I have been able to collect about clerks who worked in the Office during this period suggests that recruiting practice followed these criteria. They were in many cases more than 'respectable for their Birth'. There was, unsurprisingly, a fairly high social qualification for office in this period. One of the clerks was the son of a nobleman, two were sons of clergymen, nine were sons of gentlemen, and five were sons of parents from the business and professional classes. The patronage system produced, as is suggested below, inevitable fluctuations in the social background from which clerks were recruited, but it looks as if the Home Office became socially more exclusive after 1822 than it had previously been. The Hon. Arthur Dillon, the only nobleman in the Office during the period, and Wyndham Smith, son of Sydney Smith, Canon of St Paul's, were both appointed after

---

[21] *Select Committee on Miscellaneous Expenditure*, 1848, P.P. 1848, XVIII, pt. 1, p. 311.
[22] P.P. 1848, XVIII, pt. 1, p. 225.

1822, and in contrast to the earlier period, none of the clerks whom I have been able to identify who were appointed after 1822 had a recent background of trade.

The educational standard of the clerks was not apparently very high. They included, it is true, two graduates, Sydney Streatfeild and Wyndham Smith, but Streatfeild died very soon after appointment, and Smith left the Office after only a very short term as a clerk. None of the other clerks was apparently educated at the more prominent public schools. Two clerks, Alexander and Samuel Redgrave, who entered the Office in Sidmouth's time, initially as supplementary clerks at the ages of thirteen and fourteen, were educated at night school, predominantly in the fine arts. They were among the most successful recruits to the department.[23]

The clerks clearly regarded themselves as professional men, but the civil service was a profession which did not require expensive education. Sir George Cornewall Lewis, writing to Sir Charles Trevelyan in 1854 on civil servants in general, emphasized that it was a profession which could be entered very cheaply. There was, Lewis said, no need to have taken a university degree 'or to have gone through an expensive education. No outfit is required; [a clerk] is not compelled to procure uniforms or horses, to hire chambers or to buy books.'[24] Against this, the Home Office clerks, in a memorandum on the subject of a new salary scale,[25] argued that they were fully comparable with the ordinary professions.

> Many of us have accepted situations in this office in preference to Professions which we should have undoubtedly selected had we supposed it possible that the future Advantages we were taught to look forward to in the event of the faithful discharge of our Duties could have been thus withheld from us.

Whatever they said, however, most of the clerks would probably not have succeeded in the open professions. Very few of them

---

[23] See below.
[24] Lewis to Trevelyan, 20 July 1854. This memorandum is an incomplete draft. The sense is clear, however, in context. Lewis Papers, Harpton 3621.
[25] Peel Papers, B.M. Add. MSS. 40347, f. 295.

were sufficiently expensively educated, and some came from backgrounds where it was probably impossible to bear the expense of training and equipment necessary for a career in the open professions.

The biographical information also illustrates the fact that in their choice of clerks, Home Secretaries recruited men drawn from the fairly narrow circle in which they moved. This is particularly evident in the cases of Sidmouth and Peel. In Sidmouth's case personal interest was evident, since he appointed two relatives to clerkships. Sidmouth may have been affected in the case of Henry Knyvett, a clerk who came from a family of court musicians, by pressure from the court. The other men he appointed came from families in business and finance in London, circles in which Sidmouth himself moved. All the appointments which Peel made were of men from well-established gentle families. They were all men whom he had met while at the Irish Office, either Irishmen or clerks in the Irish Office. The case of Wyndham Smith, who was probably appointed in an effort to reconcile his father, Sydney Smith, to the abolition of the Deaneries, is similar to these in that he came from a circle of society in which Lord John Russell was accustomed to move. Since Home Secretaries came from different areas of society, the Home Office had a fairly polyglot and politically mixed composition.

Nevertheless, more than one member of a family sometimes served in the Office, although they seem to have been appointed by the same Home Secretary. Peel, for example, appointed three members of the Streatfeild family one after the other, and the Redgraves were also examples of this practice. There was another similar case, since John Capper, the criminal clerk, had a brother in the Aliens Office, where the clerks were appointed by the Home Secretary. There were also various other clerks with brothers and other relatives in departments where the patronage did not lie with the Home Secretary. The Northcote–Trevelyan Report complained that the patronage system often gave employment to the untried son of a good public servant. This was not the case at the Home Office either during this period or earlier. Apart from Henry Knyvett, whose father was Chief Paymaster at the Isle of Wight Depot, no identified clerk was the son of a civil servant.

Although, as I have said, the Office was collectively efficient in terms of its response to its work goals, the achievement of individual clerks was, nevertheless, very varied: some held posts which were almost sinecures, others could probably have fulfilled more demanding roles within a more dynamic bureaucracy. This disparity in achievement was especially evident at the end of the period. Three or four of the clerks were constantly under-employed and did not make an effective contribution to the work of the Office. Frederick Mills, for example, the librarian and précis writer, had an insufficient amount of work as librarian and did nothing as précis writer, even though Sir George Grey thought it would be useful to have an efficient précis writer in the Office.[26] The clerk who did the aliens work was not fully employed in 1848, nor was Richard Dawson, whose work it was to prepare answers to the Queen's Addresses. The most extreme example of an under-employed clerk, however, was Francis Walpole, the military clerk. Grey wrote of him: 'he has long been employed in business connected with the Yeomanry and Militia . . . This business is of a trifling and formal nature and is clearly insufficient to occupy the whole time of a clerk, still less of one of the standing and experience of a senior clerk.'[27]

These cases were outnumbered by those in which the clerks proved efficient and useful members of the Office. Henry Knyvett and Charles Erskine, promoted on Plasket's retire-ment, had Grey's confidence. 'I have received very satisfactory testimony to the efficiency of both these gentlemen and they appear to me fully entitled to their promotion.' Charles Fitz-gerald 'of whose competency for that responsible duty I am perfectly satisfied' was, Grey said, to become head of the domestic department. Samuel Redgrave, who was Keeper of the Criminal Register in 1848, produced statistics 'of great value and utility', and Grey said that he entertained a high opinion of the value of his services. George Everest, who since the retirement of John Capper had become criminal clerk, had Grey's entire confidence. 'Mr Everest,' he wrote, 'though there are objections to placing him over the heads of others on the Establishment will be hereafter considered to hold the rank of a

---

[26] P.P. 1848, XVIII, pt. 1, p. 314.
[27] Grey's minute of 1849, HO 36/29.

Senior Clerk, to which his long and meritorious services and the responsible nature of his duties entitle him.'[28]

Although it is necessarily impossible to speak with certainty on the subject, it looks as if a few of the successful clerks were capable of a more dynamic role than was allocated to them: even before reform there was already a pool of surplus talent in the department. Samuel and Alexander Redgrave, for example, seem to have been men of considerable ability. Apart from proving his usefulness in the Office, Samuel used his experience to write two books. He compiled a narrowly factual account of the rights and duties of the Home Secretary, which was the first of its kind. He also wrote Murray's *Handbook of Church and State*, which outlines the various contemporary governmental and church institutions, and contains speculative as well as strictly factual material. As well as this, he published several books on art, jointly with his brother, Richard Redgrave, the painter, including a definitive dictionary of nineteenth-century British artists. Alexander Redgrave, his brother, left the Home Office to take on more demanding work in the Factory Inspectorate. He too published a number of works, and some of his guides to the Factory Acts went into several editions.[29] Charles Fitzgerald, who rose quite quickly to become actual, if not titular, head of the general department, and George Everest, who was conspicuously successful in the criminal department, were probably also capable of more demanding roles. It is interesting that the Redgraves, who entered the Office when they were thirteen-year-olds, came from a manufacturing background, and that their parents could probably not have afforded to educate them for the open professions.

It is difficult, and perhaps not very useful, to speculate on how the Home Office might have developed without the Northcote–Trevelyan Report, but arguably men like these, who would have been employed in the open professions had they come from a social background which equipped them with a university or professional training, were well suited to the present and any foreseeable future situation in the department. The Home Office secured in their cases men easily capable of all the demands the business could make on them, and perhaps of equal calibre to later graduate clerks. Men from non-gentle middle-class backgrounds, intelligent but not expensively educated, were in many respects the best fitted for clerical posts. Civil service salaries had fallen appreciably between 1822 and 1848 and this movement was accompanied, at the Home Office, by an increase in the amount of work expected from the clerks. The introduction of graduates of a comparable standard to those in the open professions would inevitably reverse the trend towards reduced salaries, while at the same time the work expected of them in such a department as the Home Office was not of a kind to employ their skills and intelligence adequately. Men like Samuel Redgrave, with lower job expectations, were more satisfactory in this, as in the financial, respect.

The clerks' view of the department

The Northcote–Trevelyan Report, as it applied to the Home Office, was unfair to the old system. It failed to describe the system accurately, it defined non-existent problems and proposed new clerical roles of doubtful utility. At the same time the Report failed to identify the actual defects of bureaucracies like the Home Office. Yet, in the case of the Home Office, these defects were not only a threat to efficiency in terms of present work goals, but they prevented flexibility or innovation. Whatever system of recruitment was adopted, whatever system of promotion, so long as these defects remained, little effect would be achieved. The main problem area, in this respect, was the bureaucratic character of the Office, something difficult to analyse, but which was composed of factors like the clerks' definition of their roles, their concept of the department and of the civil service, and the historical perspective which dominated their attitude towards the business. It is easy to get the impression, from the Northcote–Trevelyan Report, that unreformed departments lacked cohesiveness and were demoralized and without *esprit de corps*. But the type of problems which afflicted the Home Office were significant only because the clerks formed a highly cohesive and well-integrated body, well-equipped to prevent change.

There were rigid conventions about what constituted appropriate business, how the work should be organized, and how the work should be evaluated for the purpose of awarding status. Most of the departmental norms were based on a view of the department which was traditionalist and quasi-legal. This was not surprising. The Office was a very ancient one, its methods scarcely disturbed by the introduction of different business in 1782, and not reformed since the 1790s. It always had old or elderly men in its senior clerical positions, and its functions encouraged respect for precedent, and for legal types of thinking. But it is curious that the more inconvenient of the department's conventions should have remained undisturbed for so long. Most of the Home Secretaries of the time were capable and industrious, and in theory they could organize the business as they wished, but the conventions of the Office delimited their sphere of action very narrowly, and Home Secretaries seem to have accepted them.

The clerks were regarded and looked upon themselves as gentlemen. Outsiders agreed with this: Torrens, for example, referred somewhat scathingly to 'the fine gentleman clerks of the Home Office'.[30] Some of the department's conditions of service reflected their gentlemanly pretensions; the office hours were from 11 a.m. to 5 p.m. and clerks were entitled to two months' leave per annum. There were no attendance books, an institution which was resisted for many years. But the self-image of clerks had more important implications than this. Clerks tended to grade occupations in social terms, and in some cases a job which demanded responsibility and intelligence was held in lower esteem than a completely mechanical one. Anthony Trollope noticed this attitude at the Post Office. He remarks in his autobiography that when he resigned from his clerkship in London to accept an assistant surveyorship, a post which was more entertaining, more responsible and better paid, his fellow civil service clerks considered it a move downwards, demotion rather than promotion. He had lost status in their eyes.[31]

Similar attitudes existed at the Home Office. Status was held by the clerks to inhere in particular posts and departments

[30] J. M. Torrens, *Memoirs of Viscount Melbourne* (1878), vol. I, p. 368.
[31] A. Trollope, *Autobiography*, World's Classics ed., p. 49.

without reference to factors like the nature of the work or the rate of pay. This can be seen in the different status accorded to the various departments in the Office. The chief clerk's department, which arguably had the most formal and essentially unimportant work of any of the major departmental subdivisions, was held to have precedence over the larger general department, which conducted most of the correspondence, and this, in turn, took precedence over the other departments. The criminal department, despite its importance, was the Cinderella of the Office. Historical considerations were the crucial determinants of status in these cases: the chief clerk's department was the oldest, the general department the second oldest and so on. It is an indication of the strength that vested interests and traditionalist attitudes had in the Office, that as new business was added to the Office, status was not revised to account for shifts of importance in the various parts of the business. Resistance to such changes probably accounted for the Home Secretary's not bringing some of the most important new business, factories, mines or Poor Law, for example, into the Home Office proper.

The same factor operated at an individual level. There was, for example, a rigid distinction made between established and unestablished clerks. In some offices, and in the Home Office later in the century, such a distinction was valid, since supernumerary clerks were employed on very mechanical work, and on a strictly temporary basis. But, particularly in the case of the clerks engaged on criminal business, the distinction was not related to the nature of their work. They had as much responsibility as the ordinary established clerks, their work was as important, and their appointments were, in practice, as permanent. John Capper and George Everest, for example, both worked in the Office for about forty years. The position of the criminal department had been recognized in 1822, although its clerks were not put on the establishment. Despite this recognition, they occupied an inferior position in the bureaucratic structure of the Office. They were not included in the ordinary promotion arrangements of the Office, and none of them could aspire to become chief clerk. They were also, in theory, dismissible instantly and without pension. In addition, the established clerks would not in any circumstances assist the unestablished clerks in their business, whereas they did, in exceptional circumstances, assist fellow members of the establishment. This had resulted in a scandalous situation in the 1840s when, on several occasions, the criminal department had had more business than it could cope with, and established clerks with little to do had failed to help them. Even in 1849, when other office conventions were under serious attack, this one remained very powerful. Grey's action in deciding to have Everest 'considered' a senior clerk was unprecedented, and his choice of wording shows that he did not consider himself at liberty to discard, even in a special case, the rules of the Office with regard to the establishment.

Similar rigid and formal principles governed the clerks' conception of their offices. Their attitudes towards their posts were based on a system of thought which had probably originated when places were bought and sold, and when the buyer also bought the duties and the promotion prospects with the place. Established clerks, once appointed, considered themselves to possess almost a proprietary claim to their places. Although Le Marchant told the Select Committee on Miscellaneous Expenditure that he knew of cases in which Home Office clerks had been dismissed for incompetence, there is no evidence to support the idea that dismissal, even for incompetence, was usual.[32] If they were honest and diligent they did not expect to be dismissed and were not, whatever the exigencies of the business.

The feeling of proprietary right also extended to promotion. An Order in Council in 1822 gave the Home Secretary the right to promote clerks from one class to another and to the post of chief clerk according to merit, rather than by seniority.[33] But although several vacancies occurred between 1822 and 1848, promotion was made according to strict seniority. Le Marchant said that nothing prevented the establishment of a more useful system of promotion 'except the general understanding of the office. I think it would be considered a grievance, for I believe that many gentlemen in the office are not aware that the Secretary of State has the power.' He, like Grey, thought that 'If he is unqualified there would be no hardship in his being passed over, but when a gentleman has done his best, has been

[32] P.P. 1848, XVIII, pt. i, p. 216.   [33] P.P. 1822, XVIII, p. 148.

regular in attendance and has been able to get through the business decently, it would be considered a hardship if he was passed over; yet some of his juniors may be very superior to him.'[34] Thirty years later this attitude was dying out, but it still existed. A report of the Office, made in 1876, referring to several elderly clerks, said, 'These gentlemen were just as certain of passing into a higher class when their turn arrived, as if their promotion had been a legal right of which they could not be dispossessed.'[35] The notion of a proprietary right to promotion was, like the proprietary claim to the place itself, probably based upon attitudes which originated at a time when a place and its prospects could be acquired by purchase on the open market. It had the force of a customary law, and bound the Home Secretary to promote according to seniority regardless of legislation to the contrary and the convenience of the Office.

The same attitude applied to the work. The absolute distinction made between established and unestablished work was one of a number of restrictive practices. The criminal work was excluded from the ordinary business because it was relatively new and the clerks were powerful enough to resist the addition of new subjects to their work. It was the principle of the Office that each clerkship had a more or less strictly defined amount of work attached to it and that whether the clerks had time for it or not, this could not be exceeded regularly without extra staff being appointed, or without an allowance being paid for the new business.

The result of this convention was that the allowance system flourished in the Office. When, for example, extra correspondence occurred on Irish matters, or relative to the County Courts Act, a clerk was given an allowance to take charge of it. There were several clerks in receipt of allowances. At best, the allowance system was a doubtful procedure. Grey denounced it in his reforming minute in 1849:[36]

The practice of granting additional salaries of this nature to Clerks on the Establishment of the Office appears to me

[34] P.P. 1848, XVIII, pt. 1, p. 226.
[35] See Sir H. A. Strutt, *The Home Office 1870–96: the Modernization of an Office* (privately printed, 1961), p. 57. I am grateful to Sir Austin Strutt for lending me his own copy.
[36] Grey's minute, HO 36/29.

to be objectionable. The whole time of the Clerks during Office hours with the exception of the holidays allowed them ought to be at the disposal of the Government in return for the regular salaries they receive . . . the placing this [additional] business in the hands of an existing clerk with an Extra Salary for the performance of it entails the same increase of expense as employing an extra clerk while it withdraws a clerk to a certain extent from the duties in which he was before occupied.

An allowance gave a clerk a proprietary claim to the work his allowance paid for and in more than one case its claims were allowed to supersede those of his ordinary business. Richard Noble, for example, who had an allowance for conducting the Secret Irish correspondence, was fully employed and took on all the Irish correspondence. He advanced through the ranks of the Office to become a senior clerk and head of the general department, but even in this rank he ordinarily did only Irish business and left the more important English correspondence to Fitzgerald. Francis Walpole's, however, was the most extreme case. When his allowance was given him in 1820, the work he was allocated was probably adequate and he may have done it in addition to other clerical work. At some time he evidently ceased to do any except military work, while continuing to rise through the ranks of the Office. When the Militia was abolished in 1827 and his work was considerably diminished, he seems to have been treated in the same way as contemporary sinecurists were when their offices were abolished and the income left to him. Walpole took on no new duties and did not resume his old ones, and by 1848 had reached the position which Grey criticized.

These attitudes and conventions had originally been justifiable, and some of them were still to some extent useful. Indeed, if the functions of the department had remained unchanged, as they had by and large till the end of the eighteenth century, its structure, even with this ethos, would still have been satisfactory. The attitudes and conventions had originally been devised for, and were suited to, departmental divisions like the chief clerk's department, where experience and precedent were the most important types of expertise, justifying promotion by seniority, and the exaggerated reverence for long-established functions, and where because fees had originally been charged for all the business, it was reasonable to allocate functions very precisely.[37] But this type of ethos was less suitable to the newer business, or indeed to any dynamic as opposed to static bureaucracy, and the attitudes and conventions of the clerks had become actual or potential obstacles to efficiency, however efficiency was defined.

At the most basic level, they had resulted in an unfair distribution of the Office's workload, most notably with respect to the criminal business. But they had also helped to make the department rigid and ill-adapted to respond to new demands and duties. The extreme respect for tradition and for vested interests gave the department a strong bias against innovation. The Home Secretary could do little to help the integration of new subjects into the department's business, since he was a constitutional rather than an absolute head of the department, his actions closely circumscribed by custom and precedent. To correct the ills of the department, departmental norms needed to be altered to permit the Home Secretary to allocate status (rank, pay) according to responsibility, to endow important new subjects with a respected position in the bureaucratic structure, to move clerks freely about the Office, and above all, he needed to establish the right to innovate. A happier balance between tradition and innovation was necessary.

It is easier to state the type of reforms which were necessary than to suggest how they might have been effected. Sir George Grey, with the reform of 1849, began to dismantle the old structure, and to construct, tentatively, a new and more appropriate style of bureaucracy. He was probably able to do so without open revolt because the solidarity of the clerks was by chance weakened, the chief clerk, the first senior clerk and the librarian retiring at about the same time. But bureaucratic attitudes were only modifiable to a limited extent by structural reform, and there was no certain way of identifying which structural features underpinned which of the clerks' attitudes.

---

[37] A fee was charged for any instrument prepared in the Home Office. By 1822 the fees had been pooled in a fee fund, but clerks had previously received personally the fees for instruments which they had prepared. Hence the origin of a precise work division.

The sale of clerkships had, by 1848, been abandoned for at least thirty years, and direct payment out of fees at about the same time, yet attitudes which seem to have originated from these structural features survived them apparently undamaged. The problem was the more acute in that the older clerks were able to transmit these values as part of the training process to new recruits, and because it was the clerks themselves who had to implement, and so to interpret, schemes of reform. Grey did not succeed, in a broad sense, in destroying the conservatism of the Home Office, nor did competitive examination. Within the limits that its functions permitted the Home Office remained, and remains, a profoundly conservative bureaucracy.

Administrators in education before 1870: patronage, social position and role

A study of Education Department staff before 1870 suggests hypotheses about the development of the civil service as a whole.[1] Since the typicality of the Department's experience is certainly not established, 'hypothesis' is preferred to 'model'. There may indeed be no common pattern. As more departments are scrutinized and as comparisons are drawn between them, a typology may well emerge. Common features may be shared by all if only in so far as departments were subject to some common controls. But it would certainly be surprising not to find deep differences of development, or anyway of sequence, between departments founded in the 1830s in response to some of the problems of industrialization and, on the other hand, departments like the Treasury or Foreign Office with longer histories and with less direct relationships with social and economic change. The Education Department, dating from 1839, belonged firmly to the former type and the development of an educational civil service is most likely to resemble patterns of evolution within the Poor Law Commission and Board, within the 'transformed' Board of Trade and within the younger branches of the Home Office.

Within such a typology, departments will show idiosyncrasies of development arising out of the nature of the matter to be

[1] This article is an expansion of part of an unpublished thesis. See J. R. B. Johnson, 'The Education Department 1839–1864: A study in Social Policy and the Growth of Government', Cambridge Ph.D. (January 1968), esp. pp. 323–36. Cited below as 'Education Department'.

administered and out of personal and political contingencies. It is important, of course, to describe these idiosyncrasies. Yet questions of a broader scope are important, too: how to account for instance, if the historical assumptions of the Fulton Report are correct, for the curiously inexpert character of English bureaucracy. Exploring particular departments, historians of government have somehow to reach out to these larger questions.

An attempt is made here to move from specifics towards the study of uniformities and to do so in a particular way. Attention is concentrated on one department, but this examination suggests relationships of a more general kind between the mode of recruitment of the civil servant, his social position and the role he assumes within government. These relationships may supply tools for describing how the civil service developed during the nineteenth century and for explaining why it developed as it did.

The Department's internal crisis from 1847 to 1849 serves as a point of departure. By March 1849 it consisted of about fifty persons—in Charles Greville's words, 'a very gigantic affair'.[2] This number included an 'assistant secretary', two 'examiners', twenty-one inspectors and a large number of clerks with widely differing responsibilities and prospects.[3] Excluded from this count are the Lord President himself and his ministerial colleagues on the Committee of Council for Education, the Department's deliberative and 'legislative' superstructure. Excluded too are members of the Privy Council Office proper who had tangential connections with education business. Education Department and Council Office shared office space, a political head in the person of the Lord President and as the title 'assistant secretary' implies, a non-political chief, the Clerk of the Council. Seventeen of the education establishment were paid from Council Office funds, the remainder from the annual parliamentary vote for Public Education.

As its structure suggests the Department's growth over ten years had been haphazard. The Committee of Council had

---

[2] *Select Committee on Miscellaneous Estimates*, P.P. 1847–8, XVIII–I, q. 3182. Cited below as Misc. Ests.
[3] For inspectors, see P.P. 1861, XLVIII, p. 338; for office staff, Privy Council Outletter Books, P.R.O., P.C. 7/7, p. 300.

grown out of the frustrated educational ambitions of the Whig ministry in the complex religious politics of 1838. Unable to devise an acceptable plan for national education, Russell and his colleagues were committed to some action by promises given to their educational allies. They were also steeled to act by fears of a militantly Anglican initiative. They therefore delegated to four ministers the tasks of carrying through a few modest measures and of seeking a more comprehensive solution. The device of Order in Council lent some constitutional propriety to this expedient, but the Committee was, and remained, a constitutional oddity, neither Board nor Ministry, rather a Board of Ministers.

Around this curious body the Department itself, as an administrative agency, gradually grew. At each stage additions of staff followed the accumulation of functions. There was little prior planning of administrative arrangements. Administration was very personal, very unbureaucratic. In February 1839 Lord Lansdowne required an expert educational adviser. He chose Dr James Phillips Kay, made him assistant secretary to the Committee and located him in the Council Office. When building-grant business which dated from 1833 was transferred thither from the Treasury in August, Dr Kay became the administrator of a system. This transfer of functions marked the inception of the Department. Shortly afterwards, Harry Chester, a second class clerk in the Council Office, was co-opted as 'acting assistant' to the 'assistant secretary'.[4] Co-option on this pattern under the eye of the Treasury and Clerk of the Council became the standard means of recruiting non-specialist staff. Specialists—counsel, architect and inspectors—were appointed directly through the Lord President's patronage, usually on representations from Kay and, in the case of inspectors, subject to negotiation with religious bodies.

The informality of these arrangements and the accelerating dynamism of Kay's administration soon produced a gross imbalance between responsibilities and resources, particularly in periods of rapid expansion in the mid and late 1840s. On each occasion, ill, overworked but obsessed with growth, Kay broke through established routines of recruitment and secured sub-

[4] P.R.O., P.C. 7/9, p. 67.

stantial increases in staff.[5] These were, however, never adequate, and the crisis of the late 1840s was the result of an accumulation of anomalies in Kay's own position, of a massive accession of business associated with the Minutes of 1846 and of the refusal of the Treasury to allow a major reorganization. The crisis culminated in Kay's physical and mental collapse and his departure from office.

So despite its size, the Department of 1849 was the outcome of a chronic failure to match means to ambitions or *vice versa*. The reasons for this failure lie deeper than this cursory history reveals, but the Department of 1849 is interesting and significant in another way. For in its personnel, not excluding the Council Office contingent, it seems to straddle three stages in the development of a civil service. It contained three quite distinct tiers of staff coexisting within the same organization. Moreover, each tier exemplifies distinctive modes of recruitment —that is of patronage—and each group (or its most eminent representatives) bore a characteristic relationship with those political aristocrats who appointed them, and enjoyed, or suffered under, a characteristic social position. Further, circumstances of appointment and of social position appear to be related to the individual's conception of the role he should play within government. It may be that these three tiers represent an evolutionary sequence characteristic of the nineteenth-century civil service as a whole, a sequence that is both social and political in character. The passing of influence from one generation to another marks, at least in one sphere of government, the growth of a bureaucracy of a particularly British kind. This growth and the relationships upon which it depended can best be traced by looking in turn at the themes of patronage, social position and role, applying these to each of the generations.

Historians of government increasingly recognize the inadequacies of contemporary stereotypes in relation to methods of recruitment. The contemporary antithesis of 'patronage' and 'corruption' on the one hand and selection by 'merit' and by 'competition' on the other is now often seen as a gross simplification. It is clear that patronage, partly no doubt in response to criticism, became quite early in the century a much

[5] For example, the expansion of 1845, P.R.O., P.C. 4/19, pp. 279–81.

more flexible and in some senses more defensible device than many of its contemporary critics wished to believe. In this respect the history of the Education Department tends to confirm the work of Professors Finer and Hughes and of Dr Kitson Clark.[6]

Only in the case of the oldest stratum of office staff did patronage work in its classic, eighteenth-century form. Chester, Harrison and Bayly were all appointed to the Council Office before 1839, being subsequently co-opted to education business. The details of most of these appointments remain obscure, but we know that Chester was the youngest son of Sir Robert, Master of Ceremonies to three successive British kings. Presumably, after a routine education at Winchester and Trinity College, Cambridge, he was well placed to benefit from family connections. But the appointment of his superior officer, Charles Cavendish Fulke Greville, is better documented.

There is no doubt that 'connections', in the person of his maternal grandfather the Duke of Portland, were critical in Greville's career.[7] At the age of ten he was made Clerk Extraordinary (extraordinary indeed!) in the Council Office, becoming automatically Clerk of the Council in 1821. He owed his place to birth into a cadet branch of the aristocracy, not at all to his haphazard education, the shortcomings of which, like many aspects of his tolerably agreeable life, he frequently bemoaned. At first, before the growth of education business, he was not ill-qualified to supervise a department in which, as he put it, 'almost everything is a matter of ancient usage and practice'.[8] But like his department and the form of patronage that put him there, he belonged to a pre-industrial, pre-reform, pre-revolution in government era. His memory stretched back to 1808 when office staff were paid from fees and Clerks of the Council dis-

[6] S. E. Finer, 'Patronage and the Public Service: Jeffersonian Bureaucracy and the British Tradition', *Public Administration* XXX (1952); G. Kitson Clark, 'Statesmen in Disguise: Reflections on the History of the Neutrality of the Civil Service', *Historical Journal* II (1959); Edward Hughes, 'Civil Service Reform 1853–4', *Public Administration* XXXII (1954).

[7] Roger Fulford, ed., *The Greville Memoirs* (London, 1963), p. xi. Most of the material on Greville throughout this essay is drawn from this source.

[8] Misc. Ests., P.P. 1847–8, XVIII–I, q. 3191.

posed of their own patronage. Forty years later he still preferred the old system, though with the power of survival typical of the class whose doings he chronicled, he adapted quite well to the new.

Professor Finer has defined patronage as 'the recruitment of public servants by private recommendation',[9] and this remained of course the means of entry over the whole period with which we are concerned. But the nature of patronage changed and the change can best be appreciated by distinguishing two aspects of any patronage system. First, patronage requires some personal link, however indirect, between patron and client, and systems of patronage may vary according to the nature of this nexus. Secondly, patronage may, in practice, be exercised more or less functionally for the job in hand. The criteria used in placing a man may be intrinsic to the job (e.g. appropriate expertise) or may rest on extrinsic considerations (e.g. the needs of the client or the private and political interests of the patron).

In both respects, so far as the evidence goes, appointments after 1839 differed from those before. Older links had been those of family, or possibly of social dependency. After 1839, the nexus was of an expert, professional or latterly of an educational character. Contact between patron and client was often mediated through a civil servant already located in the Department. Moreover, only in a very few cases can extrinsic considerations be said to have been decisive. Man was matched to job with remarkable accuracy.

Between 1839 and 1849 there were thirty-one appointments to posts more exalted than that of clerk, eight to the central office and twenty-three to the inspectorate. Twenty-two of these are fairly well documented and, of these, only four are likely instances of the operation of social dependency. Three of Lord Lansdowne's appointees were recruited via his own social circle. Josiah J. Blandford was Curate of Calne, near Bowood, Lansdowne's own country seat. Two other Anglican inspectors, Henry Brookfield and Edward Tinling, owed their appointments to the good services of the Hallams, in Brookfield's case through his wife who was the Whig historian's niece.[10]

Inspection was no sinecure but at least one cleric gravitated

[9] Finer, *loc. cit.*
[10] Nancy Ball, *Her Majesty's Inspectorate 1839–49* (Birmingham, 1963), biographical notes.

to it impelled by genteel penury. As Perpetual Curate of Stock-port, Henry Walford Bellairs found himself isolated 'amid an awfully demoralised population'. His unsolicited letters of dis-tress (to none other than W. E. Gladstone) survive. By April 1842, having lost a private fortune in a Chancery suit and speculation in the West Indies, he foresaw disaster for himself and an inexorably expanding family: 'All that appears left to me is Emigration, which to a person of delicate health and literary habits is indeed but a doubtful prospect.'[11] Could even Gladstone have resisted such a plea? In the event Bellairs got the job, a more comfortable home in Cheltenham, and a salary not relinquished until 1872.

These cases, however, were exceptional. Most of the second 'generation' in the Department were men of early middle age (the group averaged thirty-six years of age on appointment) who had often already made some mark in the world of educa-tional action and inquiry.

Dr Kay (or Kay-Shuttleworth as he became in 1842) is the best example of appointment for expertise. From the 1830s he and the Whig ministry trod convergent paths that met at the famous interview with Lansdowne early in 1839. At the time of the Reform Bill crisis Kay was active in Radical middle-class politics in Manchester. During the cholera epidemic of 1831 he drew lessons about the working-class population of the city that were partly 'moral' (and therefore led to educational concerns) and partly 'physical' (hence contributing to the early public health movement). His famous pamphlet of 1832 may be seen as the real starting point of his educational career.[12] In the year (1833) when public money was first granted for building ele-mentary schools, he was busy organizing the Manchester Statistical Society which pioneered surveys of urban educational provision. Two years later he entered government service as a very zealous practitioner of the New Poor Law and was soon in touch with Russell over a pet scheme for pauper emigration.[13]

[11] Gladstone Papers, B.M. Add. MSS. 44359, f. 97.
[12] i.e. J. P. Kay, *The Moral and Physical Condition of the Working Classes employed in the Cotton Manufacture in Manchester* (London, 1832). The main source for Kay's life remains Frank Smith, *The Life and Work of Sir James Kay-Shuttleworth* (London, 1923).
[13] His activities within the Poor Law can be traced in his corres-pondence as Assistant Commissioner, P.R.O., M.H. 32/48–50.

While, after 1837, the Whigs were summoning up courage to act in education, Kay was developing parallel ideas in pauper education. In the campaign of 1838 he played a discreet but influential part in co-operation with the Whig MP, R. A. Slaney. At this stage, perhaps earlier, he was 'on intimate relations' with Russell, being one of three advisers who injected some political realism into the Home Secretary's educational plans.[14] Lansdowne's choice of Kay in 1839 must be reckoned one of his most astute in a long career of patronage.

Once appointed Kay used his influence over successive Lord Presidents to draw in men very like himself: avowed educationalists, social investigators, statisticians, members of official inquiries, public servants from associated departments. The process was similar to that which Professor Finer has termed 'permeation',[15] though Kay's links were not essentially those of a Benthamite circle. Thus W. G. Lumley, the Department's lawyer, was a member of the London Statistical Society recruited from the Poor Law Commission. Joseph Fletcher was the Society's secretary, a pioneer social statistician and a veteran servant of Commissions of Inquiry. J. C. Symons and E. C. Tufnell were also experienced educationalists, Tufnell being rescued from the increasingly bitter internal politics of the Poor Law Commission. Hugh Seymour Tremenheere, like Fletcher and Tufnell, was a member of the Central Society for Education, an important Whig/Radical pressure group of the late 1830s. Of the clerical inspectors, Muirhead Mitchell and Alexander Thurtell were connected with Kay's educational projects at Battersea and Norwood, while Henry Moseley was appointed on Kay's recommendation. The secretary's long association with William James Kennedy dated from their co-operation in drawing up the notorious management clauses in the mid-1840s. Like Frederick Cook, Kennedy was recruited from the Church's own 'educational civil service'. Cook had been an inspector at the London Diocesan Board of Education; Kennedy had been secretary of the National Society.[16]

14 Russell Papers, P.R.O. 30/22, 3B, Kay to Russell, 29 October 1838.
15 See above, S. E. Finer, 'The transmission of Benthamite ideas 1820–50'.
16 For the early association, see Kennedy to Kay-Shuttleworth,

Clerical recruitment, however, necessarily limited the secretary's influence. Quite apart from the need to choose men who were *persona grata* with the Bishops, it opened the way to informal ecclesiastical preferment on the Brookfield–Bellairs–Tinling–Blandford pattern. Hence Kay's insistence on the professional character of the inspectorate, best seen in his 'Scheme for Periodical Inspection' of 1843.[17]

The link with the clergy is a revealing symptom of the transitional character of the educational civil service, but this form of recruitment was not inappropriate to Kay's educational ideas or to the conditions of the 1840s. A dual allegiance to church and state, while involving some strain of roles as in the case of Rev. John Allen, could be an asset while secular and religious authority, piloted by Dr Kay, sailed together on a crusade of 'civilisation'. The clergy were to education what retired naval officers were in the control of emigration—a source of partly trained recruits.[18]

The third tier of the departmental sequence consisted of those central office staff who were recruited between 1847 and 1849. They were younger than the rest, on average ten years younger than their colleagues on appointment. But they also had a common educational origin—that circle of friends and protégés that gathered around Benjamin Jowett, tutor of Balliol College, Oxford.

At first sight this liaison with Balliol looks odd. The college was certainly already acquiring a formidable intellectual reputation, but its products hardly possessed a knowledge of the condition of the poor, nor a very deep commitment to social action. Yet both creators of the link stood to gain from it. For Jowett, devoted to his friends and his students, the civil service in general and the Education Department in particular provided a sort of adjunct to the college, an honourable outlet

---

31 May 1851, an open letter in *The Times*, 24 June 1852. Much of the rest of the biographical material in this paragraph is drawn from the biographical notes in Ball, *Inspectorate*.

[17] *Minutes of the Committee of Council on Education, 1841–2*, pp. 23–36.

[18] Cp. O. O. G. M. MacDonagh, *A Pattern of Government Growth 1800–60: the Passenger Acts and Their Enforcement* (London, 1961), pp. 333–4.

as prestigious and as useful as the Bar, the Church or teaching in some big public school. For Lansdowne and for Kay (though his role here is obscure) the Jowett circle was a handy source of able men with Liberal political opinions and undogmatic religious beliefs.

It is difficult to say exactly how the link was forged. We know that in the summer of 1846, Ralph Robert Wheeler Lingen, Fellow of Balliol and one of Jowett's closest friends, was studying without much enthusiasm for the Bar. By October he had been chosen to serve on the Welsh Educational Commission, the patronage for which lay in Lansdowne's hands. But whatever its origin, the link was certainly strengthened by 'permeation', or, in plainer language, by an 'old boy network'.

Lingen was joined by Matthew Arnold (as Lansdowne's private secretary) seven months later. It is suggestive, to say the least, that Lingen had been Arnold's tutor and had been, in the young man's words, 'a genius of good counsel to me ever since'.[19] In July 1847, Lingen completed the Welsh report and accepted an offer of the chief examinership, probably on Jowett's advice and certainly with his lasting approval.

Balliol's greatest coup, however, was Frederick Temple's appointment as prospective Principal of Kneller Hall—a training college for teachers in public institutions. Lingen's influence was decisive in persuading Temple to apply.[20] The plan soon bore fruit: Temple, a man of genuine educational interests, scored a great hit with Kay and the Whigs and was appointed in February 1848. Since he was unwilling to 'fight about money matters', his friends haggled over his salary with what Jowett called, rather disparagingly, 'these official men'.[21]

The second examinership remained to be filled. Predictably the Balliol pipe-line was again in operation. It was now so well established that there were two rival candidates: Arnold espoused the cause of his fellow poet Arthur Hugh Clough;

[19] G. W. E. Russell, ed., *The Letters of Matthew Arnold 1848–1888*, 2 vols (2nd ed. London, 1901), I, p. 16.
[20] E. G. Sandford, ed., *Memoirs of Archbishop Temple*, 2 vols (London, 1906), II, p. 489.
[21] Hutton Papers, Jowett to Lingen, *c.* 18 October 1847. This letter is part of a collection of letters between Jowett and Lingen which are now in the possession of Mr R. C. Hutton, who kindly let me see them.

Lingen and Jowett favoured Francis Sandford, ultimately Lingen's successor as secretary. Clough (not a Balliol man) had recently resigned his Fellowship at Oriel on religious grounds and was tempted by Arnold's suggestion of '£500 a year, and no oaths'.[22] It was Sandford, however, who was despatched to the Department with Jowett's blessing in November 1848: 'I think [Jowett told Lingen] you will find him a useful man—a good head and sound sense. It would be difficult to find here a better man for the post.'[23]

By the end of 1848 the first Balliol influx was almost complete—almost, for in 1849 Francis Turner Palgrave entered the Department's orbit as Temple's Vice-Principal, John Osborne Morgan, another Balliol graduate, having declined the offer.[24] In 1853 Clough at length got his examinership. Thereafter the invasion slowed, though under Lingen's paternal eye young men from Balliol were exceptionally well placed for entry.

With the possible exception of Temple, the claims of the Balliol men were very different from those of our second 'generation'. Lingen's experience of elementary education was limited to the Welsh Commission, to which he brought a rather cynical objectivity very different from Kay's obsessive concern. Arnold's educational enthusiasms were, as Connell observes, a late growth of his inspectoral experience. As Lansdowne's secretary he affected nonchalance, using his post for 'comparative leisure for reading'.[25] Sandford and Palgrave too were very raw recruits. The Balliol contingent indeed shared a detachment from the concerns of practical men which, in Jowett and Lingen bordered on despair:[26]

> As you say [wrote Jowett to Lingen in 1846] it seems affectation to suppose oneself seriously affected by the current of affairs in general—I wish one could have the results of a state of self-consciousness without the thing itself.

[22] H. R. Lowry, ed., *The Letters of Matthew Arnold to Arthur Hugh Clough* (Oxford, 1932), p. 89.
[23] Hutton Papers, Jowett to Lingen, 17 November 1848.
[24] For Palgrave's career see G. F. Palgrave, *Francis Turner Palgrave* (London, 1899).
[25] W. F. Connell, *The Educational Thought and Influence of Matthew Arnold* (London, 1950), p. 17.
[26] Hutton Papers, Jowett to Lingen, *c.* 22 September 1846.

Jowett escaped from this intellectual *anomie* through his commitments to university and civil service reform and through his obvious glee in placing young men in positions of influence and watching them prosper. Yet despite his formidable intellectual interests, his practical influence seems rather sterile—social and religious agnosticism combined with intellectual élitism. For most of his protégés, on their entry at least, the Department was either a financial prop for their intellectual interests or a way of getting on in the world. As Jowett told Lingen in 1849:[27]

> There is no one that I have known in Oxford more likely
> to succeed in life, and be useful, or attain high rank and
> position than yourself. There is no one I should be so glad
> to see at the top of the tree—as it seems natural to me that
> you should be ten or twenty years hence.

The significance of the Balliol influx is obvious enough. Years before the Northcote–Trevelyan Report and decades before its implementation a direct link was forged between a department of government and an Oxford college. Of necessity, in a system of patronage, the link was essentially personal, but it foreshadowed, in many ways, the competitive entry of young men into a profession directly from their educational institutions. Though Lingen was later to express doubts about competition, during his years as secretary he sought appointment 'by personal selection from among the very best men that can be found at the Universities'.[28] The claims of such men rested on no special expertise, rather upon what Northcote, Trevelyan and Lingen described as a 'high university education'.[29] Patronage, in short, was now being exercised through the educational institutions of the mid-Victorian intelligentsia, initially through a college well emancipated from aristocratic and ecclesiastical ties. And this change of patronage, of course, redefined in subtle ways what it was to be a civil servant in both a social and political sense.

[27] *Ibid.*, Jowett to Lingen, *c.* 18 July 1849.
[28] Granville Papers, P.R.O., 30/29, Box 23, part 1, bundle marked '1857 May, June, July, August and September—Russia', Lingen to Granville, 16 May 1856.
[29] *Reports of Committees of Inquiry into Public Offices*, P.P. 1854, XXVII, p. 230. Lingen collaborated in the drawing-up of this report.

The social character of the transition may be clearer if a few theoretical points are made first, linking the theme with patronage.

In a 'classic' form of patronage, the civil service will tend to be merely an extension of the social world of the politically active metropolitan aristocracy. Civil servants will tend to be the social peers, or possibly the social dependents, of the men they serve. Their private and public worlds will coincide; there is unlikely to be tension between the status they enjoy by virtue of their office and their private standing.

In a society in which land still confers status, in which politics is aristocratic in personnel, the man recruited on account of expertise may find himself in a more ambiguous situation. He owes his job not to a particular location within landed society but to particular knowledge, particular skills, a particular sense of commitment. If he is bourgeois in origin (as is likely with such a man) his relations with aristocratic superiors may well be uncertain. In the absence of clearly defined codes of official behaviour, working relationships will depend more on personal rapport (or suspicion) than upon social convention. Yet it is likely that aristocratic patrons themselves will carry into a more functional relationship some of the attitudes appropriate to earlier patterns of recruitment. Especially where the civil servant is also a social aspirant, these ambiguities may reveal themselves in a tension between his status as a private individual and his official persona.

These transitional anomalies in the social position of the public servant may be resolved when the service comes to be recognized as an appropriate career for men with common educational patterns and when the service as a whole becomes part of a wider (i.e. a professional) grouping in society at large. This in a sense is a return to the relative stability of the first stage but with this important difference: that the civil servant is now identified with a social stratum that carries status independent of its connections with an aristocratic élite (though with cultural affinities).

Certainly Charles Greville was very much a member of a metropolitan social élite. His interests were those of unregenerate aristocracy: a love-hate relationship with the Turf and the gambling fraternity, an eternal, rather melancholic round of country-house visits, recurring love affairs, passionate, bored, mostly the latter. In more puritan moments he deplored court gossip, but was an entertaining retailer of it. His Journal records 'the maze of politicks', that incestuous, face-to-face politics of early nineteenth-century London, concerned with personalities, distrustful of abstract and general principles. He loathed the intellectual as heartily as the social aspirant. 'Nonsense and folly gilded over with good breeding and *les usages du monde* produce more agreeable results than a collection of rude, awkward intellectual powers.'[30] Among politicians with some claim to intellect he dismissed Poulett Thompson as 'an ultra communist and himself in trade'.[31] As a principle of social organization he preferred 'feudality' to either 'the greatest happiness of the greatest number' or 'some abstract political rights'.[32] His social horizons were limited, more limited perhaps than those of many of his class for he lacked non-metropolitan roots in landownership. His reaction to a looming working-class presence in a cosier political tradition veered from a fear and loathing of the mob (and a desire to 'put them down') to an uneasy acquiescence in the politics of reform. His model of national bliss was 'a state of repose'.[33]

If he is to be believed, his relations with leading politicians were those of complete equality. The Clerkship gave him access to court, cabinet and parliament. He was a friend of successive Lord Presidents. His duties were hardly onerous: work in his office began at 11.0 a.m. and ended in mid-afternoon.[34]

For Kay, subordination to a gossiping dilettante must have been insufferable. The two men differed radically in their origins, aspirations and attitudes. Kay belonged firmly to the urban sector of Victorian society; Greville was parasitic on its rural half. Greville was rescued from a witty obscurity by birth; Kay was upwardly mobile in a typically early Victorian way. His family was Lancastrian, Dissenting and manufacturing. He was trained as a doctor at Edinburgh outside the aristocratic English tradition. His early social attitudes were shaped by class-conscious Manchester, as the tone and content of the 1832 pamphlet reveals. His self-identification with 'the enlightened manufacturers' with whom he worked underlay his

[30] Fulford, ed., *Greville Memoirs*, p. 61.   [31] *Ibid.*, p. 59.
[32] *Ibid.*, p. 144.   [33] *Ibid.*, p. 102.   [34] Misc. Ests., *loc. cit.*

rather envious scorn for the landowner and has the authentic ring of middle-class Radicalism. He saw 'commercial society' itself in terms of an antithesis between its potential saviours— the employers of labour—and the potent threat to its success and stability—their dangerous and barbarized work-force. The pamphlet is not without genuine sociological insight (which might be traced to his 'philosophical' education at Edinburgh) but is shot through with class loyalties and animosities.[35]

This perception of class relations was worked out in his official and private lives.[36] His relationship to the working class was developed in his odyssey of educational ideas, his relations with political aristocracy through fourteen years of loyal service and his relation with landed society as a whole through eventual absorption within it. In 1842 he married the heiress of an old and well-endowed family, changed his name from plain Kay and inherited an estate worth more than £10,000 a year—decidedly aristocratic by F. M. L. Thompson's criterion. In later life, relieved from the torture of public service, rewarded with a baronetcy, but not yet disengaged from the education question, he became 'bucolic in my tastes', weaned from politics by his farms and mines.[37]

His social *métier* is difficult to re-create, for it was fragmented and always changing. Born into a world of chapel-going and Sunday-school teaching, his social world at Gawthorpe and in London seems mainly to have consisted of allies and fellow enthusiasts: the educational circles of Battersea and Norwood, some members of the office staff, some inspectors, public philanthropists like Dickens and Angela Burdett Coutts, sympathetic Whigs like Morpeth, colleagues like E. C. Tufnell. He lacked Greville's *'usages du monde'* and was an awkward, unattractive man. Dickens pronounced his prose style dreary; Morpeth found his dinner parties 'long and not lively'.[38] As

[35] For a more extended analysis see 'Education Department', pp. 25–37.
[36] The main source in what follows is Frank Smith, *op. cit.*
[37] Chadwick Papers, University College, London, Kay-Shuttleworth to Chadwick, 14 March 1857.
[38] Pilgrim Trust Collection, Dickens to Miss Coutts, 1 April 1853. I am grateful to Mrs House for showing me a copy of this letter; Lady Caroline Lascelles, *Extracts from the Journals kept by George Howard, Earl of Carlisle*, entry for 1 July 1848.

Arnold put it in a famous comment that also handsomely acknowledged his educational zeal: 'He did not attract by person or manner; his temper was not smooth or genial, and he left on many persons the impression of a man managing and designing, if not an intriguer.'[39]

This social unease had a further dimension more closely associated with his official work. His rather lowly official position was clearly resented by his wife's relations who would have preferred to see him in parliament.[40] Though not himself an ambitious man in the conventional sense, he became acutely aware of the discrepancy between his private standing and his inconspicuous official post. This tension helps to explain his curious refusal of the Prince Consort's new civil service honour. His refusal, the reasons for it, his subsequent embarrassment and attempts at self-justification highlight the social ambiguities of his position.[41]

These difficulties were uniquely destructive of Kay's peace of mind, but other educational administrators of his 'generation' faced similar problems. The clerical inspectors' difficulties have already been mentioned, a symptom of rather haphazard recruitment from a cognate profession. There was a social dimension too in Tremenheere's tussles with the Office: as inspector he expected to exercise a gentlemanly freedom of action which 'Red-Tapism' inhibited.[42] Lumley and Westmacott, respectively counsel and architect to the Department, had similar troubles: Lumley repeatedly stood on his professional dignity as a lawyer to secure more pay;[43] Westmacott resigned in 1854, claiming compensation and, according to Trevelyan, in 'very peculiar circumstances'.[44] All this is symptomatic perhaps of a lack of definition in the public servant's social position which, in turn, was related to the recruitment of different kinds of outside 'experts'.

[39] From Arnold's essay on 'Schools' in T. H. Ward, *The Reign of Queen Victoria* (London, 1887).
[40] Kay-Shuttleworth Papers, Manchester University Library, Kay-Shuttleworth to Trevelyan, 18 January 1848.
[41] *Ibid.* the series of letters on this in January 1848.
[42] E. L. and O. P. Edmonds, *I Was There: The Memoirs of H. S. Tremenheere* (Windsor, 1965), p. 57.
[43] P.R.O., P.C. 1/2949, correspondence between Kay and Lumley.
[44] P.R.O., Treasury Papers, T. 9/9, p. 138.

How then did Kay, radical doctor turned would-be aristocrat, fare with his aristocratic patrons? Certainly Russell,
Lansdowne, even the Tory Lord Wharncliffe came to respect his
expertise, so much so that they were often spokesmen for his
ideas. On the whole Kay was lucky with his Lord Presidents,
even if Wharncliffe did treat him rather like a servant. But
other politicians, lacking a respect that grew from working with
the man, were much less amenable. It is easy to see a social as
well as a political animus in Sir James Graham's hostility,[45] and
Kay's official enemies, of whom there were many, were unre-
pentant: Greville, the Duke of Buccleuch, Spring Rice, Sir
Charles Wood and, above all, John Parker of the Treasury.
Parker, who hated all 'philosophers and wise men' in government (including Senior, Chadwick and George Lewis), had no
patience with Kay or his policies and wished heartily 'to get rid
of this gentleman'.[46]

The occasional fit of rebellion apart, Kay, for his part, was
intensely loyal, especially to the Whigs. Indeed an obsequious-
ness runs through much of his correspondence, reaching a peak
of flowery subservience in a series of letters to Henry Brougham.[47] This quite disproportionate self-effacement associated
with his social and perhaps religious origins seriously weakened
his hand when his services were dispensed with in a very shabby
way in 1849.

A more harmonious pattern emerges with the Balliol men.
In particular they harmonized their public and private lives.
Balliol itself, the Council Office and Temple's Kneller Hall
formed centres of a widening sphere of influence embracing the
civil service itself, middle- and upper-class education and the
literary and artistic worlds. Fully to anatomize this important
social milieu requires a separate study but some of the ramifications of the Balliol circle require mention.

Apart from their hold on the Education Department, that
secretarial succession from Lingen, via Sandford, to Cumin and

[45] See Graham Papers, Cambridge University Library (microfilm),
bundle 52 B, Graham to Kay-Shuttleworth, 30 August 1842; see also
'Education Department', p. 123.
[46] Hickleton Papers, York City Library, A 4/52, Parker to Wood,
4 April 1847.
[47] Brougham Papers, University College, London; Letters from Kay-
Shuttleworth, August 1859 to May 1861.

Kekewich, Balliol was associated with the movement for civil service reform. Northcote was a Fellow of the College and Trevelyan worked closely with Lingen on the reorganization of the Education Department in the early 1850s. This project, long overdue, raised many of the issues dealt with in a more general way by the Northcote–Trevelyan Report itself. It might even be regarded as a sort of pilot scheme, a test-bed for the kind of recruitment advocated in the general Report.[48] Moreover, in so far as matters extrinsic to the efficiency of government may have influenced Trevelyan himself or have otherwise shaped the Report, Jowett and Temple, with their characteristically educational view of reform, are the strongest candidates for influence. Gladstone and Trevelyan thought them the fittest men to serve on the Commission, and when Temple refused the offer, Theodore Walrond, another Balliol Fellow, was recommended by Jowett.[49] Although Lingen's attitude to competition proved to be lukewarm, his temporary conversion was regarded by Northcote as a significant victory.[50]

The wider educational contribution of the group was marked —but more marked in the education of their own class than in the official sphere of the Department itself. Professor Roach has indicated some of the group's wider ramifications: the association with Edward Cardwell and with Robert Lowe, the link with the Board of Trade, the involvement of Jowett himself in the Indian civil service.[51] But Jowett, Temple and their friends formed a real power-house for the reform of Oxford in the 1850s,[52] and Temple and Lingen were involved in founding the Oxford examinations for grammar schools and, with Arnold, in the planning and performance of the Taunton Commission.[53]

[48] *Reports of Committee of Inquiry into Public Offices*, P.P. 1854, XXVII.

[49] See Edward Hughes, 'Sir Charles Trevelyan and Civil Service Reform', *English Historical Review* LXIV (1949), esp. letters printed on pp. 229–31.

[50] *Ibid.*, pp. 80–1. I am grateful to Jenifer Hart for her criticisms of an earlier, cruder assessment of Balliol influence on civil service reform.

[51] J. P. C. Roach, 'Victorian Universities and the National Intelligentsia', *Victorian Studies* III (December, 1959), p. 149, n. 56.

[52] Their roles can be traced in the Gladstone Papers.

[53] 'Education Department', p. 430.

Arnold himself always wrote more convincingly on the education of his own class than on the schools which he professionally inspected. This diversion of departmental enthusiasms away from the working class was capped by Temple's move to the Headmastership of Rugby (his inevitable destination) in 1857.

Socially the Balliol men were a cohesive group albeit with close connections with other sections of the mid-Victorian intelligentsia. The office staff formed, as Kekewich observed, 'exactly the same sort of society that is to be found in any college Common Room': 'they were scholars, poets, philosophers and musicians etc., and they were ready to discuss—and discuss well—any subject under the sun except education'.[54]

Kekewich was prone to exaggeration, but the array of departmental talents was certainly formidable, with Clough, Palgrave, Sandford, Arnold and Lingen himself (an amateur philologist and incurable writer of Greek verse) having considerable literary interests.

Their other centres of social gravity included Kneller Hall and Robert Morier's Cosmopolitan Club. Temple was visited regularly at weekends by Jowett, Arnold and on occasion by Tom Taylor (another civil servant/writer). The Tennysons, Brownings, A. P. Stanley, Scott, Lake and Walrond were also visitors. When a 'feast' was held there in honour of the christening of one of Tennyson's children Morier noted that 'poets [were] there as thick as black-berries'.[55] The Cosmopolitan Club was, in effect, an extension of university intellectual life, of Jowett's vacation reading-parties and the famous Decade Society at Oxford. Palgrave, Temple and Lingen among others attended its twice-weekly meetings.[56] At Brookfield's house at Portman Street the Balliol men dined with the HMI's contemporaries at Cambridge, including Thackeray, Tennyson, Arthur Hallam, Kinglake and Monkton Milnes.[57] The company there and at Kneller Hall shows how, by the mid-century,

[54] Sir G. W. Kekewich, *The Education Department and After* (London, 1920), p. 8.
[55] Rosslyn Wemyss, *Memoirs and Letters of Sir Robert Morier*, 2 vols (London, 1911), I, p. 116.
[56] *Ibid.*, pp. 113–14.
[57] C. H. E. and F. M. Brookfield, *Mrs Brookfield and Her Circle*, 2 vols (London, 1905), II, *passim*.

the worlds of literature, public service and higher education overlapped.

Membership of this kind of élite bred in the Balliol men a lack of awe for their political superiors. They plotted and planned self-assertively for their just rewards in terms of salary or position, Lingen being a sort of career-guidance officer in such matters. Critical of the sparse talents of the Derby administration, they were unimpressed by the educational competence of the Aberdeen coalition: as Temple put it 'they have not, no not one of them, the slightest vestige of a notion of what ought to be done'.[58] In his dealings with Lord Granville, a kindly but rather ineffectual man, Lingen wielded a whole armoury of 'advisory' phrases, from, in ascending order of strength, 'I beg leave to point out to your Lordship' to 'I protest against this proceeding'. When the Lord President wished to appoint an examiner against Lingen's advice, he received a protest of twelve pages and thirteen paragraphs. Having replied in mollifying terms, he was rocked by a second blast and gave up the drafting of a reply in despair.[59]

Bearing in mind these social differences, it is not surprising that the Education Department was a rather uncomfortable place to work in. Greville was inclined to regard Kay as a nuisance both to government and to himself. After Kay had been violently attacked in *The Times* for publicly discussing his educational philosophy, Greville told Henry Reeve that he should be 'muzzled'—'for it will not do to have the Council set up to be pelted with the ridicule and ribaldry of the Press'.[60]

Though the Balliol men came to admire Kay as an administrator,[61] in the 1840s they did not really regard him as an educated man. His interest in university reform was greeted with an arrogant scepticism: 'he is,' wrote Jowett, 'as unfit as

[58] F. L. Mulhauser, ed., *The Correspondence of Arthur Hugh Clough*, 2 vols (Oxford, 1957), II, p. 373.
[59] Granville Papers, Box 19, bundle marked '1859', Lingen to Granville, 20 July 1859, and the letters that follow.
[60] A. H. Johnson, ed., *The Letters of Charles Greville and Henry Reeve, 1836–65* (London, 1924), p. 71.
[61] See, for example, Kay-Shuttleworth Papers, Lingen to Lord Shuttleworth, 26 May 1877. But this was true while Kay was alive too!

the two barbarians Hengist and Horsa to reform the University.'[62] Lingen in particular chafed under his control. He swung from 'attacking Shuttleworth in very vigorous English' to keeping quiet, on Jowett's advice, so as not to appear 'an impracticable man' for the succession.[63] These underlying personal tensions contributed substantially to the Department's internal difficulties between 1847 and 1849.

How, then, may the social position of the civil servant affect his role within government?

Where public offices are tied to the political aristocracy by 'classic' patterns of patronage, the distinction between civil servant and politician will tend to be unreal. The term 'civil servant' itself, with its connotations of professionalism, will be inappropriate. Administration will tend to be an adjunct of politics. It will lack a dynamic of its own. The public servant will conceive it as a means of support in a style of life to which he is accustomed or perhaps as a means of day-to-day involvement in political manœuvre.

The 'expert' in government will tend to conceive his role as the pursuit of a cause, defined less as political partisanship, more by the imperatives of his expertise. His administration will tend to be dynamic, expansive and creative. He will seek to create new functions, to make policy, to be, in Sir James Stephen's phrase, a 'statesmen in disguise'. He will work on 'law-making opinion'—Members of Parliament and the particular public appropriate to his field. These commitments will be all the more intense where public service itself lacks social self-justification and may be easier to exercise where there are few precedents to guide and limit modes of action. Dr Kitson Clark's concept of an 'heroic generation' of public servant is a useful one, but it has social, even psychological dimensions as well as constitutional.

The non-expert but professional administrator will tend to see his job less as the pursuit of a cause, more as the honourable performance of prescribed duties. This may arise, in part, from the legacy bequeathed to him by the expert; he will enter an already complex administrative system with inherent tendencies towards bureaucratization. But these tendencies will be

[62] Hutton Papers, Jowett to Lingen, 'Sunday Evg.', 1847 or 1848.
[63] *Ibid.*, Jowett to Lingen, *c.* 18 July 1849.

strengthened by the interlocking patterns of his recruitment, motivation and social position. His concerns will be with the mechanics of administration, with the conditions of service of the profession he has made his own. A commitment to expansion in pursuit of policy goals may be replaced by the efficient application of rules (a 'Code'); flexibility by uniformity; propagandizing by anonymity; policy-making by precedent-following. Fresh initiatives may have to come from outside administration altogether—from parliament, from politicians, from groups of experts outside. Within the Department itself a policy-making function may wither away. A differentiation of functions will emerge between policy-maker/politician on the one side and administrator/civil servant on the other. When politicians abrogate their function, administrative convenience alone will tend to determine policy.

The experience of the Education Department helps to pin down these abstractions. While Greville epitomizes that aristocratic style of administration, Kay belongs, of course, to the statesmen in disguise, to the 'zealots' as Henry Parris has called them.[64] His regime was certainly marked by a dynamic process of growth and most of the other characteristics noted above. Growth was quantitative but also qualitative: more grants given, more schools reached, but also a progressive intensification of control over the essentially voluntary agencies of elementary education. A system of annual grants dating from 1846 acquired for Department, government and for authority in general an army of strategically located dependents (the elementary schoolteachers). The achievement was all the more remarkable for the absence of any statutory sanction and the fierce though fluctuating force of public opposition.

But was this a question of style in administration or rather a fairly automatic consequence of administrative process? There are certainly elements of this growth that fit MacDonagh's notion of self-generation.[65] An accent upon process is a useful corrective to the naïvely biographical approach of Frank Smith and the thoroughly autobiographical account of Kay himself.[66]

[64] Henry Parris, *Constitutional Bureaucracy* (London, 1969), p. 138.
[65] Cf. O. O. G. M. MacDonagh, 'The Nineteenth Century Revolution in Government: A Reappraisal', *Historical Journal* I (1958).
[66] B. C. Bloomfield, ed., *The Autobiography of Sir James Kay-*

It is true that once launched the Department showed certain built-in tendencies to grow, though dynamism in this case was based on the grant system not on the progressive enforcement of legislation. Local agents needed money; the Department was prepared to provide it on certain conditions. Qualitative growth was also, in a sense, the result of a process: the establishment of a dynamic *rapport* between an inspectorate eager to influence policy and a secretary who directed their inquiries, used their reports to influence opinion and made coherent recommendations to politicians.

Yet this process of growth, if 'process' it is to be, rested in the last analysis (within necessary political limitations) on the value systems of its agents and upon their will to act. Dynamism was essentially personal and essentially purposive—though the results were not always those that were predicted. But policy *was* made and followed, and growth occurred, and occurred in the way it did in large part because its principal agent combined a rigid fixity of purpose with a tactical skill bordering on political genius. But Kay's strategy was always guided by his concern with a particular kind of educational progress, the origins of which would lead deep into the hinterland of early Victorian class realities and attitudes.[67] In this sense the Minutes of 1846 were as unpragmatic as Chadwick's New Poor Law. Kay's expertise was really an intense personal involvement deriving from a particular social vision. That vision—of the elementary school as a functioning centre of 'civilization' amid a dangerous and degraded population—in turn rested on a personal perception of early nineteenth-century social structure and in particular on the 'need' (as perceived by Kay) for new kinds of social discipline and control. The relation between this vision and any contemporary body of theory and doctrine (Benthamism for instance) is far from clear, and it may well be that the fashionable divorce between 'ideas' and 'facts' has led historians of government astray. A better formulation (though too general to take us very far) might be this: the motive force in much government growth was an historical social structure

---

Shuttleworth, University of London Institute of Education, Education Libraries Bulletin, Supplement 7 (1964).
[67] For an analysis of attitudes see 'Education Department', pp. 25–35.

(or aspects of it) as perceived through the eyes and minds of men strategically located within it. Kay's location was both geographical and social: his capacity to be at the significant place at the significant time is as striking as his social mediation between urban society and its problems and a rurally based élite. And it is because of this importance of personal vision growing from personal experience that modes of recruitment and the general social characteristics of the men who are recruited are vital in any adequate explanation of the growth of government.

Kay's style of administration lacked something of the verve and the high-powered salesmanship of Chadwick's noisy campaigns and disclosures, but it fits the Chadwick–Simon–Trevelyan–Porter–Hill *modus operandi* very well. Kay aspired to be, as the Duke of Sutherland (an ally) and Greville (an enemy) noted, a 'Minister', if possible a Minister of Public Instruction.[68] He was fount of policy, chief executant of it, secret negotiator in chief, public apologist, stimulator of public pressure, former of public opinion. In a constitutional view of things there is little to add to the analyses of this style by Dr Kitson Clark and Professor Finer,[69] except to say that all the uncertainties (and therefore opportunities) surrounding this generation of public servants were present with double force in the Education Department. The explosiveness of the education issue was the main limitation, but that quality helped to shape a department whose constitutional arrangements were more than usually inexact. There is no doubt that this gave the permanent official an enormous influence, supposing he wished to wield it.

In January 1850 Lingen inherited all the policy-making discretions of his predecessor and even, at first, the same set of politicians to deal with. Yet the contrast between the two regimes is sharp. If Kay belonged to an 'heroic' generation, Lingen exemplifies bureaucracy. We know less of this unexciting type (at least historically), though parallels could be drawn with John Lambert, Sir John Simon's enemy.

---

[68] Kay-Shuttleworth Papers, Duke of Sutherland to Kay-Shuttleworth, 24 January 1846; Johnson, *Letters*, p. 71.
[69] Kitson Clark, 'Statesmen in Disguise', *loc. cit.*; Finer, 'The Individual Responsibility of Ministers', *Public Administration* XXXIV (1956).

After 1850 qualitative growth was replaced by control, latterly by reaction and retrenchment. Quantitative growth continued: more schools reached, much more money spent, many emendations of and accretions to the Minutes. Yet, until the Revised Code, this was largely working-out the implications of the Minutes themselves which were originally planned as a phased, progressive system. But the principles of government action remained unchanged and until 1870 there was no major legislation, though the need for legislative breakthrough was more apparent every year. Even the Revised Code was barely a new departure. Though it subverted the aims of the Minutes of 1846, it was a pruning operation devoid of any creative educational or social alternative.

Again MacDonagh's categories take us some way in explaining a process which in terms of the model looks decidedly pathological. If qualitative dynamism rested on *rapport* between inspectors and the central office, a failure to grow can be traced to mutual alienation. Inspectors trained in the Shuttleworthian tradition continued to act as educational statesmen, but faced an impenetrable block at the centre. The secretariat abrogated policy-making but also sought to shape the inspectorate in its own image, making the Department instrumental not suggestive. This objective, rigorously pursued after 1858, reduced the inspectorate to an administrative agency, the Department to a rather efficient machine.

Yet Lingen's control was quite as deliberate as Kay's fostering of growth. In a way it was quite as difficult. The period of expansion had created expectations that proved difficult to disappoint. A denominational educational public had been habituated to rather generous aid and pressed for more; inspectors had grown used to recommending policy and expected to be heard. Formidable talents were needed to wage war on both.

As we have seen, the social experiences underlying Kay's passion were foreign to the Balliol men. Lingen's Wales was very different from Kay's Manchester, mid-century Oxford very different from social medicine at Edinburgh. Jowett was no counterpart to Professor W. P. Alison, nor Greek verse and philology to Political Economy and the Scottish tradition of historical sociology. Lingen's most memorable educational experience, his friendship with Jowett apart, was his arrival at Oxford in 1837 from a provincial grammar school to sit for a Trinity scholarship.[70]

As the knowledgeable man who wrote his obituary put it, 'his mind was essentially logical'.[71] He was more a man of principles than enthusiasms, more of rather conventional ambition than a crusader. On some things he felt very strongly—jobbery, special pleading, university reform, Oxford ecclesiasticism (opposition to which was a ruling passion of his life). But the education of the poor was not among his enthusiasms. His coolness (and efficiency) was noted by W. F. Cowper, the Department's first Vice-President in 1857: 'This office is moving with its usual clock-work regularity. Lingen will go on leave next week—he meditates a journey to Rome, I suppose to get as far as he can out of the reach of Education.'[72]

So to his analysis of the mid-century educational situation Lingen brought the virtues of a logician. His view was acute, subtle, entirely dispassionate. It cannot be recapitulated in full here,[73] but briefly he saw the Minutes of 1846 as a palliative, but the best that could be got. He looked forward to the 'substitution of a final settlement' along lines which in contemporary jargon were 'secularist': properly constituted local authorities, separation of secular and religious instruction, a reduction in the responsibilities and costs of central government. In the meantime he saw himself as caretaker of the principles of 1846. His job was to stem the growth of a system of subsidies and to control the expansionist tendencies of inspectorate and educational public. Though he reigned supreme in the office, his control over departmental 'legislation' by Minute was incomplete. He therefore failed to prevent a large increase in expenditure in the mid-1850s and was obliged to lend rather reluctant support to the Revised Code. He used it, however, to discipline the inspectorate.

No man was more convinced of the deficiencies of the system he administered and his alternative was notably perceptive.

[70] George Marshall, ed., *Osborne Gordon: A Memoir* (Oxford, 1855), p. 4. Lingen's contribution is mainly about the Oxford episode.
[71] *The Times*, 24 July 1905, p. 8.
[72] Granville Papers, Box 19, bundle marked '1857', Cowper to Granville, 22 September 1857.
[73] For a fuller account see 'Education Department', pp. 418–25.

The paradox was that he did so little to change the one and move towards the other. He simply did not believe that policy-making, still less policy-pushing, were within his province. These belonged to the politician, not to the office staff, emphatically not to the inspectorate. The Department was there to administer and administer it would.

He therefore assumed a role which he described as 'passion-less bureaucracy'.[74] He was a creator of civil service attitudes which are now (rightly or wrongly) proverbial. His stance was essentially neutral and anonymous. He rarely disclosed his views on policy; his statements to Commissions and Select Committees were guarded. He never engaged, except occasionally in self-defence, in anything like public controversy. He treated all parties with an equal severity, insisting on the uniform application of all rules. Accountability and economy were his watch-words.

Even so, 'passionless' is a little misleading. For he was deeply concerned with the techniques and the ethics of public service: with career structure, with incentive and merit, with *esprit de corps*, with proper procedure and discipline. Unlike many of his group who sought their deeper satisfactions outside their work, he identified fully with the 'permanent service' he helped to shape. So much is clear from the letter he wrote to Arthur Helps after his move to the Treasury in 1871:[75]

> Power is not strutting . . . nor titles . . . but work, service,
> self-denial and self-devotion, quite as often in resisting
> the cry 'something must be done' as in doing. No such
> preaching should ever appear in minutes, but in example,
> if it can be set.

These interlocking patterns of change can most usefully be seen as a progressive professionalization of an important branch of the civil service. It was a process not dissimilar to the emergence of other professions with a common matrix in the social hierarchies of landed society. By changes in the pattern of

[74] Memorandum: The Representation of the Committee of Council on Education in the House of Commons, 6 June 1855, P.R.O., Ed. 24/53, p. 10. This document is in Lingen's hand.
[75] E. A. Helps, *The Correspondence of Sir Arthur Helps* (London, 1917), p. 317. The omissions indicate quotations in Greek.

recruitment, links with landed society were severed, educational and cultural criteria ultimately replacing those of birth. Of course, educational opportunities themselves were socially stratified and no very egalitarian recruitment emerged. Yet the change was significant and, in one department at least, predated the Northcote–Trevelyan Report and the coming of competition. After a period of fluidity and unusual opportunities, the new social pattern formed around the educational institutions of the mid-century intelligentsia. These men permeated the service and gave it much of its modern character. It acquired an autonomous professional standing. Tensions arising from a rather haphazard and open recruitment were resolved as the service was less tied to repositories of expertise outside. The professional ethic that was formulated centred more upon the job of the civil servant *qua* administrator than upon imperatives of particular fields of social action. The ethic was transferable within government: Lingen's attitudes were as applicable to the Treasury as to the Education Department. But this development of a professional ethic was associated with a narrowing of the definition of what it was to be a civil servant.

How, then, are we to account for this process? Education Department experience suggests that the Northcote–Trevelyan Report was not too important. It seems to signpost change rather than cause it. The process was longer, more complex, more subterranean. Changes in the pattern of recruitment also predated open competition; they occurred first under a system of reformed patronage. Whether the Education Department was (as seems likely) a leading sector in this respect only further research will reveal. But it could be that the report is best seen as a *post hoc* rationalization of the position of the new kind of civil servant and an attempt to mould the whole service in the same image.

A deeper explanation may lie in an analysis of interaction between processes within government and outside, particularly in the educational system. This study tends to confirm the truism that the character of the service will depend, in large part, on the types of men recruited—on their predispositions and the social, educational and experiential forces which shaped them. Patterns of recruitment depend in turn on two sorts of conditions: the needs of government as perceived by those responsible for recruitment and the sources of potential recruitment outside. One might add a third condition: the responsiveness of methods of recruitment to governmental needs. This study suggests that reformed patronage was a particularly sensitive form of mediation.

On the rash assumption that the Education Department was typical it is possible to construct a hypothetical explanation of professionalization bearing these general points in mind. The acceptance of new responsibilities by government, growing from particular perceptions of social and economic problems, created a need for kinds of expertise. This need was recognized by those aristocratic patrons who controlled recruitment. Patronage was modified to recruit from precisely those groups most active in the identification of problems, whether medical men, social investigators, statisticians, 'Benthamites' and so forth. These groups were already urging government to act and formed a natural source of innovating policy-makers. They often fitted uneasily into a still traditional political world, but drew in more men like themselves. Their activities built up increasingly large and complex systems of control, and scale and complexity itself produced pressures towards professionalization and bureaucracy. The innovators could not continue to control *and* direct their own creations, the more so since in a developing system of representative government they had to be seen to be responsible to parliament, at least for their policy-making functions. But government growth also created a 'need' for a new kind of élite, men of more general abilities who might make administrative rationalization and control their main objectives. A fund of such men was available in the old universities where some teachers had an eye on the service as an honourable destination for their graduates. It may well be, as Musgrove has argued, that opportunities for such men in the most élitist of the professions were in decline relative to educational supply.[76] Young men recruited almost straight from an upper-middle-class education looked upon the service as a career and shaped it as a unified profession. The 'professional amateur' had arrived.

[76] F. Musgrove, 'Middle-class Education and Employment in the Nineteenth Century', *Ec.H.R.*, 2nd series, XII (1959–60). The argument here is more convincing than Musgrove's critics have allowed if attention is focused on the low growth rates of the relatively prestigious professions—especially the church and the Bar.

The Colonial Office and its permanent officials 1801–1914

Unlike many other government departments, the Colonial Office has not been neglected by historians. In recent years, a large number of works have appeared which have closed the gaps in our knowledge and allowed us an almost complete picture of the development of the Office from the beginning to the end of the nineteenth century.[1] Some of the drawing has been merely outline, some extremely detailed and expertly coloured. It becomes possible to examine the broader perspective and to suggest what might be the unique or the distinctive features in the history of this important government

[1] Recent works on the subject include R. R. Nelson, *The Home Office, 1782–1801* (Durham, N.C., 1969); D. M. Young, *The Colonial Office in the Early Nineteenth Century* (London, 1961); D. J. Murray, *The West Indies and the Development of Colonial Government* (Oxford, 1965); T. J. Barron, 'James Stephen, the Development of the Colonial Office and the Administration of Three Crown Colonies', Ph.D., London 1969; W. P. N. Tyler, 'Sir Frederic Rogers, Permanent Under-Secretary at the Colonial Office, 1860–71', Ph.D., Duke University, N.C., 1962; John W. Cell, *British Colonial Administration in the Mid-Nineteenth Century: The Policy-Making Process* (New Haven, Conn., 1970); Brian Blakeley, 'The Colonial Office, 1870–1890', Ph.D., Duke University, 1966; R. V. Kubicek, *The Administration of Imperialism: Joseph Chamberlain at the Colonial Office* (Durham, N.C., 1969); R. Hyam, *Elgin and Churchill at the Colonial Office* (London, 1968); J. A. Cross, 'The Dominions Department of the Colonial Office: Origins and Early Years, 1905–1914', Ph.D., London, 1965. We are grateful to the authors of unpublished theses for permission to consult their work. An even larger number of works dealing principally with colonial policy contain invaluable material on the Office.

department.[2] This essay seeks to understand one small, though perhaps significant, part of the Office's development—that which concerned the role played by the civil servants themselves.

The importance of creating an efficient secretariat was early appreciated by the political heads of the Colonial Department, particularly by Earl Bathurst and Henry Goulburn who have been described as the real founders of the Office. Bathurst may have been old-fashioned, Goulburn fastidious, but they were both adept at shaping an administrative machine and conscious promoters of a departmental *esprit de corps*. Goulburn's successor as parliamentary under-secretary, Robert Wilmot Horton, a restless, creative, dynamic administrator, was even more influential. Under his influence the first full-scale reorganization was made in the 1820s of the composition and structure of the Office. A large number of new posts were added to cope with an increased workload, rapid promotion was promised to attract better clerical candidates, grades were introduced to encourage clerks to remain beyond a few years and to acquire experience, and pensions were provided to persuade the older, less competent clerks to withdraw and make way for younger men. Horton's greatest skill, perhaps, was his ability to detect and to exploit potential administrative talent. He brought on to the establishment men with some intellectual pretensions, like James Stephen, Henry Taylor and Thomas Hyde Villiers who, by various means, were pushed over the obstacle of seniority promotions and found their way rapidly to positions of influence. Horton also invited a number of clerks to assume responsibility for conducting various technical if subordinate parts of the daily business. In 1825 his reforms reached their apogee with the creation of both a new permanent under-secretaryship and a permanent counselship, demonstrating the importance of the work of the non-political personnel.[3]

Behind the statistics of an expanding clerical staff and a

[2] One pioneering attempt at a general history of the office deserves attention, viz. R. B. Pugh, 'The Colonial Office, 1801–1925' in E. A. Benians, Sir James Butler and C. E. Carrington (eds), *The Cambridge History of the British Empire*, vol. III (Cambridge, 1959), pp. 711–68. See also R. B. Pugh, *The Records of the Colonial and Dominions Offices* (Public Record Office Handbooks, no. 3, London, 1964), pp. 3–16.
[3] Both Young, *op. cit.*, pp. 47–83 and Murray, *op. cit.*, pp. 109–26, deal extensively with Goulburn's and Horton's reforms.

growing volume of office business were developments which were altering the functioning of the office machine. The Secretaries of State in other departments were expected to handle the bulk of their office business personally, but this proved impossible in the Colonial Office. There the political heads were required to be almost a cabinet council in themselves, being responsible for a broad field of administration in each colony rather than for one particular subject. The distance and unfamiliarity of the colonies aggravated this difficulty. An understanding of many colonial problems necessarily required either a local knowledge or a sustained study and interest which the average aristocratic politician of the period simply could not muster. In terms of the sheer volume of work which they had to perform the Colonial Secretaries also became victims both of the formal expansion of empire and of the parliamentary demands for greater imperial supervision of colonial policies on questions of slavery or land and emigration policies. By the end of the 1820s the Colonial Office was coping with a volume of correspondence which was approximately twice as large as it had been in 1815 and considerably more complex and technical.

The embarrassment of the secretaries of state does not in itself explain the solution which emerged. Much of the burden of correspondence was a product of internal administrative initiative rather than external pressures. The permanent officials in the Colonial Office became influential not only because of an increasing demand for their work, but because they themselves seized the opportunity created by this demand to expand the range and depth of their activities. The Office was acquiring a memory and the ability to plan, and here the role of the permanent official was crucial. It was the expertise of the permanent officials derived from years of study of particular problems and their specialist knowledge, forensic, economic, literary, which determined that the conduct of much of colonial business should be relinquished by the parliamentary heads in favour of them.

In some ways this contribution by the permanent staff was merely accidental, a product of a political crisis. After eight years in the Office Henry Taylor could write:[4]

[4] Taylor to Howick, 6 February 1833, Taylor correspondence, Grey Papers, Durham University.

From the first year that I was in this office I have been
employed not in the business of a clerk but in that
of a statesman. So far as the West Indian colonies have
been concerned I have at all times since that period done
more for the Secretary and Under-Secretary of
State for the time being of their peculiar and appropriate
business than they have done for themselves. I have
been accustomed to relieve them from the trouble of
taking decisions and of writing them. In ninety-nine cases
out of a hundred the consideration which had been given
to a subject by the Secretary of State has consisted
in reading the draft submitted to him and his decision has
consisted in adopting it, and the more important the
question has been the more have I found my judgement
to be leant upon.

But these were years of crisis on the question of West Indian
slavery and it is clear that Taylor's services were volunteered
quite as much as they were requested. He later admitted that
he was never again employed so strenuously or with such
singular authority after 1833.[5]

None the less Taylor's experience, though more dramatic
than that of other officials, was not unique. James Stephen,
whose first connection with the department had been in the
humble capacity of an occasional legal counsel, was in many
ways even more influential. In 1827 William Huskisson found
Stephen's services and assistance in the Office 'indispensable'.[6]
Two other civil servants who served outside the normal clerical
ranks, T. F. Elliot, who was précis writer, and W. H. C. Mur-
doch, who was a supernumerary clerk, were said in 1832 to
have 'powers and aptitudes of such a nature as would in any
profession in which competition had free scope ensure them
success and even eminence'.[7] And both of them were given
duties in the Office which apparently allowed them to show

[5] Taylor to Gladstone, 8 May 1846, Gladstone Papers, B.M. Add.
MSS. 44,363. ff. 79–80.
[6] Huskisson to Wilmot, 18 October 1827, Huskisson Papers, B.M.
Add. MSS. 38,751, f. 267.
[7] Stephen to Howick, 10 February 1832, Stephen correspondence,
Grey Papers. Both clerks had served on commissions to Canada and
so acquired an extra-official reputation.

their abilities. When contemplating a reform of the establishment in the same year, the young Lord Howick noticed the great importance of the senior clerks, 'how much depends upon their fitness for their situations and how much is expected from them'.[8] These leading officials were proud of their achievements which, they were convinced, had raised the public reputation of the Office, and they were determined that they should stand in status and salary on a par with their opposite numbers in the major offices of state, the Treasury, Home Office and Foreign Office.

Not all clerks in the 1820s and 1830s were as talented or as influential as these. There may have been, as Stephen maintained, considerable jostling on the dispatch-writing line as clerks scrambled for the responsible duties. But many of the daily tasks for clerks below the first class were purely routine, often little more than copying and doubtless irksome to men of ability. Moreover, promotion to the leading positions in normal circumstances was a slow process. Absolute seniority was not officially countenanced, though vacancies had to be filled from the clerical rank immediately below. The increase in the number of clerical positions—there were nine in 1822, twelve in 1824 and eighteen in 1825, after which the number remained fairly constant until the 1840s—inevitably lengthened the ladder which the new clerk had to climb. Clerks appointed after 1825 found their advance blocked by the large number of young men who thronged the upper echelons of the Office as a result of the Horton reforms. But these subordinate positions were not designed for the exclusive preoccupation of aspiring bureaucrats. They were given to 'gentlemen, drawn from a rank in society to which a liberal education and a cultivated address belong as a matter of course' and they involved a maximum attendance at the office of seven hours a day, from 11 a.m. till 6 p.m. with breaks for meals. Stephen's picture of the junior clerks as 'twelve young gentlemen copying papers in the interval between their morning rides and their afternoon dinner parties' must have been reasonably accurate in the 1820s and 1830s.[9]

[8] Memorandum on the C.O. establishment, February 1832, C.O. memos no. 2, Grey Papers.
[9] Stephen's memo, 30 March 1832, C.O. 537/22, f. 7; see also Hay to Spring Rice, February 1831, C.O. 324/133, ff. 94–9.

Below the clerks on the establishment were varying numbers of copyists, hired as required and paid by the week. They had no security of tenure and no guaranteed prospects of promotion or salary increments, and consequently theirs were not positions to which fashionable gentlemen aspired. Rather they were sought apparently by men who depended entirely on what they earned as clerks for their livelihood. Some of them were initially attached to an under-secretary or senior clerk and were required, as were their superiors, to work at extraordinary hours, from early in the morning perhaps or till late at night. Their eagerness to accept any extra work, however unelevating, marked them out from the gentlemen clerks. A number of copyists, like Peter Smith, George Wilder and George Mayer, were eventually given positions on the establishment and rose by dint of application and energy to leading clerical positions. Others were employed for years on end outside the establishment, but they too acquired the good opinion of the leading officials, who invariably preferred them to the junior clerks as assistants.[10]

Clerks complained both of having too much and too little to do. This was not entirely a matter of individual status or even of personal energy but stemmed in part from the nature of colonial government itself. The mushrooming growth of the Empire throughout the nineteenth century involved the supervision of new, remote, heterogeneous colonies with weak local institutions of government. This growth was accompanied by the concession of responsible government to the white settlement colonies from the 1840s onwards which, if it did not remove, at least altered the nature of metropolitan initiative and control. A kind of permanent see-saw was created between the Office's authority on any particular problem and its capacity to deal with it, making the achievement of any degree of equilibrium in staffing and organization extremely difficult. The creative civil servant was continually hampered by this concurrence of growing and dwindling responsibilities. Issues like slavery on which the Office could take a moral stand were few. More pragmatic questions tended to be affected either by ignorance of local detail or by a faith in the progressive ab-

[10] Taylor to Villiers, 2 April 1832, memo on the C.O., item 8, Grey Papers.

dication of central control. The resultant hesitancy, the need to wait on events, made the Office peculiarly prone to political upheavals.

To add to their other difficulties, the permanent officials seldom escaped the public controversy to which colonial policy seemed condemned. Not only were there parliamentary charges of extravagance or of sinecures in the creation of the Office but there were two particular charges which appear to have gained some public favour in the period before 1830. It was maintained that the Colonial Office, in asserting the use of the imperial executive, acted as a barrier to traditional political decentralization within the Empire which would have devolved executive powers on to the colonial governments. Secondly, it was felt that the Colonial Office civil service in the 1820s had become dominated by men who were anti-slavery enthusiasts.[11] The one clerical advocate of the West India interest, Major Moody, was manœuvred out of office in 1828. Pro-slavery spokesmen asserted that the Colonial Office permanent officials were partisans who used their offices for political ends and exercised a pernicious influence over their parliamentary superiors. These arguments were developed between 1827 when Bathurst resigned and 1835 when Charles Grant, later Lord Glenelg, succeeded. In this period the Office sustained no less than seven separate secretaryships. Political instability made the minister too elusive for the critics and pointed to the clerks as the real perpetrators of colonial misrule. By the end of the 1820s it was publicly maintained—and even one Prime Minister was prepared to believe it—that civil servants ruled the politicians in the Colonial Office.

That Office business got into arrears or that policy vacillated in these years should not occasion surprise. Though political instability did put the onus for maintaining continuity and co-ordination on to the permanent officials, they were not equipped to carry such a burden. Business had been shared out

[11] E.g. the speeches by Tierney & Marryat, *Parliamentary Debates* XXXIII, 3 April 1816, cols 892–9, 905–6; by Grosvenor, *P.D.* XXXIV, 13 June 1816, cols 1094–5; by Tierney & Marryat, *P.D.* XXXVI, 29 April 1817, cols 51–64. See also Joseph Marryat, *An Examination of the Report of the Berbice Commissioners* . . . (London, 1817). Journals like *John Bull* and *Blackwood's Magazine* carried many articles in the 1820s in this vein.

too widely, amongst many individuals, clerks as well as senior men, the parliamentary as well as the permanent under-secretary. That colonial questions were dealt with as efficiently as they were between 1827 and 1835 and that a major piece of legislation like the Slavery Abolition Act of 1833 could have been successfully launched, is a tribute to the industry and ability rather than to the irresponsibility of the permanent staff. They were not blind to the Office's defects but, more acute than their critics in their analysis, they insisted that the root cause lay not in a slavish devotion to routine but in an inability to offset the violent political fluctuations which resulted from ministerial instability. For every Huskisson and Lord Aberdeen who knew how to utilize and benefit from a civil service there was an E. G. Stanley and a Lord Goderich at the helm who spent their time trying to relegate the civil service to the function of copyists or avoiding the necessity of taking decisions on questions submitted to them.[12]

If there was no lack of spirited criticism of the Office in these years there was no deficiency of proposals for reform. R. W. Hay, the permanent under-secretary, Taylor, Stephen and James Spedding, another talented clerk, each produced his own set of suggestions.[13] Their objects were, in Spedding's words, 'to ensure for the public service both a more plentiful supply of able men and a fairer scope for the exercise of their abilities'.[14] They sought not to curb or obliterate the civil service but to give it the status and authority which would allow it to contribute most effectively to the business of govern-

---

[12] The reformers' views are brought together in Henry Taylor, *The Statesman* (London, 1836), a work which derives from lengthy debates within the Office dating back to at least five years before its publication. The details may be traced in the Grey Papers at Durham and Taylor Papers in the Bodleian.

[13] Their views are found in Stephen to Howick, 10 February 1832, Stephen correspondence, Howick's memo, February 1832 and Taylor to Villiers, 2 April 1832, memos on the C.O., Grey Papers; Henry Taylor, *The Statesman*; James Spedding, review of 'Henry Taylor's *The Statesman*' reprinted from *Edinburgh Review*, October 1836, in James Spedding, *Reviews and Discussions* (London, 1879), pp. 1–34; Hay's memo, 2 April 1832, C.O. 537/22, f. 17; Stephen to Taylor, 16 November 1835 in C. E. Stephen, *The Rt Hon. Sir James Stephen: Letters with Biographical Notes* (Gloucester, 1906), pp. 42–3.

[14] Spedding, *op. cit.*, p. 1.

ment. They wanted in the main to do so by decreasing the number of officials to the point where each man would have to be both diligent and able to get through his duties. In this way the misuse of patronage would be impossible since politicians who appointed incompetents would themselves immediately suffer when office work broke down. These views, more astutely phrased, they repeatedly pressed on their superiors after 1832 and not without results. In 1834, when an assistant under-secretaryship was created in the Colonial Office to ensure that 'the steady and continued prosecution of colonial objects' should be protected from 'the inevitable fluctuations of political events', the emergence of the modern secretariat was already foreshadowed.[15]

Between 1827 and 1835 the progress of reform was slow. Eight years of rapidly changing ministries was not a propitious time to suggest major reforms. But the political turmoil of these years was itself an important factor in what followed. The civil service under Bathurst, Goulburn and Horton had been built up during an era of Tory dominance. It took its roots from an eighteenth-century concept of King's Friends, of disinterested service to the person of the monarch. The debate over the Reform Bill shattered this administrative calm as the Whigs began to appreciate the value and importance of the civil service. Howick, as Secretary at War, wrote in December 1835 to remind his Prime Minister of 'the necessity of losing no time in getting steady friends of our own into the most important of the permanent official situations'.[16] R. W. Hay, an impeccable Tory, was said to be clinging to his office after 1832 though ill and incompetent in the hope of finding a successor of the same political complexion. The ruse, if such it was, proved fatal. In 1836 he was removed to make way for a man of more Whiggish views and pretensions—James Stephen.

To Stephen fell the task of interpreting and implementing the views on Office reform which he, Spedding and Taylor had

[15] Order in Council, 17 September 1834, C.O. 878/1, ff. 107–9.
[16] Howick's journal entry, 22 December 1835, Journal, C.3/1B, Grey Papers. In June 1833 Howick wrote that 'Hay and Toryism have recovered their ascendency' and that 'the old Tory system of Colonial Policy is to be resumed in all its rigour'. Journal entries, 20 June 1833 and 30 June 1833, Journal, C.3/1A, Grey Papers.

been debating. He had come to the conclusion that any reform must depend on establishing a new relationship between the permanent officials and the politicians. He wrote in 1833:[17]

> In every branch of the public service subordinate officers will not seldom be able to form more accurate opinions, and even to act with more wisdom than their superiors. Yet no one would thence infer that subordination is to be disregarded in favour of higher intelligence or skill when it may happen to be found in an inferior rank. Superior competency must be presumed in favour of those who fill the highest offices; and, accordingly, with them the chief and sometimes the only responsibility resides.

But how could the skilled subordinate be made really responsible to his superior? Stephen had a solution:

> I would observe that in the distribution of political power . . . there must always be a danger of abuse, and that the utmost which can be accomplished is to establish such a gradation of authority . . . as may diminish that danger to the lowest degree which is compatible with the efficiency of public officers in their different stations.[18]

In other words, some chain of command should be evolved by which the expertise of the civil servants would define and limit the actions of the politicians and the public principles of the politicians would guide and check the activities of the civil servants. The dangers of either political vacillation or bureaucratic irresponsibility would thereby be avoided.

When Stephen became permanent under-secretary in 1836, he proceeded to implement these ideas in a series of measures which required no formal authorization and so have been largely overlooked. Despite their obscurity, the Stephen reforms constitute the most thorough overhaul of business procedures which the Office received in the whole of the nineteenth century. The most important change was the separation of functions in the work of the permanent and political staffs. The political heads were saved the drudgery of office business by being confined to the work of deliberation and decision on

[17] Stephen to Hay, 12 August 1833, C.O. 158/78, Stephen.
[18] Stephen to Hay, 9 September 1833, C.O. 158/78, Stephen.

proposals submitted to them by the permanent officials. This dichotomy of roles was established simply by introducing a hierarchical method of handling correspondence. In-coming letters were first examined by the permanent officials, the senior clerks taking the responsibility for consulting past papers and other preparatory work before handing the materials on to the permanent under-secretary. The permanent under-secretary then, if he could, suggested a course of action and passed the papers to the parliamentary under-secretary who, in turn, forwarded them to the Secretary of State. When a final decision was reached the permanent under-secretary again took over to ensure that out-going dispatches were correctly prepared and signed. In this way the expertise gained by the clerks and the permanent under-secretary was made the basis of the political decisions while the final control remained in the hands of the politicians. The scheme was based avowedly on the view that a civil servant was an apolitical figure whose public personality was submerged in that of his superiors.[19]

A similar procedural change was adopted in regulating the conduct of the colonial civil service in its relations with the Colonial Office. In 1837 an official set of rules and regulations was published on subjects ranging from the distribution of crown lands to the summoning of legislative councils. This, it was hoped, would 'form a basis for future improvements and . . . tend to the immediate introduction of a better method and of greater certainty in the despatch of the duties of the governors and other public officers'.[20] A similar set of rules was adopted to govern the relationship between the Office and the public at home, especially on the reception of appeals, the handling of patronage questions and the interviewing of callers at the Office itself. Behind these moves was a desire to establish uniformity of principle and action by standardizing procedures and channelling all correspondence into a single path between governors and the Secretary of State. All in-coming letters

[19] Edward Hughes, 'Sir James Stephen and the Anonymity of the Civil Servant', *Public Administration* 36 (1958), pp. 29–36.
[20] Colonial Office, *Rules and Regulations for the Information and Guidance of the Principal Officers and Others in His Majesty's Colonial Possessions* (London, 1837), p. iii. This work was revised and reissued on a great many subsequent occasions.

from the colonies, whether from private individuals, officials of government departments outside the Colonial Office, or its own personnel, were to be sent first to the governor and were not to proceed to the Colonial Office without an accompanying dispatch from the governor recommending some course of action on them. Certain established forms of correspondence were to be used to allow the Office to determine at a glance the contents and importance of each in-coming dispatch. In Whitehall the consultation of other departments, individuals and authorities was to be done by the Colonial Office before communicating with the governors.[21]

Partly to relieve the pressure of work on the political heads and the leading officials, special office duties of a responsible nature were increasingly devolved on to junior clerks. T. F. Elliot was promoted in 1837 to the post of Chief Agent or Agent General for Emigration, a position which had been foreshadowed within the Office by clerical specialization at least as early as 1834 and which, in turn, anticipated by several years the creation of a separate Land and Emigration Board in 1840. James Spedding was assigned the supervision of parliamentary correspondence and acted for a time as a kind of public relations officer in providing parliament with a picture of the Office's work. Peter Smith handled military questions and questions relating to the conferment of colonial honours. Legal business, too, though dealt with by Stephen until 1846, was kept as a separate concern of a technical nature. The position of chief clerk, resurrected in 1839, was designed as an umbrella under cover of which many of these new specialist functions could shelter.[22] In these ways uniformity of proceeding was wedded to professionalism.

The most striking development of the Stephen era was undoubtedly the evolution of a copyist class and the virtual creation of two clerical grades, the 'intellectual' and the 'mech-

[21] e.g. circulars to governors, 1 November 1841 and 1 December 1841, C.O. 323/227, ff. 329, 334.
[22] Stephen to Smith, 29 September 1834, C.O. 323/218, f. 202B; Stephen to Spearman, 9 January 1837, C.O. 324/147, pp. 312–37; Stephen to Wilder, 30 April 1838, C.O. 537/22, ff. 47–8; Ordnance to C.O., 28 March 1838, Stephen's minute, 29 March, C.O. 323/224, f. 180; Russell to Treasury, 17 December 1839, C.O. 537/22, f. 89.

anical'. Again the changes were made quite informally without arousing the attention of parliament. An arrangement was made by which two of the longest serving 'occasional' copyists were employed full time as heads of a new sub-section of the department and given responsibility, in consultation with the permanent under-secretary, to engage copyists as the work required, paying them by the piece rather than weekly to provide a work incentive. The funds for this new departmental sub-section were made available out of the contingencies grant. This, it was claimed, was cheaper than putting clerks on the establishment and also more efficient in that piece-work was performed more industriously. The new system was not entirely successful. One of the first head copyists misappropriated the funds and, when faced with the fact, committed suicide to the scandal and concern of the whole Office. But the practice was a sound one and was specifically commended by the Commissioners who investigated the Colonial Office in 1849.[23]

Not all of the Office personnel were entirely pleased by the reforms. The Stephen system utilized for the 'intellectual' grade only the senior clerks, their chief assistants and a small number of specialist clerks. The junior clerks of the third and fourth classes and the probationers, though above the 'mechanical' grade, were intended to be merely backstops, required to take over when illness or holidays carried off their superiors but otherwise seldom extensively employed. Since, however, the Office coped with an increasing volume of correspondence from 1835 onwards, complaints of under-employment were few. What was more galling was the fact that pay was low for junior clerks and did not rise after the 1820s although prospects of promotion lessened with the abolition of a number of senior posts in the early 1830s and the cancellation of all extra fees and perquisites. Pensions were dependent upon length of service and senior clerks tended to remain much longer as a result, instead of giving way to younger men. One junior clerk estimated in 1846 that, on average, a clerk appointed after 1833 would take eighteen years to advance from the bottom of the fourth to the top of the third class. To get to the bottom

---

[23] Stephen's memo, 4 November 1839, C.O. 537/22, f. 87; Stephen to Russell, 2 November 1839, C.O. 537/22, ff. 83–6; P.P. 1854, XXVII (1715), pp. 47–65.

of the second class took twenty-two years and to get to the bottom of the first class thirty years. Not until forty-six years of service, with his best years long flown and his energies exhausted, would a clerk reach his maximum salary of £1,000 per year. In the mid-1840s the junior clerks persistently but unsuccessfully pressed for a redistribution of the clerical establishment which would increase the numbers in the senior classes and decrease those in the junior.[24]

The Office's critics were not slow to appreciate that changes had taken place. Throughout the 1830s and 1840s the Colonial Reformers, a group even more vociferous than the pro-slavery men, impugned the government policies on colonial land sales, emigration schemes and constitutional development. Their principal spokesmen were Edward Gibbon Wakefield and Charles Buller, though a host of lesser figures joined in the chorus. These critics built on the ideas of their pro-slavery predecessors and presented a clear and sustained attack on the growing influence of the Colonial Office's 'bum-bureaucracy'. Their charges included not only the exercising of a dictatorship over the political heads of the Office, over parliament and over the colonies themselves, but also more modern-sounding assertions of suppressing initiative, opposing change and being insensitive to public requirements and demands.[25] These charges were usually completely unsubstantiated and far from unprejudiced, but they were believed and may have contributed something to the later public image of the civil service.

During the Secretaryship of Earl Grey from 1846 to 1852, the Colonial Office's achievements began to be better appreciated, at least within professional circles. The size of the Office staff again began to grow, no less than three posts (a permanent under-secretaryship, and assistant under-secretaryship and a

[24] Unwin to Stephen, 27 March 1846, and Chapman *et al.* to Gladstone, 13 March 1846, C.O. 537/22, ff. 155–64, 143–54.
[25] These views are most conveniently found in E. M. Wrong, *Charles Buller and Responsible Government* (Oxford, 1926); Saxe Bannister, *On Abolishing Transportation and Reforming the Colonial Office* (London, 1837); E. G. Wakefield, *A View of the Art of Colonization in Letters Between a Statesman and a Colonist* (London, 1849); and Peter Burroughs, ed., *The Colonial Reformers and Canada, 1830–49* (Toronto, 1969), pp. 80–92. The attack was presented principally in periodicals such as *The Spectator* and *The Colonial Magazine*.

précis writership) being created out of Stephen's office on his retirement. An experiment was made, though largely unsuccessfully, with a Privy Council colonial committee composed of experts on colonial problems.[26] The Office's ideas on bureaucratic reform were impressed on the Commissioners of 1849 and perhaps even had an influence on the Northcote–Trevelyan Report itself. But already the Office was falling away from the standards which Stephen had set for it. The zealots of empire had tended to disappear, as with Stephen who finally relinquished all contacts in the early 1850s, or to remain only as shadows of their former selves, as with Taylor who conducted his official correspondence from his convalescent home in Bournemouth. The new men of the mid-nineteenth century, like Herman Merivale or Frederic Rogers, were much more academic in their approach, much less the enthusiasts who burned on questions of the morality of slavery or colonial rights to self-government.

The Office was no longer in the van of reform. A limited scheme of competition for clerical posts was introduced in 1856, but the numbers of junior clerks were not reduced and their pay was not increased. The copying class, less rigorously supervised, began to degenerate into a bottom-rung junior clerical class. The progress of responsible government in the settlement colonies meant a slow working-out of the ideas which the Colonial Reformers had hoped, probably justifiably, would weaken the authority of the Colonial Office by moving the centre of administrative initiative overseas. A belief in separatism became part of the new Office outlook, along with an aloofness and detachment from the problems of the non-settlement colonies which was sometimes frankly racialist at base. How completely things had changed in thirty years is obvious from William Baillie Hamilton's description of the department in the 1860s: 'a sleepy and humdrum office, where important work was no doubt done, but simply because it had got to be done, where there seemed no enthusiasm, no *esprit de corps*, and no encouragement for individual exertion'.[27]

[26] J. M. Ward, 'The Retirement of a Titan: James Stephen, 1847–50', *Journal of Modern History* XXXI, 3 (1959), pp. 189–205.
[27] Baillie Hamilton, 'Forty-four Years at the Colonial Office',

Professor K. Robinson maintained a few years ago that 'we know much more of the Colonial Office in the earlier decades of the nineteenth century than in any later period'.[28] This generalization still holds good, although detailed studies in recent years have gone some considerable way towards filling the gap.[29] The development of bureaucratic techniques, however, has not been fully treated and the role of the permanent official has not attracted the attention which it deserves. Whereas in the Stephen era there is no lack of information on the leading personalities, the picture of the latter half of the century is much less full. Considering its importance, even the administrative career of Joseph Chamberlain at the Office has been accorded remarkably little systematic assessment.[30] This is doubly surprising since a detailed survey of the administrative structure of the Colonial Office in the immediate pre-1914 age could well provide a parallel to and a contrast with the history of the Foreign Office at that period.

The changes made in the early 1870s when the Liberal government was in office are often thought to have inaugurated a new era of purposive and dynamic administration. The introduction of open competition for almost all clerical appointments, the increases in pay to equal the Treasury scale, the reduction of the upper division of clerks from twenty-six to eighteen positions and the arrival of two new senior administrators (Robert Herbert, as permanent under-secretary, and Robert Meade, as assistant under-secretary) whose periods in office coincided with the rise of the 'new imperialism', all suggest important changes. But this can be easily over-stressed. The preparations for implementing open competition had been begun, albeit reluctantly, while Frederic Rogers was still per-

---

Nineteenth Century LV (April 1909), p. 601; see also W. D. McIntyre, *The Imperial Frontier in the Tropics* (London, 1967), pp. 46–79.

[28] K. Robinson, review of R. Heussler, *Yesterday's Rulers, Journal of Commonwealth Political Studies* II (1963–4), p. 170.

[29] B. Blakeley's 'The Colonial Office, 1870–1890' and R. Hyam's *Elgin and Churchill at the Colonial Office* are particularly impressive in this regard.

[30] R. V. Kubicek's stimulating study *The Administration of Imperialism: Joseph Chamberlain at the Colonial Office* provides the basis for a full-scale reassessment.

manent head; the clerical reductions partly sought to clarify
the old distinctions between intellectual and mechanical work;
and the two new senior officials were no more than cautious
innovators in colonial policy.[31] Both Herbert and Meade were
experienced administrators whose appointment to the public
service reflected their close connections with the governing
élite. Herbert, a cousin of Lord Carnarvon, had been private
secretary to Gladstone as well as premier of the colony of
Queensland; Meade had served in the Foreign Office and in the
entourage of the Prince of Wales.

Such changes as did take place stemmed from the considerable increase in the volume of office business after 1870 without
a corresponding growth in the size of the staff.[32] The senior
permanent officials found difficulty in coping, whereas at the
lower levels the work was still predominantly routine with
very little scope for initiative. The political heads tended to
favour further devolution and a broadening of responsibility
inevitably followed. Carnarvon complained that he had had
business thrown upon him that was of no concern to the
Secretary of State.[33] In 1872 Herbert tried to come to grips
with the problem when he directed that minuting should not
be restricted to any particular class of clerks. This gave the
junior clerks the opportunity of joining the intellectual clerical
cadre, though it was some time before they did so fully. The
old tradition of how the Office should function survived even
after the first arrival of the open competitors in 1877. The
secretariat of permanent under-secretary and assistant under-
secretaries still controlled the formation of policy and were

[31] Minutes by Rogers, 24 December 1869, 17 February 1870; by
Monsell, 21 February 1870; and by Granville, 22 February 1870, on
Treasury to C.O., 23 December 1869, C.O. 323/297. Herbert correctly
felt that the C.O. in 1870 could promise clerks both good pay and
responsible duties and so would 'command about the best of the
competitive market'. See Herbert's minute, 23 July 1870 on C.S.C. to
C.O., 9 July 1870, C.O. 323/301.
[32] See Herbert's evidence to the Childers Commission, P.P. 1873, VII,
pp. 162–7. Herbert told the Commissioners that one man in the C.O.
would henceforth be expected to do the work of two. He also virtually
pledged himself against further increases in the establishment.
[33] Carnarvon to Disraeli, 9 December 1866 (private), Disraeli Papers,
Hughenden, B/XX/He/5.

responsible for advising the Secretary of State; the clerks worked harder and on more important tasks but were still cast mainly in the form of experts, rapidly assimilating the contents of dispatches, writing memoranda, preparing difficult drafts.

An attempt was made at this period to transfer some correspondence from the geographic divisions to the General Department. But Herbert's attempt to reduce the number of geographical departments was not successful and was quickly abandoned. The retention of clerical divisions, each concerned with a particular set of colonies which were related to one another by geographical proximity alone, remained a characteristic of Colonial Office methods from its earliest days until 1907.[34] The deficiencies of this system were manifold. In theory each group of clerks were specialists on the administration of their area, but in practice the wide range of problems with which they had to deal ensured that, for example, matters of precedence and ceremonial had to be as familiar to them as the details of colonial hospital administration.

A subsidiary problem was the provision of adequate recruits by the open competitive method. The new scheme was not in fact required until 1877, when the two candidates selected were products of Winchester and Oxford. The Office felt elated at the results of this pioneering experiment. Meade told Disraeli's private secretary, Algernon Turnor, that the system had provided exactly the class of men that it was designed to elicit.[35] Thereafter the Office successfully relied on its examination challenge to attract very high calibre competitors, mainly of public school and Oxbridge backgrounds. Amongst the entrants in the period between 1877 and 1890 were two future permanent heads of the department and two future Cabinet Ministers. A large number of the new entrants were Fabian sympathizers and it seems probable that a sense of mission towards subject races induced them to prefer the Colonial Office to other departments of state. Sidney Webb, G. W. Johnson and Sydney Olivier were the most prominent Fabians, radicals in British politics and paternalists towards the Empire.

[34] Sir John Bramston, 'The Colonial Office from Within', *Empire Review* I, 3 (April 1901), pp. 280–2.
[35] Meade to Turnor, 23 October 1877, Disraeli Papers, Hughenden, B/XII/M/32b.

But none of them, significantly, were of the stuff of which bureaucrats in their generation were made and they soon moved on or failed to attain high rank. Both Webb and Olivier found office work deadening to initiative. According to Olivier the chief problem apart from the inefficiency of some of the senior clerks, was one peculiar to imperial administration—the lack of contact with realities induced by dealing with the problems of a far-flung empire from the security of Whitehall.[36] Local knowledge could have been secured by service in the colonies, but civil service conservatism was such that when Olivier applied to be transferred overseas he was faced with difficulties in securing his pension rights from a reluctant Treasury.

Some idea of the condition of the Colonial Office as an administrative machine can be gained from the reaction of the staff to the Ridley Commission of 1888. The Commissioners felt that the Office, with its three assistant under-secretaries at this time, had more senior staff than its work required. Within the Office itself, matters were seen in a rather different light. Despite the progress of devolution, the assistant under-secretaries complained of having too much to do. The junior clerks were prepared, as ever, to assume more responsibility. But only Meade of the superiors believed that such a move might be desirable and the Secretary of State, Lord Knutsford, categorically refused to allow clerks 'signing power'.[37] In practice, however, the clerks did receive more and more responsible duties as time passed though their work was countersigned by others. One of the major results of increasing pressure of business after 1890 was the gradual abandonment of detailed minuting. This, too, tended to increase the discretionary power of the clerks who received the incoming dispatches first and assessed them.

According to a well-propagated myth, the arrival of Joseph

[36] S. Olivier, *Letters and Selected Writings with a Memoir*, ed. M. Olivier (London, 1948), p. 36.
[37] R. Antrobus's rough memo marked 'D' on draft C.O. to Treasury, 15 May 1888, C.O. 323/374; Meade's evidence, P.P. 1888, XXVII (5545), pp. 73–85; minutes on Treasury proposals by Herbert, 11 May 1888, Meade, 10 May 1888 and Knutsford, 14 May 1888, draft C.O. to Treasury, 15 May 1888, C.O. 323/374.

Chamberlain at the Colonial Office revolutionized its functioning and activities. This alleged mastery has been attributed to
Chamberlain's supposed ascendancy over the Treasury. But an
examination of the Edward Hamilton diaries would almost
entirely disprove this theory. Unofficial contacts had become
of great importance in the relationship between the two departments. Robert Meade, a Gladstonian Liberal, conducted
most of the correspondence with the Treasury and resolved
difficulties by personal consultation. After he retired in 1897
relations were much less smooth. Chamberlain's ambitious and
expensive projects required liaison of the highest order which
he signally failed to obtain. He antagonized his Treasury colleagues not only by his improvidence but also by attempting
to appropriate two of their outstanding officials, Alfred Milner
and George Murray.[38] Milner went from the chairmanship of
the Board of Inland Revenue to the High Commissionership
at the Cape, but Murray was not enticed, as Chamberlain had
hoped, into the Colonial Office. As a result no adequate replacement was found for Meade. Within the Office there was a
serious crisis of confidence at this period over the circumstances
surrounding the inquiry into the Jameson Raid, in which the
Office was inevitably implicated.[39] The officials consequently
felt weak and vulnerable and this affected the conduct of
business.

The main fallacy of Chamberlain's thinking was his un-
swerving belief in the efficacy of reasserting British supremacy in
South Africa as well as extending British commitments in the
tropics, despite his recognition that the colonial service was
'lamentably weak both at home and abroad'.[40] He failed to
see that it was useless to propound new policies from Britain
without altering the administrative structure of the Empire.
Chamberlain contented himself with inadequate attempts to

[38] Hamilton Diary, entries for 15 January 1897, 25 January 1897 and
5 February 1897, B.M. Add. MSS. 48670.

[39] Jeffrey Butler, *The Liberal Party and the Jameson Raid* (Oxford,
1968), pp. 127–9, 256. Sir Edward Wingfield, who succeeded Meade,
suffered a stroke in 1899 and Robert Herbert had to be called out of
a seven-year retirement to replace him—an extraordinary position for
the Office to be in on the eve of the South African war.

[40] Hamilton Diary, entry for 28 July 1896, B.M. Add. MSS. 48669.

unify the colonial service itself. His grandiose schemes involved the Colonial Office in activity which, by the 1890s, had become almost foreign to its nature. As Olivier had earlier observed, it could not act as a creative machine in deciding policies. Its officials were from the first brought up in the work of control. The influence exerted by the men on the spot had to guide the office in its actions because problems of distance, unfamiliarity and complexity (imperial interests were now world-wide) proved to be too great for the Office itself to overcome. Chamberlain did appreciate, however, the importance of allowing Colonial clerks to acquire personal experience of colonial conditions. He arranged for the secondment of three junior clerks to Milner's staff at the Cape, partly to strengthen the colonial government, partly to supply the Office with much-needed field experience. The same reciprocal benefits were sought by requiring a number of colonial civil servants on leave to serve for short periods in the Colonial Office. But these were merely palliatives which could not entirely overcome the difficulties.[41]

To some extent Chamberlain's hands were tied by the need for financial retrenchment. Parliamentary criticisms reinforced a real concern throughout government service to reduce administrative costs to a minimum. To go against these ingrained procedures, to seek not only to expand the Office but to mould it into a creative agency, was to court catastrophe. Chamberlain only averted this by phenomenal personal efforts and by throwing every clerk with any ability into the dispatch-writing line. A kind of minor administrative revolution did in fact occur in the functioning if not in the structure of the Office. Liberal observers saw this as a dangerous development and unfairly attributed Chamberlain's aggressive policies to the advice of jingoistic officials. But the climate of jingoism created by the South African war did unquestionably communicate itself to some members of the Colonial Office staff,

---

[41] Chamberlain convened an office committee to look into internal reorganization: Ommanney to Chamberlain, 2 January 1903, Monk Bretton Papers, Bodleian, Box 85. He also deputed Selborne to conduct an inquiry into conditions in the colonial civil service: Papers on the Proposed Re-organisation of the Colonial Service, Monk Bretton Papers, Box 86.

and Chamberlain did rely heavily on his subordinates. In some over-worked divisions of the Office even the newest recruits were employed on intricate tasks; in one sub-department it became normal practice for the junior member to conduct business on his own account.[42]

From 1896 work fell into arrears and clerks were given more discretion to deal with the less urgent business. In a letter to the Treasury of September 1898, it was stated that the Office required an extra assistant under-secretary since the principal clerks were disposing of between 30 per cent and 50 per cent of the correspondence, whereas before 1895 the secretariat had been responsible for almost everything.[43] It was this pressure of business which allowed the able clerical entrants to make their marks rapidly. The number of papers received in the Office had been only 23,306 in 1895; in 1897 the figure was nearly 28,000. Even this was small compared to the figure of 42,000 reached three years later. Fortunately, the clerical candidates after 1877 had both the will and the ability to take up the slack. H. E. Dale, a 'bright young university prizeman', was virtually running the Australian business of the Colonial Office only six years after entry.[44]

After 1900 an important change occurred in the status of the permanent under-secretary. Robert Herbert was the last of his line to have serious pretensions to the title 'Mr Mother Country'. Meade, who succeeded him in 1892, only nominally filled the same functions but he had worked too long in the Office to be in favour of drastic changes. Ommanney was appointed in 1900 on the strength of his vast knowledge of the work of the Crown Agent's Office, which dealt with loans, public works and other utilities. This reflected in part a change of emphasis from the

---

[42] Ripon to Campbell-Bannerman, 30 September 1899, Campbell-Bannerman Papers, B.M. Add. MSS. 41224. See also Sir A. Hemming, 'The Colonial Office and the Crown Colonies', *Empire Review* XI, 66 (July 1906), pp. 501–12.

[43] Draft to Treasury, 30 September 1898, C.O. 323/438. Before 1895 clerks who by-passed their official superiors and submitted drafts directly to the parliamentary under-secretary warranted a note of censure from the permanent under-secretary: see Meade to Ripon, 11 October 1892, Ripon Papers, B.M. Add. MSS. 43556.

[44] Sir John Bramston, *op. cit.*, p. 280; Sir A. Hemming, *op. cit.*, pp. 502–4.

previous concern with the affairs of the self-governing dominions. Since Ommanney was more of a bureaucratic than a colonial expert it also allowed for a more pragmatic approach to the problems of the devolution and co-ordination of office work. When Ommanney was due to retire in 1907 Elgin favoured Sir John Anderson for the post, laying stress on his experience of colonial affairs at home and abroad. But bureaucratic expertise was preferred to professional knowledge and largely for political reasons Sir Francis Hopwood, an accomplished public servant at the Board of Trade, was selected instead.[45] Hopwood and his successors differed considerably from their nineteenth-century predecessors. Like modern senior civil servants, they were (to utilize Professor W. J. M. Mackenzie's description) 'forced by their experience and situation to think primarily in terms of the internal state of the organisation'.[46]

Hopwood was a meticulous bureaucrat renowned for his businesslike approach. In his appreciation of the powers of patronage and persuasion which the post conferred, he was second to none. He was also a representative of the band of new men who attached themselves to King Edward in an advisory capacity. Hopwood's impact was considerable: he acted as a kind of diplomatic intermediary between the Secretary of State and the real policy-makers, the assistant under-secretaries, often reconciling their various views. Harcourt was sorry to lose him in 1911, appointing Anderson in his stead. Anderson, acting on Harcourt's prompting, reduced the number of assistant under-secretaries from four to two to provide the senior clerks with more responsibility.[47]

Elgin's administration from 1905 to 1908, though much less ostentatious than that of Chamberlain, made a contribution of at least equal importance to the way in which the Colonial Office officials functioned. The creation of a Dominions department recognized the need to dissociate the business of the

[45] Elgin to Campbell-Bannerman, 10 November 1906, B.M. Add. MSS. 52515; Ommanney's & Hopwood's obituaries in *The Times*, 25 August 1925, and 18 January 1947.
[46] W. J. M. Mackenzie, *Politics and Social Science* (Harmondsworth, 1967), pp. 359-60.
[47] Sir John Anderson's evidence to the MacDonnell Commission, 17 May 1912, P.P. 1912-13, XV (6535), pp. 133-45.

self-governing colonies from that of the dependencies. This development was more than a paper concession to the wounded
susceptibilities of dominion statesmen: it was the beginning
of a trend towards bifurcating the Office into two quite distinct
units.[48] The dominions side of the work, which required diplomatic skills, seems to have attracted the more cerebral of the
clerks, but the crown-colony work was not neglected and may
have benefited from the division to some extent. Specialization
was certainly enhanced since there was little interchange of
personnel between the two branches.

Elgin also determined on a partial abandonment of the
scheme of Office organization that had existed almost unchanged since 1870. The position of the senior civil servants
had become invidiously burdensome. Elgin pointed the way
towards reform: the re-allocation of business by subject
matter, not area; the use of advisory committees to bring
in local knowledge; and the adoption by the Office of a more
streamlined structure in keeping with the demands made
upon it. But in one sense he was returning to the Victorian
tradition of strictly practical superintendence by eschewing
creativity. Elgin had, in fact, more in common with his Liberal
predecessors than with the Liberals of his own generation.
Chamberlain's innovations came under fire and Elgin felt
compelled to take steps to reassert his authority over officials
who had been allowed too much freedom of expression since
1895.[49] The staff was expanded numerically to keep pace with
the mounting volume of work which had now to encompass a
considerable addition of African correspondence transferred
from Foreign Office or chartered company rule. It could no
longer be said of the Office in 1907 that it remained what it had
been in 1870—a close-knit unit in which every member shared
to some degree the same confidences. Indeed the earlier *esprit
de corps* had waned. Many clerks soon departed for fresher
pastures and the ability of the Office to attract the best civil
service examinees had become a thing of the past.

In the years prior to the outbreak of World War I, growing
dissatisfaction with the Colonial Office manifested itself in

[48] J. A. Cross, 'The Dominions Department of the Colonial Office:
Origins and Early Years, 1905–1914', London Ph.D. thesis, 1965.
[49] R. Hyam, *op. cit.*, p. 484.

some influential circles, notably that of the *Round Table* movement. The disciples of Milner, the arch-enemy of dictation from Downing Street, hoped to form an unholy alliance with the old Dominions to provide sufficient ammunition for a reformist platform. That they were so unsuccessful was partly due to the capacity of the Office staff to influence their superiors against reform of any kind. Pressures from many sides were growing as problems of international security, economic development and trusteeship piled high in the Secretary of State's in-tray. The Imperial Conferences, in which statesmen from the dominions came face to face with their British counterparts, threatened to make the Colonial Office's jealously guarded status as an imperial post office a complete anachronism. In defence questions there was a conflict of interest between grand strategy, as defined by the service departments, and colonial defence, as defined by the dominions with the help of the Overseas Defence Committee of the Colonial Office, which was itself engulfed in the Committee of Imperial Defence after 1904.

The Colonial Office tended to lose popularity within Whitehall as a consequence of its role as a mediator between other government departments and the colonies themselves. Where the influence of the Colonial Office over other departments had once been marked, as on questions of establishing protectorates, the Secretary of State was now reduced to a subservient role. Such progress as was made in these years concerned a greater awareness of the importance of securing better recruits for the colonial service and the introduction of scientific specialists to cope with problems like the extirpation of disease in the tropical dependencies.[50] The Colonial Office in the early twentieth century was assuming a multiplicity of technical functions combined with a palpable decline in its authority within Whitehall on overseas questions. It was no longer providing a platform for the enthusiast or the reforming politician; neither was its staff exercising control over proconsuls and governors who created their own policies and recruited

[50] For a list of the numerous advisers, committees and bureaux utilized by the Office to tackle the problem see Pugh, *C.H.B.E.*, III, pp. 761–2.

their own aides. It seemed increasingly likely that the Office would become a mere cipher in the government of the Empire.

The Colonial Office throughout the nineteenth century faced a constant battle with the public purse over matters great and small, including that of the well-being of the Office itself. On one occasion in 1840, the Treasury had demanded a saving in stationery expenditure by insisting that short communications should be written on half sheets of office paper. Vernon Smith was indignant: 'No gentleman', he minuted on the proposal, 'writes to another on half a sheet of paper.'[51] But the Colonial Office itself could impose equally niggling restrictions on expenditure.[52] What was sought internally by the reforms of 1823–5, 1833–6, and 1869–72 was increased efficiency without greatly increased cost and in each case this was successfully achieved. By the late nineteenth century, however, the structure of the Office was no longer conducive to the efficient discharge of business. As the Empire grew in size and brought in ever more remote regions, the increase in work doomed the Office to expand to a larger size than was compatible with the concentration of authority in the hands of a small secretariat. Yet the division between the secretariat and the body of the clerks remained. The under-secretaryships were generally filled by men who, on first appointment, could boast a high social standing and legal experience but little direct knowledge of colonial administration. The first assistant under-secretary to emerge from the ranks of the clerks was Edward Fairfield and he did not attain that position until 1892.

The Office's much vaunted minuting procedures also came in for a good deal of criticism in the latter part of the nineteenth century. The pace of technology, bringing with it the use of telegrams and cable messages, was destructive of the

[51] Smith's minute, 4 March 1840 on Trevelyan to Stephen, C.O. 323/226, f. 140.
[52] A recent work argues that the Treasury's influence over colonial policy declined in the second half of the century though the general concern for retrenchment did not: A.M. Burton, 'The Influence of the Treasury on the Making of British Colonial Policy, 1868–1880', Oxford D.Phil. thesis, 1960. We are grateful to Dr Burton for permission to refer to her thesis.

routine method of handling correspondence. Both Herbert and Ommanney, permanent heads with little else in common, re' garded minuting procedures with misgiving. The operatio had become ritualistic in its emphasis on the preservation of an orderly sequence of minutes corresponding with the status or seniority of each individual.[53] But, excessive though it was, the formalism had its value. The files constituted the precedents on which policy was formulated and as such were rightly regarded with respect. The minutes are, of course, invaluable for the historian who can divine from them the outlook and attitudes of the civil servants. But though it is clear that the Office harboured clerks with widely differing viewpoints, from Little Englanders to rabid imperialists, in general pragmatic solutions to problems offset any commitment to ideology. The staff did not have the leisure to speculate on the future of the empire; they rarely had the opportunity of consciously moulding developments. Nor, perhaps, would they have welcomed such responsibility.

By the outbreak of World War I, the Colonial Office in some ways stood apart from the other branches of the civil service. Colonial policy was still of great concern to a wide section of British opinion, intellectuals and philanthropists, businessmen and concession-hunters. But the Office, with its agents in five continents exercising power within a very large number of subordinate governments, could never control and master the formulation of policy as other departments might hope to do. It continued to stand up for its position within Whitehall as the department which co-ordinated the implementation of colonial policy and served as the special representative of colonial rights. This difficult role gave it an influential place in government while also making it the recipient of much animadversion and satire. The Office survived the criticisms. Over the composition and functioning of the Office machine the Secretary

---

[53] Meade to Ripon, 11 October 1892, Ripon Papers, B.M. Add. MSS. 43,556, ff. 75–8; Herbert's minute, 11 May 1888 on Antrobus's memos April and May 1888, draft C.O. to Treasury, 15 May 1888, C.O. 323/374. Milner, as Secretary of State, wrote in 1919: 'I am rather intolerant of the minute upon minute and nothing happens at the end methods of this venerable block of buildings.' Milner to Novar, 26 March 1919, Novar Papers, National Library of Australia.

of State continued to exercise much independent initiative. The impact of the various Royal Commissions on the Office was negligible. Calls for retrenchment or for a decrease in the size of the secretariat were ignored. But if the Office in the early twentieth century could claim acknowledgment as an important government department, this was no longer because of its peculiar problems or its zealous and creative administrators. It had simply become part of a much wider sphere of administration in which the senior permanent officials occupied a position in the governing world irrespective of their particular offices.

The Foreign Office before 1914: a study in resistance

The administrative history of the Foreign Office illustrates the wisdom of the cliché-makers. Well into the twentieth century, this department remained the stronghold of the aristocracy, 'the last choice preserve of administration practised as a sport', and a place which was 'just easy enough to be agreeable, just ceremonious enough to possess distinction, and just industrious enough to do its work'.[1] Such tags, of course, disguise those changes which did take place for even the Foreign Office was not totally immune from the pressures which created the administrative revolution of the Victorian era. Yet these pressures were never so great nor the responses so complete as those which affected many of the domestic departments; thus the Foreign Office, in administrative terms, remained the 'lame duck' of Whitehall. Even in periods when the Office was subject to considerable external pressure from members of both Houses of Parliament as in the 1850s and '60s, it was far better equipped for resistance than the home departments. The phrases 'within the royal prerogative' and 'not in the public interest' were regularly and conveniently deployed.[2]

[1] A. Cecil, *British Foreign Secretaries* (London, 1927), p. 229.
A. W. Ward and G. P. Gooch, *Cambridge History of British Foreign Policy* (Cambridge, 1923), vol. 3, p. 599.
[2] V. Cromwell, 'The Private Member of the House of Commons and Foreign Policy in the Nineteenth Century', *Liber Memorialis Sir Maurice Powicke: Studies presented to the International Commission for the History of Representative and Parliamentary Institutions* XXVII (Louvain/Paris, 1965), pp. 202–5.

There are a number of somewhat obvious generalizations which can be made about the nineteenth-century Foreign Office. First of all, its political head was one of the most powerful figures in the Cabinet. For most politicians, only the office of Prime Minister ranked higher than that of Foreign Secretary: Palmerston, Salisbury and Rosebery all went to the 'top of the greasy pole' with obvious reluctance. In return, only the Foreign Office was considered an important enough post for an ex-Prime Minister—e.g. Lord John Russell in 1859. Within the Cabinet, the Foreign Secretary enjoyed a very special position. His colleagues intervened only sporadically in the affairs of his department, and the Cabinet, as a whole, proved to be an insufficient and ineffective check on his powers. Since the Prime Minister alone could exercise the kind of daily supervision necessary, the relationship between the Prime Minister and Foreign Secretary remained a crucial factor in the formulation of foreign policy throughout the century. At the same time there was usually a small core of interested ministers who were kept informed of daily proceedings. The ministerial confidential print was introduced in 1878, though few ministers had the desire or the time to go through this compilation of despatches and telegrams. Within the Cabinet a group of men, the Colonial Secretary, Secretary for War, First Lord of the Admiralty, Secretary for India and the Chancellor of the Exchequer and sometimes a senior statesman or two usually took a special interest in foreign issues and might be individually consulted. The Foreign Office tended to be a cheap department and Treasury intervention was normally restricted to petty matters (the appointment of one or two additional second division clerks, a third assistant under secretary) and points of detail.[3] Treasury attempts to encourage administrative change in the Office

[3] Ward and Gooch, *op. cit.*, p. 617. In 1869 the cost of the Foreign Office was £63,079; and in 1900–1 £79,000 (Expenditure, Civil Government Charges, Accounts and Papers, 1901, P.P. 1913–14, XXXVII, I). The story of the relations of the Foreign Office with the Treasury is given in R. A. Jones, 'The Administration of the British Diplomatic Service and Foreign Office, 1848–1906' (unpublished Ph.D. thesis, London, 1968), especially in ch. I.
Dr Jones has kindly permitted us to quote material from his thesis, which is to be published as *The Nineteenth-Century Foreign Office: An Administrative History* (London, 1971).

were usually blocked by firm objections on the part of the Foreign Secretary. The Treasury occasionally proved obstructive as it did in 1850, but the force of resistance to be found in the Foreign Office is indicated by the fact that after extensive pressure it was only in 1870 that the agency system disappeared and the Treasury found itself involved in the payment of heavy compensation.[4] It was only towards the end of the century, when the government modified its traditional laissez-faire stand with regard to loans and concessions, that the Chancellor of the Exchequer took a more important role.

The Foreign Secretary, with a few exceptions, not only enjoyed a large measure of independence in the Cabinet; he was also relatively free from parliamentary control. Almost all Foreign Secretaries sat in the House of Lords between 1800 and 1914: between Canning and Grey, only three sat in the Commons. Thus, in general, they were free from the stresses of criticism in the lower house, but that did not mean a quiet parliamentary life. The nineteenth century was a period of intense public interest in the conduct of foreign policy and much parliamentary time was consumed by debates on foreign affairs.[5] Constitutionally, however, parliament had and has only trivial powers in this sphere and despite much noisy criticism and censure, few instances of real interference can be found. This is not to say that parliamentary opinion could be ignored and indeed it often proved a useful diplomatic excuse. The number and size of parliamentary papers on foreign affairs provided a vast range of information, but the contents were always those approved by the Office and motions for papers were regularly repulsed by the words 'not in the public interest'.[6] Easy relationships between Members of Parliament and diplomats abroad, together with the existence of a number of Members in both houses with experience of office, ensured that debates proved regularly demanding for the Foreign Secretary in the Lords and his parliamentary under secretary in the Commons. At all times the special nature of the work done by the Office was emphasized and thus it is always necessary to see the

---

[4] *Ibid.* ch. V.   [5] Cromwell, *op. cit., passim.*
[6] V. Cromwell, 'The Administrative Background to the Presentation to Parliament of Parliamentary Papers on Foreign Affairs in the Mid-Nineteenth Century', *Journal of the Society of Archivists* II, 1963.

Foreign Secretary in a rather special position. To complete the picture of the Foreign Secretary, it should also be noted that Foreign Secretaries usually stayed in office throughout the life of a ministry and generally returned to this same position when their parties were returned to power.[7] There were fewer politicians at the Foreign Office than in any other administrative department.

Before considering in detail the structure and composition of the Foreign Office two points must be made. Firstly, it must be remembered that the functions of even the most senior officials remained relatively trivial until late in the nineteenth century. Decisions affecting Britain's foreign policy remained very much political and the work done in the 'political' departments of the Office was primarily of a file-keeping and information-providing nature. Of course there are hints of pressures occasionally building up within the Office, but rarely are instances of important influences on decisions to be found. An indication of this situation is to be seen in the character of the political departments within the Office. Until the 1840s and '50s the administrative departments retained a higher status than the political. During Palmerston's earlier years the former were headed by senior clerks, while the latter were run by clerks assistant. Only under Hammond did the political departments establish their importance in the work of the Office and the Office begin to taken on its twentieth-century shape.

Secondly, when considering the Foreign Office in the nineteenth century, it must be emphasized that for almost all purposes the Office was seen as separate from the Diplomatic Service. Even in the early years of the twentieth century, exchanges with the Diplomatic Service, despite pressures from various outside committees, were still relatively rare. The appointment of Charles Hardinge from the embassy at St Petersburg to the permanent under secretaryship in 1906 was the first such appointment since the days of Addington and was the subject of considerable comment. Sanderson had spent his entire forty-seven years in the Foreign Office with the exception of two special (and short) missions abroad. The initiative had to come from the clerk or diplomat concerned, private arrangements had to be made and then the private secretary's approval

[7] Between 1854 and 1914 there were only fourteen Foreign Secretaries.

sought before such exchanges could be arranged. The life of the diplomat was far more costly than that of the clerk and even at the second and first secretary level diplomatic pay barely covered expenses. There were, moreover, no inducements in terms of pay or promotion to encourage these exchanges. It was only under Hardinge that the numbers began to rise; in 1908 and 1909 there were ten exchanges, a record figure.[8] At the highest levels, it had become customary for under secretaries to be rewarded with an embassy. Julian Pauncefote and Philip Currie (1882–9 and 1889–94), successive permanent under secretaries, Francis Villiers, Francis Bertie and Martin Gosselin (who came originally from the Diplomatic Service), all assistant under secretaries under Lord Salisbury, went as ambassadors or ministers. Occasionally a senior diplomat was brought back to the Foreign Office. Charles Hardinge (1907–10) was followed by Arthur Nicolson (1910–16); Martin Gosselin and Ralph Paget were brought in as assistant under secretaries. Nevertheless, even on the eve of the war, there was some degree of antagonism between the two services and little sympathy with outside proposals (e.g., the Commission of 1890) for amalgamation. The division between the Office and the Diplomatic Service often aided the former in their resistance to external pressures for change. The issues were often confused. When arguments about retrenchment were being floated in the middle of the century, the target of the critics more often than not was the Diplomatic Service. The Foreign Office itself was, as has been shown, a relatively cheap department. And from its own standpoint the Diplomatic Service could always point out their dependence on the services of unpaid attachés whose replacement could only mean greater expenditure. The Foreign Office clerk tended to consider his overseas counterpart a social butterfly, while the diplomat thought the clerk a drudge pinned to his desk and papers. Both services treated members of the Consular Services as Cinderellas.[9] The gap between the Diplomatic Service and Consular Service (particularly the General Consular Service) was particularly noticeable. An occasional consul (William White, Ernest Satow, John Jordan)

[8] D. Collins, *Aspects of British Politics*, (Oxford/London, 1954), p. 115.
[9] D. C. M. Platt, *Finance, Trade and Politics in British Foreign Policy, 1815–1914* (Oxford, 1968), pp. xx–xxx.

moved into the Diplomatic Service, but these were outstanding exceptions. Diplomats and consuls joined different clubs in London and did not mix abroad. Thus when considering the Foreign Office we are looking at one very limited aspect of the machinery for the conduct of foreign policy.

From the start of its history, the Foreign Office was a small secretarial office whose functions were determined by its chief. Changes in size and function came very slowly. Canning's staff came very close in number and classification to that which served Sir Edward Grey. His Office consisted of two under secretaries, a chief clerk, three senior clerks, thirteen junior clerks, a librarian and sub-librarian, a private secretary, a précis writer, a translator, a Turkish interpreter and a collector and transcriber of papers. The Office remained virtually static throughout the second half of the nineteenth century. The permanent establishment numbered thirty in 1853 and, after a period of expansion under Clarendon, rose to forty-three in 1858. The number was forty-one in 1902–3.[10] In 1905 the introduction of the Registry system increased the number of second division clerks from eighteen to fifty-nine.[11] In 1914 Grey had two under secretaries, three assistant under secretaries, one controller of commercial and consular affairs, one chief clerk, seven senior clerks and twenty-eight junior clerks.[12]

Most of the changes which were forced on the Office in the nineteenth century arose from acute pressure of work; the number of incoming and outgoing despatches was rising continuously. As well as forcing a modest increase in the Office establishment, pressure of work in the 1850s also determined the organization of the Office in the second half of the century. The first change concerned the development of the 'political' departments. Faced with a large increase in the number of despatches to be handled, Palmerston tried to get the senior clerks in charge of the administrative departments to share in this political business. His failure to achieve this meant a redistribution of power within the Office. The heads of the

[10] Foreign Office Establishment, July 1903, P.R.O., F.O. 366/760, cited in Jones, p. 76.
[11] P.P. 1914–16, Fifth Report of the Royal Commission on the Civil Service, Cmnd. 7749, Appendix LXXXVI.
[12] *Ibid.*

existing political departments were increased in status and pay, and their departments began to rise in importance and prestige. The second change related to a differentiation in function between the 'permanent' and 'parliamentary' under secretaries within the Office and the growing power of the former. By 1860 the permanent under secretary had established a pre-eminent position within the Office. Although Palmerston did not like it, it was in his administration that the permanent under secretary began to establish his dominant position within the Foreign Office. After a sharp quarrel in 1848 with the chief clerk, at that time head of the administrative departments, he had become the recognized head of the Office:[13] at the same time most of the intra-office correspondence appears to have been in his hand. Under Palmerston however there were still many blurred lines and the purely political character of the parliamentary under secretary was not yet firmly established.

It was really Edmund Hammond (1854–73) who gave the Office its permanent shape.[14] Hammond was an 'insider' with a long previous career in the Foreign Office and had been chosen only when Clarendon failed to secure an outsider for the post. Hammond's exact role in the policy-making process depended on his relationship with the Foreign Secretary (he was close to Clarendon and Granville but not to Russell), but he was the first permanent under secretary to feel that 'he was bound to advise and to recommend to the secretary of state what he thought should be done'. On the whole, Hammond's advice was conservative, but the important point is that he felt free to offer it on a wide range of diplomatic problems. He played, moreover, a key role in the appointment of ministers and had almost exclusive control over the selection of consuls, particularly in the Far East, an area which engaged his personal interest. Within the Foreign Office, Hammond gradually ousted the parliamentary under secretary from the diplomatic business of the Foreign Office. By 1865 he supervised four of the five

[13] V. Cromwell, 'An Incident in the Development of the Permanent Under-Secretaryship at the Foreign Office', *Bulletin of the Institute of Historical Research* XXXIII (1960), pp. 99–113.
[14] For details of Hammond's career see M. A. Anderson, 'Edmund Hammond, Permanent Under-Secretary of State for Foreign Affairs, 1854–1873', unpublished Ph.D. thesis, London, 1955.

political departments and, though the parliamentary under secretary saw papers on their way to the Foreign Secretary, he spent an increasing proportion of his time on purely parliamentary affairs. It must be said that Hammond took advantage of every opportunity to expand his own powers at his neighbour's expense; he often urged the parliamentary under secretary to take vacations while he refused to leave London lest the reins of control slip from his fingers. The parliamentary under secretary was not unaware of what was happening but fought a losing battle. Before the Select Committee of 1860, Hammond was the chief witness and the obvious representative of the Foreign Office. *Vanity Fair* captioned a cartoon of Hammond in 1861 'Mr Foreign Office'.

By the time Hammond retired with appropriate honours, the position of the permanent under secretary was firmly established, and the distinction between the two under secretaries clearly delineated. Hammond's successors, Charles Tenterden, Julian Pauncefote and Philip Currie, though all very different in temperament and roles, did not fundamentally alter Hammond's division of responsibility within the Foreign Office. The permanent under secretary was responsible for the operations of his department. He headed the key political departments and took a major share in the drafting of political despatches, though almost always on detailed instructions from the Foreign Secretary. He saw that despatches and telegrams were sent to the Foreign Secretary on time and that the latter's orders were carried out. He checked that letters were promptly copied, and that the outward correspondence was appropriately circulated. As in the case of Hammond, the permanent under secretary's contribution to the actual making of policy depended very much on the Foreign Secretary and the relations between the political chief and his senior civil servant. On the whole, such interventions were restricted to minor questions, though there were informal discussions of more general problems.

While the permanent under secretary was establishing such superiority, the functions of his parliamentary partner were becoming simply those of attending sittings in the Commons and going through despatch boxes in preparation for appearances there. He had lost almost all responsibility for the internal affairs of the Office. The situation established under Hammond continued to be the regular pattern. The parliamentary under secretary knew all about the decisions reached by the Foreign Secretary and the Cabinet without having had any say in their determination. His main internal concern, apart from parliamentary business which did, of course, bring him into contact with all the departments, was with the commercial department, and in Brodrick's time even this link was severed.

The functions of the staff changed almost imperceptibly during the course of the century. Castlereagh did all his own work and ignored his staff. Canning did his own drafting but saw that despatches were accurately copied and circulated. Palmerston, while he neither sought the views of his officials nor permitted even his under secretaries to intervene in matters of policy, nevertheless wanted an efficient secretarial office and drove his clerks relentlessly.[15] Though, like Canning, he wrote all important despatches himself, he demanded factual information from under secretaries, checked that proper abstracts were made and despatches copied with speed and accuracy. By constantly badgering his clerks, he shaped the Foreign Office into an efficient office of scribes.

This is what the Office remained throughout the Victorian period. Although the Treasury was eager to bring its structure into line with that of other government departments, particularly by encouraging the introduction of a class of copying clerks, the Foreign Office maintained a firm resistance against any differentiation between intellectual and mechanical work. Its business was, as senior officials continually avowed, far too confidential to be given to copying clerks. Repeated Treasury demands were successfully resisted. Instead, after considerable haggling, the Treasury agreed to give special allowances for senior clerks and to permit a modest increase in the size of the establishment. In 1857 the Office consisted of one chief clerk, eight senior clerks, nine assistant clerks, ten first-class, nine second-class and six third-class junior clerks. This structure, created under Lord Clarendon, remained virtually unaltered until the reforms of 1905-6. A fundamental distinction was established between the Foreign Office and its

15 C. Webster, *The Foreign Policy of Palmerston, 1830-1841* (London, 1951), I, p. 58; C. Webster, *The Art and Practice of Diplomacy* (London, 1961), pp. 181-96.

domestic counterparts. Throughout the nineteenth century the clerks spent much of their time doing work of a most mechanical nature. Despite the success of its opposition to Treasury pressure, the Office permitted some innovation. Unestablished clerks were used first in the slave trade and consular departments and after 1865 in the treaty, library and chief clerk's departments. But these supplemental clerks, although generously paid, were restricted to positions where work of a non-confidential nature was performed. In 1881 an effort was made to modernize and rationalize the structure of the Office: the 'political' departments were reduced in number and increased in size. Though official opposition to the introduction of copying clerks continued, four lower division clerks were employed in the commercial and consular departments. This change was to be crucial for the future administrative development of the Office. As the pressure of work increased, the number of second-division clerks rose, and in 1889 a lady typist was introduced into the establishment. More fundamental reforms were clearly necessary if the Foreign Office was to make more efficient use of its personnel, but there seems to have been little demand from within the establishment for any change in the distribution of work. Second division staff continued to be employed in the administrative departments only.

This, then, was the outline of the organization of the mid-nineteenth-century Foreign Office. How were the staff of the Office recruited? And who were they? As is well known, during the first half of the century, patronage was the usual method of recruitment, but it must be remembered that once officials were appointed they tended to serve until the age of retirement. Between 1855 and 1857, qualifying examinations (on subjects suggested by the Foreign Secretary and approved by the Civil Service Commissioners) were introduced for candidates who had secured the Foreign Secretary's official nomination.[16] These tests were, according to Charles Spring Rice, a farce and were 'not much more than an ordinary boy of fourteen, with a poor education, ought to be able to answer'.[17] They served only to keep out the 'grossly ignorant'. The new examination

[16] See Z. Steiner, *The Foreign Office and Foreign Policy, 1898–1914* (Cambridge, 1969), p. 16.
[17] P.P. 1914–16, Cmnd. 7749, p. 75.

consisted of eight compulsory tests. These were orthography, arithmetic, English composition, précis writing, French, Latin and German translation and a general intelligence test. The optional subjects included further tests in German, a combined test in the geography and history of Europe (1783 to 1847), the constitutional history of England, Books I to IV of Euclid, ancient Greek, Italian or Spanish. Although the Foreign Office was exempted from the Order in Council of 1870, outside pressure forced Clarendon to adopt a more stringent examination in 1871. Though the system of nomination by the Foreign Secretary continued, there was a real measure of competition among nominated candidates. The latter might secure his nomination at an early age but had to be between eighteen and twenty-four or twenty-five to sit the examination. The Foreign Office fixed the number of candidates permitted to take the examination (usually three or four to every available place) and also decided the year in which the candidate was to compete. This system of recruitment remained unchanged, apart from minor modifications in examination subjects and their assessment, until Lord Lansdowne entered the Foreign Office.[18]

In the 1850s few of the clerks had reached any high academic attainment. It is often difficult to trace the educational history of the clerks, but where this can be established the general pattern appears to have been education at home rather than at public school and if a university had been attended a degree was often not taken or, if taken, a third. Palmerston's stepson, the Hon. Charles Spencer Cowper, had been educated at Eton, but not at a university as was Lord Tenterden who was recruited in 1854. William Pitt Adams, who was recruited in 1826, went to Oxford but did not graduate. Sir Henry Percy Anderson got a third in Classics before entering the Office in 1854. George Canning Backhouse failed to graduate after Harrow and Christ Church. John Bidwell Junior followed his father

---

[18] By comparison with the system of examinations for entry to the Foreign Office, that for the Diplomatic Service followed a different pattern. It began as more severe and as the century progressed became easier. The report of the Commons Select Committee on the Diplomatic Service in 1861 describes current practice, P.P. 1861, VI, 459, q. 221–70. The introduction to *The Records of the Foreign Office, 1782–1939* (London, 1969), pp. 25–6, describes later developments.

into the Office in 1842, but nothing is known of his education. Such then was the pattern before the introduction of even the simplest examination and the situation changed little until 1871.[19]

After 1871 the quality of recruits improved with the appearance of such candidates as Sir William Conyngham Greene and Sir Arthur Henry Harding with first-class degrees to their credit. But the general pattern remained very much the same until Lord Lansdowne suggested that the examination age be raised to twenty-two in order to encourage university graduates and also recommended that recruits take the normal civil-service papers, provided that a higher score be required in the obligatory French and German papers.[20] His suggestions were accepted; the entering age was raised and any number of nominated candidates could sit for the examination. Competition tended to be fierce; there were sometimes twenty candidates for one or two appointments. A second change followed in 1907 when a Board of Selection consisting of the private secretary, permanent under secretary, one or more members of the Diplomatic Service and the head of one of the political departments, was instituted. After securing permission to appear before the Board (a purely mechanical matter) the applicant now applied to the Board rather than to the private secretary for his official nomination and permission to take the examination. The creation of the Board was intended to reduce the pressure on the private secretary and, at the same time, to reduce the Foreign Secretary's patronage powers. The Board seems to have acted as a preliminary sieve; it rejected only about two per cent of those applying.[21] There seems to have been no fundamental change in the kinds of men seeking admission and the Board asked the same kinds of questions about family, interests and school as were previously asked by the private secretary. Though outside critics blamed the Board for the exclusive character of the Foreign Office and Diplomatic Service, in general only men of a particular background and schooling applied.

[19] R. A. Jones is to include a detailed analysis of the staffing of the Office in his forthcoming book.
[20] P.P. 1914–16, Cmnd. 7749, q. 38,693.
[21] *Ibid.*, p. 10.

At the end of the century, in common with other departments of government and the professions, the Foreign Office was staffed by the sons (though usually second sons) of the aristocracy and wealthy gentry, many of whom were themselves engaged in a professional career. Many were the sons and relatives of those who had already served either in the Queen's Household, at the Foreign Office or in the Diplomatic Service. One did not need a private income to enter as even a junior clerk was paid a salary (in distinction to the Diplomatic Service where the system of unpaid attaché posts long survived), but salaries were low and most junior clerks had other sources of income. Between 1898 and 1907, twenty-eight clerks entered the Foreign Office. The educational background of twenty-four of these new entrants has been traced, all of whom went to one of the major public schools, twelve to Eton. Less than half had a university education, all of course at Oxford or Cambridge. Lord Lansdowne's reforms did have some effect: among sixteen new clerks entering the Foreign Office between 1908 and 1913, nine had gone to Eton but all had gone to university.[22] Thus, the Lansdowne reforms encouraged men to take their university degrees before going abroad to learn their languages. The crammer had not been eliminated, and after his return from France and Germany, the prospective clerk finished his 'study' at Scoones in Garrick Street, where he was properly prepped-up for the coming ordeal. Despite the continued predominance of sons of the aristocracy on the establishment of the Foreign Office, the list of both successful and unsuccessful candidates suggests that a larger number of upper-middle-class families, particularly professional men, were beginning to enter their sons for the Foreign Office competitions. In 1912, for instance, two sons of merchants entered the Foreign Office. As in some other departments, there was a trend away from men trained in the classics and a wider range of Honours Schools were represented. Though Firsts were rare, it was generally thought that the Foreign Office had academically better candidates than the Diplomatic Service.

Most clerks looked forward to a lifetime at the Foreign Office. The new entrant was placed in whatever department needed assistance and some attempt was made to move him after a

[22] *Ibid.*, Appendix LXXXIV; Steiner, *op. cit.*, Appendix 3.

year or two. With few exceptions, promotion was inevitable and seniority the general rule until the senior clerk level. Men went 'Hackney coach-like from Bottom to Top, by dint of mere living'.[23] After Hammond's time, the permanent under secretaryship was usually awarded to a man who had come up the Foreign Office ladder: Pauncefote was an exception since exchanges with the Diplomatic Service remained, despite pressure from various outside committees, relatively rare.[24] The competition had little significant effect on either the responsibilities of the senior officials or the distribution of authority within the Foreign Office until the Foreign Secretaryship of Lord Lansdowne.

Since the days of Lord Hammond, the permanent under secretary was not only the recognized head of the Foreign Office but in a position to give advice on political questions. The practice varied. According to Lord Currie, Salisbury's permanent under secretary from 1889–94, his predecessor Pauncefote 'did not even read the political despatches. He merely passed them on with the departmental minutes, consequently there was no-one to submit that general view of the subjects interesting each country that you desire.'[25] Currie was more active in this respect though both he and Thomas Sanderson (1894–1905) took relatively limited views of their roles as adviser. Sanderson, in particular, thought it was his chief responsibility to get the papers sent to the Foreign Secretary in an orderly fashion and to carry out the latter's instructions with despatch. He did not consider it his duty to give advice except at those times when his opinions were solicited. The permanent under secretary was responsible for the discipline and efficiency of his office, a role which Sanderson took very seriously. Next in rank came the assistant under secretaries, the first of whom was appointed in 1859, the second in 1895 and a third in 1898, who directed the political and administrative departments not already supervised by the permanent under secretary. The latter determined how the business was to be distributed, and

[23] P.R.O. Russell Papers, Palmerston to Russell, 20 October 1839, quoted in Anderson, *op. cit.*, p. 42.
[24] Charles Hardinge's appointment from the embassy in St Petersburg in 1906 was similarly unusual.
[25] Jones, *op. cit.*, p. 123, Currie to Salisbury, 13 March 1888.

there was in practice a great deal of flexibility both with regard to departments and countries. The assistant under secretaries read the incoming despatches which, with a brief query or suggestion or without any comment at all, were passed on to Salisbury. According to the latter's instructions, the under secretaries then prepared the drafts required for the Foreign Secretary's signature. Individual departments acquired their own reputations and styles. The Eastern Department became known as the most aristocratic. The Western, the most important department in the Office, and Eastern Departments each occupied three rooms: the first room where the senior clerk and his assistant worked; a second room where the junior clerks, often men who had already been in the Office for ten years or more, kept the registers and managed the print; and a third room where the remaining juniors employed their time performing the kind of work done elsewhere by members of the second division.

Even under Lord Salisbury, the senior clerks were the office 'experts'. They were responsible for only one department and often stayed at their posts for a dozen or so years. They supplied the past papers and information needed by the Foreign Secretary and read the final drafts of outgoing letters before forwarding them to an under secretary. They were also responsible for the compilation of the confidential print and collected the material needed for parliamentary questions and Blue Books which jobs were both time-consuming and tedious. In the non-European departments, heads enjoyed a good deal of independence, but by contrast in the European departments the senior clerks had little part in the actual formulation of policy. The assistant clerks, one in each department, wrote the drafts and paraphrases and might occasionally be asked to prepare a memorandum on a particular issue. The juniors 'lived a pleasant routine existence which stultified their education, dulled their wits and deprived them of every kind of initiative'.[26] They spent their time registering, docketing, ciphering and deciphering, distributing papers and preparing the bags to be sent to the embassies and legations. Though the

---

[26] J. D. Gregory, *On the Edge of Diplomacy, Rambles and Reflections, 1902–28* (London, 1929), p. 18.

'nursery', that room in the old Foreign Office where the juniors boxed, fenced and played the piano had vanished with that building, there was still football and stump cricket in the corridors, leisurely hours and long weekends. The company of a congenial group of men similar in upbringing and taste more than compensated for the many hours spent in work of the most routine kind.

Personal familiarity as well as long years of experience contributed to the ease with which an ever-increasing flow of paper work was handled. The efficiency of the Foreign Office depended on the memory and devotedness of the permanent under secretary. The system functioned well only as long as he could shoulder his full share of the burden and the Foreign Secretary could deal with all the problems which crossed his desk. In 1890 a Royal Commission on the Civil Service had again urged that the political clerks and attachés be relieved of their mechanical work and be given a greater share of the political business, but, as before, its recommendations were not implemented and only modest changes occurred. The number of second division clerks was increased; two such clerks were even permitted to work in the political departments in order to improve the totally inadequate registers needed for indexing. As the daily correspondence increased, past papers were misplaced and the registers and indices were both incomplete and out of date. Salisbury's ill-health, clashes within the Cabinet over foreign policy issues, the expansion of non-European business, all placed additional strains on the administrative machinery. Though Sanderson kept the papers moving, his eyes and health suffered and much of his later irritability can be attributed to over-work. Some division of responsibility did occur as the under secretaries made suggestions and reached decisions which Salisbury accepted, yet little was done without his approval and on all key questions the Foreign Secretary kept the reins in his own hands.[27]

The first real steps towards reform were taken after Lord Lansdowne entered the Foreign Office. Not only did he decide to alter the system of recruitment to attract more university men but was also determined to give the younger men of the Office a greater part in the political work of their departments.

[27] Steiner, *op. cit.*, pp. 34–43.

A Treasury official commented[28] after an interview with Sanderson that

> Lansdowne wishes that all the younger as well as the older men should be specialists in some branch of their work and make it their business to keep papers up to date and to undertake to be the expert opinion on the facts of any particular question.

The senior clerks, too, were well aware of the anomalies of a system in which a few men did almost all the substantive work while a large number of highly educated men found their skills under-utilized. Even this purely routine work was not efficiently done; despite Sanderson's efforts, there were numerous complaints about the circulation of papers and the incompleteness of files.

It was Francis Villiers, an assistant under secretary in Lansdowne's Office, who made the first practical suggestions for a major reform of the department. In a letter to Sanderson of 27 April 1903, he underlined the discrepancy between the quality of the men recruited and the kind of work they were asked to do.[29] He urged that there should be a further devolution of responsibility from the under secretaries and heads of departments to the juniors and suggested ways in which the latter could be freed from some of their more tedious responsibilities. These recommendations included the creation of a ciphering room, the delegation of all non-political work to the non-political departments, the systematization of Blue Book work and the transfer of the job of preparing the bags to office keepers. Villiers raised but dismissed the possibility of establishing a general registry as 'entirely subversive to our present arrangements'. Though Sanderson defended his own past efforts to improve the existing system, he did agree to implement most of Villiers's suggestions and accordingly instructed the heads of departments. Pressed by Lansdowne, the first steps were taken which led to a greater devolution of responsibility throughout the establishment.

[28] Jones, *op. cit.*, memorandum by G. H. Duckworth, 2 July 1905, T.I. 10369/4480, quoted on pp. 241–2.
[29] Jones, *op. cit.*, p. 237, Villiers to Sanderson 27 April 1903, Department, Correspondence and Memoranda, 1848–1905, vol. 3A.

In May 1904 the Cartwright Committee, a Committee instituted by Sanderson prompted by Lansdowne, recommended
that the Foreign Office should initiate a Registry system which
would be run, as in the Colonial Office, by second division
clerks. After many difficulties with the Treasury, the additional
funds needed to implement the new scheme were secured and
the Registry system put into operation on 1 January 1906.
Its success was assured when Eyre Crowe, an enthusiastic reformer who had been instrumental in working out the details
of the new system, became temporary head of the Registry.[30]
Charles Hardinge replaced the ailing Sanderson and returned
to London early in 1906 determined to turn the 'existing cosy,
if somewhat tedious family party' into an organized Department of State.

The extent and character of the Crowe–Hardinge reforms
have been examined in some detail elsewhere.[31] The establishment of a Central Registry and three sub-registries staffed by
second division clerks transformed the work of the first division
staff. All the purely secretarial work done by the latter—the
registering, docketing, copying, printing and distribution of
papers—was now done by second division clerks. Only telegrams continued to be processed by a first division clerk and
this practice was dropped in 1911. The combined reforms of
1904 and 1905 enabled the whole diplomatic establishment to
take a part, admittedly a restricted one, in the policy-making
process. Papers were now laid flat and put in jackets on which
minutes were written not only by the under secretaries and
senior clerks but by the juniors who were for the first time
encouraged to give their opinions on many of the current issues.
Junior clerks, in addition, were often asked to prepare memoranda on special subjects and could become such experts on
these questions that the appropriate papers were first sent to
them when they came from the sub-Registry to the department.

The minutes written by the juniors were short and often
disregarded. The minute-writing process was as much, if not
more, a training device for future advisers than a source of
guidance for the Foreign Secretary. At the more senior levels

---

[30] For Crowe's role, see Jones, *op. cit.*, pp. 279–84, and Steiner, *op. cit.*,
pp. 80–1.
[31] Jones, op. cit., pp. 263–94, and Steiner, *op. cit.*, pp. 79–80.

of the Foreign Office, however, the under secretaries and the senior clerks took a larger share in the formulation of policy than their predecessors. Many questions could be settled at this stage without further reference to the Foreign Secretary. In addition, the permanent under secretary was relieved of all direct departmental responsibilities and became the main and almost exclusive channel of communication between the Office and Foreign Secretary. He saw all papers important enough to be passed on to his chief and his minutes obviously carried a special authority. John Tilley, a critical observer of the new system, wrote: 'when a subject had been thoroughly threshed out by a junior and then by a senior who knew their subject, it was often natural for the Secretary of State to accept their views and save an expenditure of time and thought which he could not easily afford.'[32] It must, however, be remembered that a large number of papers went to Edward Grey with only brief minutes or with conflicting views which he had to resolve. Secondly, though Grey did permit his subordinates a degree of independent action never contemplated by Salisbury in his prime, this was, in part, the necessary consequence of the increased workload at the Foreign Office. The daily decisions made by the permanent officials covered questions of secondary importance. All major questions went up the Foreign Office hierarchy and, with few exceptions, even senior officials were unwilling to recommend action without the Foreign Secretary's approval. They were ready to express their views and thought their advisory function to be the most important of their responsibilities, but a fundamental division of responsibility remained. An administrative reform, however fundamental, could not overthrow traditional patterns of behaviour. As before, a great deal depended on the personalities of the men involved and their relationship with the Foreign Secretary.

Apart from the changed role of the permanent officials and the increasing concentration on their advisory rather than on their clerical duties, there were other modest changes in the structure and tone of the Office. Since the second division clerks worked from ten-thirty until six, most of the diplomatic establishment was expected to arrive by eleven. Hardinge, an

[32] J. Tilley and S. Gaselee, *The Foreign Office* (London, 1933), pp. 160–1.

excellent administrator, encouraged his clerks to leave promptly at six and some of the earlier flexibility of Foreign Office life disappeared. Telephones were placed in all departmental rooms and the number of second division clerks and typists was increased. Some degree of expertise was welcome. Middle Eastern railway questions were always referred to Alwyn Parker, an assistant clerk, and German questions went to Eyre Crowe, appointed senior clerk in 1906, regardless of the department to which the original papers were sent. Though the social cohesion and exclusiveness of the Foreign Office was scarcely touched by the new broom, a different concept of the role of the bureaucrat was beginning to emerge. The Foreign Secretary not only received the views of his diplomats but the comments of his permanent officials on these views. After 1905 there was a new source of information and advice from within the walls of the Foreign Office.

The Crowe–Hardinge reforms, as the reforms of 1905–6 came to be called, barely affected the Diplomatic Service. Although by this date, diplomats were taking the same competitive examinations as their Foreign Office counterparts after the recommendations of the Royal Commission of 1890, their examination papers were separately graded and the two services independently run. The need for a private income of at least £400 undoubtedly restricted the pool of available candidates as well as the prospect of a life spent almost entirely abroad. The statistics indicate that the aristocratic bias of the Diplomatic Service was in no way modified during the last years of peace and that the domination of the Etonians became even more marked. It was not only the radicals in parliament who argued that British diplomats were more snobbish and less efficient than their European counterparts, and that inherited and outdated attitudes towards trade and traders persisted.[33] But even within the existing structure of the service, no effort was made to modernize it; diplomats still did routine work which could easily have been done by local staff or second division clerks. The typewriter did begin to replace the pen but, as late as 1914, diplomats up to the grade of First Secretary were primarily employed in clerical work. Charles Hardinge encouraged a

[33] A. J. P. Taylor, *The Troublemakers: Dissent over Foreign Policy, 1792–1939* (London, 1957), chs IV and V.

greater number of transfers between the Foreign Office and Diplomatic Service: Eyre Crowe succeeded in introducing a system of annual reports for which junior diplomats were asked to prepare special sections. Crowe's hope that transfers and promotions might be judged in the light of these reports proved illusory and such matters were handled, as they always had been, by the Foreign Secretary's private secretary. The appointment of ambassadors and ministers might involve the King and Prime Minister as well as the Foreign Secretary and permanent under secretary. But with regard to the juniors, apart from informal communication with the permanent under secretary and the relevant ambassador, the private secretary had a free hand. Promotion was slow and it was therefore essential to cultivate the private secretary if one was not to be buried in some forgotten post. There were no means for retiring the incompetent until they reached retirement age and too often a posting in South America was used as a substitute. Though there were important exceptions, this was not a career to attract the very ambitious or able and more than one junior diplomat soon transferred to the Foreign Office. Individual ambassadors, Francis Bertie, Arthur Nicolson, George Buchanan were of key importance in the moulding of pre-war British policy, but the rise of the Foreign Office had its effect on the prestige of the Foreign Service.

The introduction of a new means of circulating and keeping papers was only a clerical revolution. What made it significant for the history of the department was its accompaniment by a certain group of men coming into positions of power within the Office.[34] It was Lansdowne who insisted that, 'It is essential that the devolution which I require should take place from the top to the bottom of the Office.'[35] But it was the new Foreign Secretary, Sir Edward Grey, who determined how this new distribution of authority was to work out in practice. By nature, Grey enjoyed discussing questions of policy with his senior men and even encouraged debate and contention. As the Foreign Secretary sat in the Commons and was deeply involved in the domestic difficulties of his government, Grey often asked his permanent under secretary to take up responsibilities previously reserved to the Foreign Secretary, as for instance the

[34] Steiner, *op. cit.*, pp. 70–82.   [35] Jones, *op. cit.*, p. 260.

semi-official correspondence with diplomats abroad, and permitted other officials a good deal of independence in negotiating matters of secondary importance. Nevertheless, Grey was as much the master of his own Office as Salisbury. The responsibility for all major decisions rested with him. There were numerous times, particularly between 1911 and 1914, when Grey's actions ran counter to the prevailing opinion within the department. Office advice was only one element in Grey's deliberations and the fundamental separation between the duties of a political chief and his civil servants was never obscured.

The new reforms and Grey's willingness to seek advice did, however, encourage the senior men, many of whom had firm political views, to express themselves in minutes and memoranda. Charles Hardinge's social standing and experience placed him in a special position from the start. Freed from almost all his clerical and direct departmental responsibilities, he could give his full attention to a wide range of diplomatic problems and often influenced Grey on the particular line to be followed. This was particularly true with regard to Anglo-German and Anglo-Russian relations.[36] While the partnership of Grey and Hardinge was one of equals in a way which was almost unique in Foreign Office history, it was based on a concurrence of views and deep loyalty on both sides. If Hardinge often behaved more like a statesman than a civil servant, he never overstepped assumed lines of demarcation and always appreciated the political aspect of any diplomatic decision.

Hardinge was not only a responsible adviser but also an effective head of the Office. He never seems to have been overwhelmed by the mass of papers with which he had to deal and ruled with a firm hand both the Office and the Diplomatic Service. Far more than Sanderson, he took an active interest in diplomatic appointments and assignments and tended to favour those men who agreed with his views about Germany and the necessity of the *ententes* with France and Russia. Hardinge's close relationship with Grey and his domineering personality enhanced the reputation of his office. The importance of the personal element can be clearly seen in the contrast between Hardinge and his successor, Arthur Nicolson, who played a far

[36] Steiner, *op. cit.*, pp. 95-100.

less significant role in the actual formulation of policy although his formal powers remained the same.

Nicolson was appointed in 1910 when Hardinge became Viceroy of India, because Hardinge and Grey both knew that he shared their concern about Germany and their wish to promote the existing *ententes*. Though a successful diplomat, Nicolson proved to be a poor administrator and, within eighteen months of his arrival in London, was pressing Grey for another diplomatic appointment. Like Hardinge, he saw all papers of major importance and continued to provide the main link between the Foreign Office and the Diplomatic Service, but found desk-work tedious and the mass of administrative detail oppressive. More important, in terms of British policy, Nicolson never established a close working relationship with Grey and their personal relations deteriorated rather than improved during the last years of peace. There were a number of reasons for the permanent under secretary's relative eclipse. Grey had completed his apprenticeship and by 1912 had reached the height of his reputation both at home and abroad. And, though Grey and Nicolson started out from similar premises, there were small but important differences in their views which led Grey to look elsewhere for advice and assistance. Between 1911 and 1914, Nicolson was to complain repeatedly that he did not see Grey often enough and that when he did his advice was being ignored. There was not the same close harmony of views which characterized the Grey–Hardinge partnership and this was a crucial factor in explaining Nicolson's sense of isolation. Finally, differences of approach were complicated by Nicolson's open antipathy towards the Liberal government, a feeling which had been shared by Hardinge who, however, managed to be more discreet in his comments, and his extreme stand on Ulster. It was widely known that Nicolson was soon to leave the Foreign Office for Paris and that in the spring of 1914 he was the Foreign Secretary's chief adviser in name only.

 The new reforms not only provided new opportunities for the permanent under secretary; the assistant under secretaries and senior clerks were to make full use of their greater freedom. Louis Mallet, an assistant under secretary in the Eastern Department and Eyre Crowe, first as senior clerk in the Western Department and then as assistant under secretary, repeatedly pressed their very strong views on Grey. The Far Eastern Department had always handled a wide range of issues on its own initiative; F. A. Campbell, the assistant under secretary until his death in 1911, was the China expert and Grey generally deferred to his judgment. Yet Grey continued to see a surprising number of papers, considering the secondary importance of some of the issues involved, and even when a minute might have been read with care and approval, the advice offered was sometimes rejected and a different line of action followed. As for the more junior men, their minutes suggest that they were encouraged to express their views and expert knowledge, but their influence was minimal and their suggestions always checked by departmental heads. The devolution desired by Lansdowne was accomplished, but the burden on the Foreign Secretary was not substantially reduced and the Foreign Office remained a department in which responsibility was heavily concentrated in the hands of its senior hierarchy.

One must be careful not to infer too much from the written evidence. Minutes and memoranda do not always give a valid indication of the power structure within the Foreign Office any more than in any government department. Officially, the key figure at Whitehall was the permanent under secretary. Yet between 1912 and 1914, it was commonly known, even abroad, that the important man to see was William Tyrrell, Grey's private secretary and closest intimate. Even under Salisbury, the private secretary had been a man of some importance. He determined who was to sit for examinations; he controlled the promotions, assignments and leaves for diplomats and was generally responsible for the running of the diplomatic and consular services. But the powers of the private secretary in the opening years of the twentieth century, even when formidable, were purely administrative and secretarial. Eric Barrington, private secretary to both Salisbury and Lansdowne, did not offer advice on any substantive points of diplomacy. The first sign of a change came with the appointment of Louis Mallet as Lansdowne's précis writer and then as Grey's private secretary. Mallet used his influence to strengthen Lansdowne's support for France during the first Moroccan crisis and to assure the continuation of an *entente* policy during the early years of Liberal rule. But it was William Tyrrell, Mallet's successor, who created for himself an unprecedented position of power.[37] Sharply contrasted in personality and talents, Grey and Tyrrell became close intimates, and when Nicolson replaced Hardinge at the Foreign Office, it was the private secretary who gradually became Grey's chief adviser and unofficial ambassador. Tyrrell's power was based almost entirely on his personal friendship with Grey and not on his official position. The scattered evidence suggests that the private secretary sometimes pressed Grey to follow a policy disliked by both Nicolson and Crowe. Tyrrell went further and seems to have taken an active part in implementing this policy. 'Grey is absorbed, not unnaturally, with domestic politics,' Valentine Chirol, a good source of Foreign Office gossip, wrote in the spring of 1914, 'and leaves things (perhaps a great deal too much) in William Tyrrell's hands.'[38] The personal enmity between Tyrrell and Nicolson was barely disguised, and it was clearly the former who had Grey's ear. Yet the administrative historian might well overlook Tyrrell's crucial role as there are few minutes or memoranda in Tyrrell's hand and evidence for the private secretary's actions is scanty and not always reliable. It can only be assumed that the man closest to the Foreign Secretary is in a very special position regardless of his official title. Grey was increasingly troubled by his eyes and was preoccupied with the Ulster difficulties. His relations with Nicolson were strained and he had never been personally close to Eyre Crowe. In this atmosphere, Grey seems to have turned to Tyrrell for advice and assistance.

In the spring of 1914, an unusually calm one, the Foreign Office was operating in its usual quiet and aloof manner. Outsiders acknowledged the ease with which business was performed, the relative speed with which decisions were made and the high level of office discussion and argument. The Foreign Office seemed to benefit from all the advantages of an aristocratic élite who were also becoming professional bureaucrats. Few observers knew about the personal difficulties at the top of the structure. Grey had not yet decided to send Nicolson to Paris and, moreover, had not made a clear decision about the

[37] For a detailed description of Tyrrell's role, see Steiner, *op. cit.*, pp. 147–52.
[38] Hardinge MSS. vol. 93, Chirol to Hardinge, 22 May 1914.

next permanent under secretary. Crowe and Tyrrell were the probable contenders. As Nicolson disliked handling Office problems, these two men shared the work between them, but these arrangements did not improve the morale of the department. There were also difficulties at the bottom of the Foreign Office hierarchy. The second division staff became increasingly dissatisfied with its totally subordinate position and its limited career structure. Matters came to a head in 1913 when one of the last remaining supplementary clerks retired and his job in the Treaties department was given to a first division clerk. The second division clerks appealed to Grey, but nothing was done and the rumblings continued. The Registry system, despite some changes, was not operating smoothly. The Central Registry had proved a great bottleneck, particularly during 1912 and 1913 when the Balkan crisis led to a further increase in the daily workload. It was time for a further overhaul and modernization of the clerical arrangements.

There were also some complaints from outside the Foreign Office. In the autumn of 1911, the radical backbenchers led by Arthur Ponsonby and Labour party members headed by Ramsay MacDonald joined forces for a major assault on Grey's diplomacy and on his methods of conducting foreign policy. They were joined by E. D. Morel, whose campaigns about the Belgian Congo, though given partial support by the Foreign Office, had developed into a general attack on Grey and his subordinates. This campaign continued throughout the winter of 1911–12; thereafter the attack was pressed by the Liberal Foreign Affairs Group and the Foreign Affairs Committee. The former, active both in parliament and in the press, had two points in mind. On the one hand, they wished to see the Foreign Secretary and his Office brought under more direct parliamentary control. On the other, they wished to make the Foreign Office and Diplomatic Service more representative, more responsive to present needs and more efficient. Only a few individuals saw the possible contradiction between these goals.

These complaints were repeated before a Royal Commission on the Civil Service which was appointed in the spring of 1914 to look into the Foreign Office, the Consular and Diplomatic Services. As in 1890, the Commission, in the face of considerable opposition from the Foreign Office, urged that the Foreign Office and Diplomatic Service be merged into a single Foreign Service and steps taken to eliminate the social and financial barriers to such an amalgamation. The Board of Selection was to be broadened, the property qualifications dropped and the examination for all candidates be the same as that given Class I of the Home Civil Service. Specific recommendations were made for improving the Consular Services, though no move was made to bring these into the suggested unified Foreign Service. In the event, the outbreak of war delayed any innovations, but a series of departmental committees considered the Commission's recommendations as well as other internal Foreign Office problems. In April 1918 the key committee on amalgamation presented its report and in the following year the Foreign Office and Diplomatic Service were officially merged.[39] As had been suggested, staffs became interchangeable, the property qualification was abandoned and appropriate pay scales, still absurdly low, were introduced. The interviewing and examination system was revised and other reforms promised.

The Foreign Office emerged from the war reformed but weakened in power and prestige. Its altered position was, in part, a consequence of the war. Even before Lloyd George took over the government, Grey had lost his influence in the Cabinet and the Foreign Office frequently found its decisions overruled. Grey believed that military considerations had to take precedence over any diplomatic goals and he constantly deferred to his military colleagues. Difficulties in Turkey, in the Balkans and over blockade questions were blamed on diplomatic ineptitude. But the problem was not only one of military–civilian relations. Lloyd George's contemptuous treatment of the Foreign Office had its background in the radical attack on the 'old diplomacy'. The Union of Democratic Control, formed in 1914, continued the pre-war campaign against the methods and personnel of the Diplomatic Service. Throughout the political spectrum the view could be heard that the days of formal diplomacy were numbered and that that alliance of court and upper classes which had controlled foreign relations would vanish with the coming of peace. Specific reforms urged by writers in *The New Europe* were swallowed up in a general

[39] *The Records of the Foreign Office*, p. 9, gives the details.

denunciation of the 'old diplomacy'. At the same time at the Foreign Office, the reformers lost the initiative and a real opportunity to re-shape the structure of the diplomatic machine was lost. Even before the peace negotiations were concluded, the professional diplomats had become the villains of the pre-war world. Myth overcame reality and plots were proved where there were none. The diplomats, themselves, suffered from a loss of nerve from which they never fully recovered. They tended to earlier patterns of behaviour despite the altered circumstances. Some changes did take place, but none were radical enough to restore the Foreign Office to its pre-war position in the making of policy. In the inter-war years, the diplomats were only to play a secondary role.

Treasury control 1854–1914

Gladstone's association with the Treasury, as First Lord or Chancellor, throughout the greater part of the second half of the nineteenth century, and his identification with financial prudence and retrenchment, have helped to project and foster an image of an omnipotent and omniscient department whose prime concern was to turn down proposals made to it and to save candle-ends. Magnification of the image has produced the now familiar picture of a department exercising an inflexible and, sometimes, capricious control of public expenditure in the relentless pursuit of stringent economy, and dealing autocratically, at times despotically, with other departments about whose work it was largely ignorant or ill-informed.

In recent years this view of Treasury control has been increasingly challenged, principally on the grounds that it exaggerates both the Treasury's nominal power to control other departments and its operational effectiveness as a constraint upon the autonomy of departments to determine and pursue particular policies.[1] So far the evidence is persuasive, but conclusive only for a limited period of time and for some, not all, types of public expenditure. A great deal more work remains to be done on the Treasury and other central departments before definitive answers are possible to such key questions as: How effective was the Treasury in determining and regulating the levels of departmental expenditure? To what extent did it

---

[1] See Henry Roseveare, *The Treasury* (London, 1969), especially chs 5–7; Maurice Wright, *Treasury Control of the Civil Service, 1854–74* (London, 1969).

attempt through its financial control to influence or 'interfere' with policy?

This essay adds to what I have written about Treasury control elsewhere in two ways. First, I have extended that account both in time and subject-matter by using the evidence accumulated by the Ridley and MacDonnell Royal Commissions,[2] and such other secondary material as was readily accessible. My purpose is to see whether such an exercise confirms or denies for Treasury control as a whole for the period up to 1914 what has been said primarily about establishments' expenditure in the twenty years after the Northcote–Trevelyan Report. Secondly, recent work on the growth and development of certain central departments and the policies associated with them affords the means to look at Treasury control from a different angle: from the viewpoint of the recipient. From these sources I have constructed brief accounts of Treasury control as it affected the growth, development and policies of the Colonial Office, the Medical and Education Departments, and the Local Government Board. Finally, on the basis of the two exercises, I have formulated some general propositions about the nature and operation of Treasury control.

In 1875 the Playfair Commission had reported in favour of a strong Treasury *vis-à-vis* other departments, had recommended that it should have the means to assess the requirements and conditions of other departments, and that it should be able to exercise an 'efficient and intelligent control'.[3] The Ridley Commission, which was appointed in 1887, pursued even more vigorously the inquiry begun by Playfair into the theory, principles, practice and effectiveness of Treasury control. The concern of both Commissions with the operation of Treasury control reflected the growing feeling that the Treasury was unable to arrest the growth of establishments, and that it had been particularly ineffective in controlling the numbers of highly paid clerical officers, many of whom were felt to be

[2] *Reports of the Royal* (Ridley) *Commission on Civil Establishments,* 1887–90, and the *Royal* (MacDonnell) *Commission on the Civil Service,* 1912–14.
[3] *Reports of the Civil Service* (Playfair) *Inquiry Commission,* 1875, P.P. 1875, XXIII.

unnecessary. A recurring theme of the questions addressed to witnesses who appeared before the Ridley Commission was the need to strengthen Treasury control. From the first day of the inquiry, and Welby's admission that the weakness of the Treasury was that it lacked an independent authority, the Commission began to develop the idea that finally emerged in their report that general regulations for the organization of the civil service should be embodied in an Order in Council, which would serve as a guide to departments and the Treasury in the formulation of their establishments. More significantly, the Commission proposed the appointment of a standing committee composed of senior officials from the departments and the Treasury to consider and report to the Treasury on the establishments' proposals made by the departments. That it was felt necessary and desirable to make these recommendations, that the Treasury required to be bolstered by the independent authority of an Order in Council and a standing committee, is striking evidence of the widespread feeling throughout the service that Treasury control was not very effective.

Welby and other witnesses agreed that the theory of Treasury control was complete; and that its control of the legitimacy of expenditure was effective—'departments now hardly ever neglect to observe the rule of coming to the Treasury to sanction proposed changes before they are made'.[4] But Treasury control as a restraint upon the levels of departmental expenditure appeared to be no more effective in the seventies and eighties than it had been earlier. The greatest defect, it was alleged, was that it remained, as it had always been, a negative control which could be exercised only when a department applied for an increase. If there was no demand for increased expenditure there was 'virtually no Treasury control'.[5] The Treasury was powerless to order an inquiry to see if reductions could be made, or to see if there was waste and inefficiency in the organization and administration of the department. Welby agreed that as a general rule it was only necessary for a department to keep quiet to escape Treasury control, and that it was quite possible that there might be, without the knowledge of the Treasury,

[4] Ridley Commission, 2nd Report, P.P. 1888, XXVII, pp. xi–xii.
[5] Ridley Commission, 1st Report, P.P. 1887, XIX, Welby's evidence, pp. 1–9.

certain offices or parts of offices where men on full pay had little or nothing to do.

If the Treasury was virtually powerless to act 'positively', what of its 'negative' control when proposals came up to it? Welby's arguments emphasizing the practical difficulties in exercising control are almost identical with those conclusions drawn from the analysis of the operation of the day-to-day control in the earlier period. Briefly, Welby argued that practically, Treasury control was very much limited by the status and seniority of ministers, and by the size of departments. 'A powerful Cabinet Minister does not accept readily a decision of the Treasury which overrules something he proposes, and, in practice that is a considerable check upon the power of control,' Welby volunteered in his evidence. The Commission pressed him very hard on this and he was asked point-blank whether the Treasury was powerless against a powerful minister, to which he replied:

> One puts forward as an instance the strongest case, viz.
> that of a powerful minister, very anxious about his
> department, perhaps having some scheme to carry out
> which he wants to carry out in a particular manner, will do
> his very utmost to get his views carried out; and if he is a
> very important personage, probably, his views will be
> adopted in preference to those of what I will call the
> Departmental Treasury.

When such a situation occurred, Welby went on, the issue escalated very rapidly, and the Cabinet Minister dealt directly with his colleague, the Chancellor of the Exchequer.

This particular difficulty was exacerbated when the minister was supported by the weight of parliamentary and public opinion; in dealing with the Departmental Treasury, or his colleagues the Financial Secretary or the Chancellor, or arguing in Cabinet, his hand was immeasurably strengthened. Other limiting factors, Welby admitted, were the size, importance and technical nature of the department with which the Treasury dealt. 'The smaller the department, the more complete can be the control.'

Other witnesses confirmed the practical limitations to the exercise of control alleged by Welby. The Assistant Secretary of

the Commercial Department at the Board of Trade lent uncon-
scious but striking support to the argument that the Treasury
was constrained by the political weight of the departmental
minister. Asked whether all the most important matters were
practically decided between the President of the Board of Trade
and the Chancellor he replied: 'that must be so necessarily, and
the result is that when you have very important matters they
are much more easy to get through than the smaller matters in
which nobody takes any particular interest.'[6] Sir Thomas
Farrer, formerly permanent under secretary at the Board of
Trade, made the same point in a different way: 'The fact is, that
we can, any of us at the other offices cheat the Treasury if we
please. We can cheat them in big things; they may bully us in
small things.'[7] On the big things the permanent secretary or
minister went personally to the heads of the Treasury, and in
Farrer's experience they had no difficulty in settling matters.
Again, this confirms the analysis of the earlier period, where it
was found that Treasury resistance was invariably overcome
when the department involved the permanent head of the
department or the minister in an issue. Face-to-face negotiation
was rarely unsuccessful for the department. In the earlier
period, however, departments seemed equally willing to involve
their permanent secretaries and ministers in the 'little' as in the
'big' things. Evidence to be presented later suggests that this
might have been the case in the period after Ridley too, and
that the inference to be drawn from Farrer's evidence—that the
Treasury normally got their way in small things—is a misleading one.

   Welby's cross-examination by the Ridley Commission provides additional support for the argument that the Treasury had
greater difficulty in controlling the Admiralty and War Office
than other departments. Both Welby and Lingen, his predecessor and now a member of the Ridley Commission, confessed that the Treasury's control of the Admiralty and War
Office estimates was ineffective. Lingen admitted that in his day
(1870–85), their estimates, which were by far the largest and
most complex, used to arrive at the Treasury only a day or two
before their presentation to parliament, while those of the civil

[6] Ridley Commission, 2nd Report, R. Giffen's evidence.
[7] Ridley Commission, 2nd Report.

departments were invariably submitted by 15 December. As a result, the Treasury's scrutiny was hurried and superficial. Since Lingen's retirement, the two departments had submitted their estimates a little earlier, so that the Treasury Principal Officer now had a 'longer time' but 'not a sufficiently long time' to go through them.

Even more disturbing was Welby's admission that the Treasury attempted nothing in the way of a systematic and continuous review of either the estimates (civil and military) or of expenditure generally. From Welby's conception of what was required can be inferred a very *ad hoc*, haphazard and ineffective system of Treasury control:[8]

> Each branch of the Treasury should watch the course of expenditure of the departments under it during a series of years, keeping the facts, as shown by the expenditure for a series of years, before it. In that way it would learn whether the departments were economical or not, and it would be able to bring before the Financial Secretary, who is the final judge in these matters, cases in which it had reason to think that a department was extravagant, that it was using more clerks than was necessary, then the Financial Secretary could decide as to whether inquiry was necessary with a view to reduction. I think that, so to speak, the review by the Treasury of expenditure of departments over a series of years is not quite sufficiently systematically conducted, and that if it were more systematically conducted we should be in a better position to bring before the Financial Secretary, cases in which inquiry would be useful.

Welby's suggestion that 'the room of each Principal Clerk in the Treasury should have maps on its walls showing the financial history of each department year after year, so that he could test its progress at a glance' was a sensible one, but why had something so obvious and simple to arrange as a comparison of one year's estimates with those of previous years not been done before? Was the Treasury's scrutiny of the civil estimates as elementary and as crude as this seems to suggest?

The most important part of Welby's evidence provoked a

[8] Ridley Commission, 2nd Report, Welby's evidence.

discussion of an issue which lies at the heart of the debate on the effectiveness of Treasury control: the extent to which the Treasury could and did control 'policy'. There is little doubt that Welby was right when he claimed that he saw 'in public a tendency to speak of the Treasury control as if it were intended to be a reconsideration of the policy of another department . . . that an uninstructed department should review, and perhaps be the means of reversing the policy recommended by what I will call an instructed department.' Sir Robert Chalmers, permanent secretary to the Treasury, 1911–13, made the same point before the MacDonnell Commission twenty-five years later.[9] Whether or not it was the case that Treasury control was a constraint upon policy, many within the civil service, and more outside, believed that it was.[10] Welby, however, strenuously denied that the Treasury had any such authority, Treasury control was a 'purely financial check, instituted for purely financial purposes, and that from the moment it interferes in any shape or kind with policy it is departing from its proper sphere'.

Lingen was quick to spot the weakness in this argument and led Welby into an untenable position where he refused to admit that a financial judgment involved a judgment on the merits of a proposal. It was not, in Welby's view, the function of the Treasury 'to say whether the policy which leads to a certain expenditure is right or not'. It was, however, within the competence of the Treasury to require a department to provide '*prima facie* good grounds for incurring expenditure', but that did not, Welby hastened to add, infer or imply 'a power in the Treasury to overrule the policy of another department, on the ground of policy'. The distinction which Welby doggedly insisted upon throughout some tough cross-examination, between the right of the Treasury to demand '*prima facie* good grounds' and its inability to say whether the policy which led to expenditure was right or not, is, to be charitable, a trifle obscure. Less charitably, it could be argued that the distinction was at best an arbitrary one and unenforceable in practice; at worst, the distinction was quite meaningless. If the latter is true, then it is

[9] MacDonnell Commission, 1st Report, P.P. 1912–13, XV, Chalmers's evidence.
[10] See, for example, the correspondence in *The Times*, 7, 29, 30 and 31 January 1890, and 4 and 8 February 1890.

difficult to resist the conclusion that, by admitting it was right for the Treasury to require a department to provide *prima facie* good grounds for incurring expenditure, Treasury control inevitably impinged, to a greater or lesser extent, upon policy. This is not to claim that Treasury control was a constraint upon departmental policies, merely to assert that in practice it could not help raising, directly or indirectly, issues of policy when it offered 'financial' criticism.

Welby's purpose in making a distinction between 'policy' and the financial implications of policy was to refute criticism that the Treasury, an 'uninstructed department', reviewed the policy of other departments. Policy, Welby argued, was the concern of the departmental minister. If the Chancellor of the Exchequer chose to call that policy in question, and only he in the Treasury could do so, then 'that question he takes, as a member of the Cabinet before the Cabinet. That becomes a matter of different procedure.' Somewhat disingenuously, he argued that any control exercised there was independent of the Treasury. This is demonstrably false. Ministers spoke with the authority of their departments, as well as that which derived from their seniority, experience and political weight. If the Chancellor took a policy issue to the Cabinet he would almost certainly be briefed by the departmental Treasury, as a minister would be briefed similarly by his department. Treasury control did not necessarily leave off where Cabinet discussion began.

The contradiction into which the Commission's examination had led him was perhaps an outward manifestation of a more fundamental confusion in Welby's mind which he had expressed privately to the Chancellor of the Exchequer a very short while previously. It is perhaps no accident that the example which he gave to the Commission to illustrate the difference between 'policy' and the financial implications of policy was drawn from the case which had provoked him within the Treasury to seek guidance and clarification from the Treasury ministers on the meaning of Treasury control and how they wished the department to exercise it. In front of the Commission, Welby had argued that it was not the function of the Treasury to object to an Admiralty proposal to create an Intelligence Department on lines similar to that which had recently been established in the

War Office; it could not say 'that it is impolitic to create the department'. The proper function of the Departmental Treasury was to criticize and advise the Chancellor on the proposal 'in its financial aspects'. They, and the Chancellor, were exceeding their function if they said that the creation of an Intelligence Department was impolitic 'quite apart from its money aspect'. Again, the distinction is by no means clear. The creation of an Intelligence Department in the Admiralty might be 'impolitic' because there was very little money for new expenditure and it had a low priority, or because it was felt to duplicate an otherwise existing service, or simply because it cost too much money. A small Intelligence Department of, say, a half-dozen people might be less 'impolitic' than one with an establishment of fifty.

After the Admiralty's Intelligence Department had been set up, the War Office, which had been relieved of responsibility for Admiralty intelligence, rather surprisingly asked for more staff and an increase of expenditure of twenty per cent. The request, for which no reasons were given, drove Welby to ascertain how far his views on Treasury control met with the approval of his ministers. He assumed that the Government was serious in its declarations that it was anxious for economy, if consistent with efficiency. He understood Treasury control to mean:[11]

1 That the Chancellor of the Exchequer, who has to find the money, is to know how it is going. This is essential, but the duty of the Treasury in this respect would be fulfilled if we merely keep a register.

2 But the Chancellor is not content to be a mere Registrar, and that, further, has not in my opinion been the view taken by political authorities of his functions. He requires to be satisfied that demands are really necessary. Many things may be desirable but not imperative. The imperative ought to have precedence, and the Chancellor of the Exchequer practically decides for which of services urged upon him he can afford to provide.

3 Some one in a great service like that of the public must watch over a certain uniformity of pay and regulation, and this duty falls to the Head of the Treasury, i.e., the Chancellor of the Exchequer.

[11] Quoted in Sir Horace Hamilton, 'Treasury Control in the Eighties', *Public Administration* XXXIII (Spring 1955), p. 13.

From his 'observations over many years' Welby concluded that 'our Political Chiefs are shy of giving us general instructions how they wish the control exercised. Decisions *ad hoc* are easier, but I think that the Chiefs ought to let their subordinates know how they wish the control to be exercised', whether as Registrar or Controller. He asked for his three rules to be 'corrected, enlarged or modified'. Goschen, the Chancellor of the Exchequer, declined to define control, or to state how he wished it to be exercised, excusing himself on the grounds that he was a newcomer to the Treasury, and doubting whether it was expedient to define control 'more regularly and methodically'. It was better, he thought, to call attention to examples and concrete cases 'where I might not approve the method followed'. Goschen agreed with Welby that the Chancellor was more than a Registrar; he must be satisfied of the expediency and urgency of the proposed outlay, but it was going too far to say that he must 'be convinced that it is really *necessary*'. While this appeared to denote a qualified approval of the concept of the Treasury as Controller spelled out by Welby in his Minute, it fell far short of the general instructions which he had asked for.

Welby's belief, partly endorsed by Goschen, that the Treasury was a Controller, and that it had to be satisfied of the expediency and urgency of proposals put up to it, and his judgment that the 'imperative ought to have precedence', is difficult to reconcile with his later insistence before the Commission of a distinction between policy and its financial implications. Questions of expediency, urgency and priority lead inescapably to questions of policy. To what extent the Treasury should involve itself in policy remained undecided as Goschen and his successors declined to provide 'general instructions' for the guidance of their subordinates how they wanted the control exercised.[12] 'Decisions *ad hoc* are easier', and it was simpler to 'call attention to examples and cases' where, in the judgment of the Treasury officials, the Chancellor might not approve the method followed,

[12] That this was probably the case is suggested by the fact that Welby's and Goschen's Minutes were produced for Ministers thirteen years later when the Treasury had to brief them for a House of Commons debate on a private member's resolution criticizing the exercise of Treasury control. See Sir Horace Hamilton, *op. cit.*

than to define beforehand the circumstances in which the Treasury would intervene and those in which it was prepared to be guided by the judgment of the departmental Minister.

The evidence before the Ridley Commission provides some justification for the belief that the conclusions drawn about the operation and efficacy of Treasury control for the earlier period may have equal validity for the years 1874–90. Further than this, it is possible to hypothesize that the control of 'policy' and 'professional/technical' expenditure may have been even less effective than that of establishments' expenditure. The apparent continuity is emphasized by the remarkable correspondence of the explanations provided by Welby and other witnesses for the lack of effective control—principally the autonomy of the departmental minister and the size, technical nature and importance of the department—with those which were offered for the earlier period. More persuasive even than this is the enthusiasm of Welby and almost all other witnesses for the measures suggested by the Commission to strengthen the Treasury *vis-à-vis* other departments. The need for the periodical review of establishments led to the prescription of regulations in a subsequent Order in Council, which dealt also with some of the other Ridley recommendations. These permitted the Treasury to initiate an inquiry without first receiving a demand for an increase of pay or staff. No remedy was found for the lack of 'independent authority' of which Welby complained. Against strong Treasury objection, a Permanent Consultative Committee was set up in 1890, but it fulfilled neither Welby's need for an independent rule-making body to which the Treasury could refer in dealing with departmental proposals, nor the Commission's hope that all proposals for establishment changes would be referred to it. Lacking Treasury support, it soon lapsed, having discussed, largely fruitlessly, one or two general problems of civil service organization.

Control of Colonial Policy, 1868–80

In her study of relations between the Treasury and the Colonial Office, Ann Burton argues that the extent and efficacy of the Treasury's influence upon imperial and colonial expenditure was more limited in practice than has been generally believed, and that the image of a formidable and parsimonious Treasury was not strictly justified.[13] Nevertheless, that image was very welcome and useful to the Colonial Office, who used the threat of Treasury control as a deterrent to refuse requests for expenditure from the colonies and overseas territories. Suppliants were often refused 'peremptorily a request on the grounds that it would be folly to consult the Treasury'; or told that although the Colonial Office would be only too willing to sanction the proposal 'the Treasury would not hear of it'.

The Colonial Office would not acknowledge that the Treasury was useful to it in this way, partly because it was 'habitually resented as an obstacle to be overcome rather than regarded as a source of assistance in the co-ordination of finance'. Friction between the two departments arose from the Treasury's (layman's) criticism of the Colonial Office's (specialists') proposals, and from the delay of Treasury replies—'possibly a device to discourage requests'. Some of the permanent officials in the Treasury were personally as well as professionally disliked, and it was generally believed that the Chancellor of the Exchequer or the Financial Secretary would listen more sympathetically to their proposals than the Departmental Treasury.

Miss Burton confirms the thesis urged upon the Ridley Commission that the departments got their way with the 'big' things, while the Treasury bullied them over the 'little' things. Over relatively minor administrative matters, direct Treasury control of the Colonial Office was virtually absolute. The main reason for this was that such issues rarely enlisted public or parliamentary pressure, and upon such pressure, it is argued, depended the effectiveness with which the Colonial Office resisted Treasury control. On the other hand, the power of the Treasury to control expenditure attendant upon policy was extremely limited. Quoting a minute by Welby and Gladstone's evidence to the Select Committee on Civil Services Expenditure, Miss Burton professes to see a clear distinction between policy and the financial aspects of policy, the one subject only to

[13] 'The Influence of the Treasury on the Making of British Colonial Policy', D.Phil., Oxford, 1960. Some of the main conclusions are summarized in 'Treasury Control and Colonial Policy in the Late Nineteenth Century', *Public Administration* XLVI (Summer 1966), pp. 169–92, from which all the quotations used here are taken.

Cabinet control and the other the only proper preserve of the Treasury. This is very similar to Welby's argument before Ridley. When issues were taken to Cabinet for decision, that decision, whether favourable or otherwise to the Chancellor, 'could no longer be considered Treasury control'.[14] Such an issue occurred in a dispute between the two departments over assisted emigration to Western Australia, when Lowe refused to sanction an expenditure of £65,000, although advised to do so by his own officials. Lord Granville, the Colonial Secretary, took the case to Cabinet, but as the majority of his colleagues were either indifferent or opposed to him, he had to give way. Miss Burton is strictly accurate when she argues that this was less a triumph of Treasury control than a personal victory for Lowe, 'illustrative of his reputation as a quarrelsome Chancellor whose tendency was to encroach upon the authority of his colleagues'. But what if Lowe had been advised by his Treasury officials to refuse sanction? On this occasion, as upon those where the Chancellor was in accord with his advisers, Lowe would be briefed by the Treasury for his Cabinet battle with Granville. Moreover, to argue as Miss Burton does, following Welby and Gladstone, is to miss the point that what the Treasury did or did not do, could or could not do, was influenced as much by the personality of its Chancellor of the Exchequer (compare Gladstone and Disraeli, for example), as by other factors; in the same way, the policies of other departments were influenced by the personalities of their ministers.

Miss Burton concludes by arguing that although it was not within the power of the Treasury to interfere directly in policy decisions, its criticism of the purely financial aspects of a settled policy did enable it to have an indirect influence upon the conduct of a policy. It could distort policy by a series of minor administrative decisions, but if that distortion became too serious the department would protest. Its protest on the grounds of interference with policy would lead to the Treasury's defeat in an inter-departmental dispute—presumably because the Treasury, acknowledging that it had no *locus*, would back down. If it refused to back down, then the issue would be carried to Cabinet by the departmental minister, where Cabinet control would endorse or overrule the Treasury.

[14] Burton, *op. cit.*

The image of a powerful and antagonistic Treasury was weakened also by many limitations on direct Treasury control in the areas of both imperial and colonial expenditure. In a detailed examination of the control of imperial expenditure, Miss Burton shows that the opportunities for control were limited. Grants-in-aid, military expenditure, and imperial guarantees for colonial loans were so closely tied to policy issues that the Treasury was often merely an instrument of policy, sanctioning proposals as a formality. The Treasury's control of colonial funds was similarly constrained.

Among the factors which contributed to the limitation of direct Treasury control Miss Burton notes: the demands of policy, the exigencies of the moment, the inability to supervise closely distant expenditure, and the influence of the Chancellor of the Exchequer, Robert Lowe, who overruled his Treasury advisers in the decision to relax control of the revenue and expenditure of the Crown Colonies in 1870. The degree of control was also a function of the political strength of a colony. Here a parallel can be drawn with the existence of hierarchy among Whitehall departments.[15] Thus, those with 'first-class' status, i.e. self-government, were accorded greater respect and were better able to resist control. Those with an inferior status, the smaller Crown Colonies, were subjected to a greater degree of control which they were much less able to resist.

The growth of the Medical Department

The astonishing growth of the Medical Department from a small subordinate part of the Privy Council with a staff of one to an independent department with an annual expenditure of £16,000 is one of the many interesting subsidiary themes of Royston Lambert's biography of Sir John Simon.[16] The light that this throws upon the operation and effectiveness of Treasury control is particularly important because Lambert is not concerned to prove or disprove theories about the influence of the Treasury, and also because he is telling us what it was like to be on the receiving end of Treasury control.

[15] See below, p. 219.
[16] What follows is constructed from the evidence presented in his book, *Sir John Simon, 1816–1904* (London, 1963).

In thirteen years the departmental estimate increased thirteen-fold, and the 'fanatical economy of these years did not prevent the Treasury from accepting, if in the shape of a compromise, every important demand that Simon made. . . . It seemed as though by relying on a few regular pretexts and on Lowe's sympathy, the Treasury could now be forced to come to terms with any proposition from the Medical Department.' These are very large and important claims. What evidence is there for making them?

The politicians had interpreted the 1858 Medical Act to mean that only temporary, job-to-job staff could be appointed for the Privy Council's medical purposes. Simon, who had been appointed Medical Officer of Health in 1855, now employed the familiar tactic of 'temporariness' to prevail upon the Treasury to approve funds and appointments. Within two years he had persuaded them to agree to a vaccination inspectorate of four— 'albeit temporary and merely fact-finding'. Simon managed to hold on to his 'temporary' inspectors for six years, but he had with the support of the Vice-President of the Council, Robert Lowe, to resist regular Treasury raids to clutch them back. In 1864, armed with a very large mass of evidence, Simon, backed by Lowe, asked the Treasury to perpetuate the annual grant of £2,000 for vaccination inspection. Faced with 'overwhelming testimony and seduced by Simon's ingenious and true argument that permanent inspectors would prove less costly than continued temporary ones, the Treasury regretfully gave way'.

Two years later, in 1866, Simon employed a different tactic. With Lowe's help he primed a Select Committee to press the Treasury for an additional sum of £10,000 for the subsidizing of public vaccination: the Treasury 'succumbed to the extent of granting £5,000'. The new discretionary power to award vaccination gratuities to local authorities 'bred in Simon's ingenious hands, yet more staff'. Part of the £5,000 was used to appoint two further inspectors of vaccination. 'By exploiting every opportunity, his influence over Lowe and Bruce [who succeeded Lowe as Vice-President], and the revelations of 1861–1864, and by avoiding Parliamentary notice, Simon had quietly by 1866 secured a permanent and highly salaried staff, a new discretionary power . . . and a largely increased estimate.'

With the return of the Liberals in 1868, and his close friend and ally, Lowe, now installed as Chancellor of the Exchequer, Simon brought forward his plans for a fundamental reorganization of the Medical Department. Although Royston Lambert comments that his demands were 'deliberately moderate and minimal' and 'tactfully modest', viewed in the context of establishment applications from other much larger departments, and bearing in mind the commitment of the government to retrenchment in general and a reduction of permanent pensionable posts in particular, Simon's demands were very substantial indeed. It is not difficult to understand why both the permanent and parliamentary secretaries of the Treasury were 'appalled' at the prospect of five more staff and another £5,000 on the annual estimates. The financial secretary, Ayrton, flatly refused, but he and Lingen had counted without Simon's influence in a higher quarter. 'When the papers reached Robert Lowe, the advice of officials and the doctrine of economy, both of which he usually so closely followed, suddenly lost their cogency: "The Chancellor of the Exchequer is of the opinion", ran the decisive minute, "that these several proposals cannot be refused." ' Only trivial modifications were made to the scheme. Later, ignoring established practice, Simon appointed a legal secretary from outside the Service. Once again Ayrton and Lingen protested, but were again overruled by Lowe. 'Just to consummate the year, Simon asked, in December, for an increase, and later for the regular authorization of the grant for laboratory research, which had hitherto been provided on an insecure, temporary basis.' Yet again, Lowe personally acceded to both requests.

On a subsequent occasion the following year, Lowe was again to ignore the advice of his permanent secretary and agree to Simon's demands. The last and 'most extensive piece of self-generation' was argued in a thirty-three page letter which reached the Treasury in mid-January 1871. Backed by cogent and copious evidence, Simon called for a 'very material' increase in the staff and estimates of the Medical Department. The annual cost was put at £7,950, an increase of 50 per cent in the department's estimates. Lingen's memorandum to the financial secretary was explosive: 'This letter impresses me as extravagant from beginning to end. The Health Department is proclaiming the same sort of unlimited missionary action as has inflamed the estimates of the Science and Art Department, which now alarm the Chancellor of the Exchequer.' Yet again Lowe rejected the advice of his senior official and junior colleague. After consultations, Simon was allowed immediately three of the six new inspectors, and verbally promised the others the following year, as three 'were as much as could be expected in one year'. The three additional clerical staff he had asked for, and the gratuities to public vaccinators, were granted immediately.

Why was Simon so successful so continuously over the thirteen years 1858–71, and Treasury control so apparently ineffective? First of all, there is Simon himself, in whom there were combined the enviable qualities of ability, energy, initiative, vision and drive, enhanced at different times by his professional competence, ingenuity and cool nerve. Unaided he might have achieved something, but nothing like as much or as quickly. The key to his success lies in his influence and his personal relationships. The Treasury usually found it more difficult to resist the demands made upon it when the permanent officials were supported actively by their ministers: when the departmental minister was both sympathetic and determined the Treasury often found the combined pressure irresistible.[17] Simon set out deliberately to cultivate the goodwill of his ministers and to win their support: 'I care extremely much for being well thought of by the chief under whom I work.' When he failed, he was markedly less successful in dealing with the Treasury, as happened during the 'disastrous' Presidency of the Duke of Marlborough in 1867–8. 'Pedestrian and limited, he became the only chief since Lord Salisbury who failed to respond to the influence of his official adviser. The near calamitous consequences indicate just how critically valuable that influence normally was.'

Equally as important as his cultivation of his ministers was his enduring and firm personal friendship with Lowe and Forster, who was Vice-President under the Presidency of Lord de Grey; the latter, incidentally, 'had long supported the sanitary cause' and 'proved co-operative and amenable'. While at the Council, Lowe, Forster and Bruce were quite ready to carry the fight into

[17] Wright, *op. cit.*, ch. 15.

Treasury chambers. When Lowe was appointed to the Treasury in 1868 he used his position and authority to overrule repeatedly his official and political advisers. In Bruce, now at the Home Office, and a Cabinet member, Simon had another influential ally. In Lambert's judgment 'the constant and crucial amenability of the Treasury stemmed from the sympathy that Simon had won from Lowe inside the Treasury, and from Buckingham, Bruce and Forster outside'.

Another factor contributing to his success was the difficulty the Treasury found in denying expenditure to implement policy laid down in parliament and supported by public opinion; but Lambert believed that Simon's exploitation of public opinion and the demands of the law counted for much less than his creation of a 'reliable network of personal relationships'. The Treasury was further handicapped in dealing with a technical subject about which it knew very little. When dealing with the Treasury, Simon capitalized upon his professional status and expertise. The technical explanation and evidence which he submitted in support of his proposals for increased expenditure was difficult to evaluate. In the spring of 1871 he asked the Treasury for an assistant inspector to supervise the quality of the national vaccine supply, supporting his application with a technical explanation and a reference to the Select Committee on Vaccination. Lingen found the additional appointment unwarrantable and the proposed salary too high. 'To his, layman's, mind "only a couple of drawers" were needed for this job. But he went on: "I do not know who is to check the assertions of experts when the government has once undertaken a class of duties which none but such persons understand." ' The Treasury again gave way.

The Education Department[18]

Kay-Shuttleworth had a less well-developed network of informal relationships with ministers or officials which could be exploited to squeeze money and staff out of a reluctant Treasury

[18] The following brief account is constructed from J. R. B. Johnson, 'The Education Department, 1839–64: A Study in Social Policy and the Growth of Government', Ph.D., Cambridge, 1968; and Gillian Sutherland, 'Some Aspects of the Making of Policy in Elementary Education in England and Wales, 1870–1895', D.Phil., Oxford, 1970.

than did Simon. Until the late 1840s this did not matter too much, but as the Treasury's attitude became less benign, his isolation and vulnerability to Treasury pressure added to the difficulties of an office increasingly troubled by staffing crises. Kay-Shuttleworth was 'decidedly unpopular in Treasury circles', and got on none too well with Charles Greville in the Privy Council Office, to whom he was subordinate and through whom he was obliged to work.[19] But even had he enjoyed a status and independence comparable with Simon, the protection and support of a senior minister, and more felicitous personal relations with his colleagues in the Privy Council Office and the Treasury, it is doubtful whether the Treasury could have been successfully resisted at this time. The tougher line which was now adopted was partly the result of pressure from parliament for closer Treasury scrutiny of education expenditure, and partly due to the personal interest which the Chancellor of the Exchequer, Sir Charles Wood, began to take in the Education Department.[20]

During the period of retrenchment of public expenditure in the 1850s and 1860s, the Education Department was in the hands of Ralph Lingen. With Lowe he introduced the system of payment by results, the main financial effect of which was to keep education expenditure down to its 1861 level for nearly a decade. This made Treasury control less necessary, but the Treasury's task was made lighter still by the financial discipline which Lingen imposed on his department. It was here in the Education Department that Lingen cut his Treasury teeth, ignoring all pleas for additional staff until those already employed were demonstrably over-worked. It was rarely necessary for the Treasury to object to additions to the ranks of the inspectorate 'for the very good reason that he kept the additions to the lowest possible minimum'.[21]

After 1870 two things stand out in the relations between the Treasury and the Education Department. First, the latter enjoyed a large measure of success in its dealings with the Treasury over the annual estimates and establishments matters. Secondly, the Treasury exercised a considerable degree of

[19] Johnson, p. 331; (see also above, Richard Johnson, 'Administrators in education before 1870').
[20] *Ibid.*, pp. 332–4.   [21] *Ibid.*, p. 44.

influence over the formulation and administration of education policy. Both are attributable directly to Lingen's presence at the Treasury from 1871 to 1885. As Permanent Secretary he took a personal and close interest in all matters relating to education policy and in the administration and management of the Education Department. The substantial increases of staff which were obtained in the first few years following his arrival at the Treasury were partly the result of his reluctant acceptance that the inevitable concomitant of the spread of the system of payment by results *under the legislation of 1870* was more staff and more money. Disavowing the political principle, he conceded the administrative and financial logic of its consequences. Later the Treasury's attitude became slightly less conciliatory.[22]

Lingen's translation to the Treasury not only provided that department with an invaluable and unique source of expertise and specialist knowledge of education policy and its financial implications, it provided also the informal access to the Treasury which had been lacking in Kay-Shuttleworth's day. The arrival of the Balliol men in the last years of his regime had brought to the Education Department not only Lingen, but Lingen's former pupil, Matthew Arnold, and Francis Sandford who succeeded Lingen as permanent secretary. The importance of a reliable network of personal relationships in treating with the Treasury, emphasized by Simon's biographer, is confirmed in Gillian Sutherland's study of the Education Department after 1870.[23]

Throughout the greater part of the 1870s the Treasury was prepared to accept without much demur a sharp increase in payments to schools and in the establishment of the Education Department, but towards the end of the decade its sympathy and patience began to drain away.[24] Nevertheless, where the Education Department dug in its heels, as over the rejection of the proposed cuts in the 1878 estimates, the Treasury found it difficult to sustain its objections.[25] And even where the Treasury was prepared to take an issue to Cabinet, it could still be defeated by the skilful exploitation of personal relationships.[26]

More important than the relative ineffectiveness of Treasury

---

[22] Sutherland, pp. 379–82.
[23] For an example, see Sutherland, pp. 382–4.
[24] *Ibid.*, pp. 381–93.   [25] *Ibid.*, pp. 396–7.   [26] *Ibid.*, pp. 405–6.

control as a restraint upon expenditure and establishments after 1870 was the degree of influence which the Treasury exercised over the development of policy. The Treasury's legitimate concern with the scrutiny of public expenditure led inescapably to a fundamental reappraisal of the policy which engendered it. With Lingen in charge, the Treasury was peculiarly well placed to do this. Without his close interest and special knowledge, it is unlikely that the Treasury would have contributed as much to the reappraisal and eventual abandonment of the system of payment by results. By 1880 'any scruples the Treasury had had about pronouncing on issues of policy, had dissolved. They had to pronounce on policy if they were to exert any check at all on the multiplication of the personnel of the Education Department.'[27] The scope for Treasury intervention was widened still further when in a Minute the following year it laid down that full details of the financial effects of proposed policies were to be submitted to it before the Education Department, as represented by the Committee of Council, had committed itself to them. The Education Department objected that this was tantamount to Treasury involvement in the decision-making process, and reminded them that their function was merely to comment on the financial consequences of those decisions. The Treasury took no notice.[28]

With the appointment of Lingen's successor in 1885, the Treasury's close and continuing interest in education expenditure and policy waned. The deterioration in the relations between the two departments which marked Lingen's last years, which had led to the 1881 Minute, his attempts directly and indirectly to re-shape policy, and the Treasury's support for the Audit Office's successful campaign to curtail the Education Department's discretionary powers, was arrested. The new policy initiatives of the Tory Government which followed were accompanied by a massive increase of expenditure, the Treasury 'more-or-less gracefully acquiescing',[29] and by considerable additions to establishments which were approved with little more than the ritualistic dragging of Treasury feet.[30]

[27] *Ibid.*, p. 391.
[28] The Education Department was still able to resist Treasury control on some policy issues. See Sutherland, pp. 438–9.
[29] *Ibid.*, p. 508.   [30] *Ibid.*, pp. 597–9.

The growth of the Local Government Board, 1871–1905

Like Lambert's account of the growth of the Medical Department, Roy MacLeod's study of *Treasury Control and Social
Administration*[31] describes what it was like to be on the receiving end of Treasury control. Like Lambert, he, too, is inclined
to emphasize 'the inflexible Treasury resistance' which the
Board encountered when it asked for an increase of staff or pay.
Yet the outcome of almost all the negotiations for more staff
which he examines was a favourable one to the Local Government Board. Some of the discussions were protracted and
frustrating; others led to the appointment of committees of
inquiry; but in the end the Treasury usually conceded most, if
not all, of what the department asked for. It is true, as MacLeod
complains, that the additions to the establishment never quite
matched the increase of business.[32]

Why was Treasury control of establishments in the Local
Government Board relatively ineffective as a restraint upon
expenditure between 1871 and 1905? First, the Treasury could
not ignore or resist the implications of government policy following the report of the Royal Sanitary Commission and the
decision to merge the Poor Law Board and the Local Government Act Office. This meant that 'because the department was
in a transitional state of development, expansion was reasonable
and expected'.[33] Secondly—and here there is an extraordinary
parallel with the growth of the Medical Department—John
Lambert, the permanent secretary, was a close personal friend
of Gladstone. Between 1871 and 1882 'considerable progress was
made under extremely unfavourable conditions', writes Mac-
Leod, and attributes this progress partly to the 'quite benevolent' Treasury policy towards the Board which resulted from
Lambert's 'close relationship with Gladstone and the Treasury
staff'.[34]

A third factor was the replacement of the favoured relationship under Lambert by the developing political weight of the
department which enhanced its bargaining position. The Presidency of the Local Government Board became a more important

[31] Occasional Papers on Social Administration, no. 23 (London, 1968).
[32] See below, p. 221.   [33] MacLeod, p. 11.   [34] *Ibid.*

political appointment. Sir Charles Dilke, appointed President in 1883, was admitted to the Cabinet, and carried a 'political weight which his two worthy but not particularly influential predecessors, Sclater-Booth and Dodson, had not enjoyed'.[35] Dilke's position in the Cabinet gave him an opportunity to press upon his colleagues the importance of local government work. The effectiveness of a sympathetic and influential minister was shown in 1883 when, after the Treasury had refused the permanent secretary's request for a complete reappraisal of the department's staff, Dilke intervened, saw Lingen personally and urged upon him a Treasury committee of inquiry. Although Lingen thought such a decision a mistake, he acquiesced in the demand for an inquiry. It resulted in a substantial increase of staff, pay rises for some of the clerks, and a redistribution of the work—'recommendations wholly accepted by the L.G.B. and the Treasury' at an annual cost of between £6,000 and £7,000.

Fourthly, MacLeod emphasizes that informal consultations and inquiries were an important and effective means of overcoming Treasury resistance in the 1880s and 1890s. Fifthly, the ineffectiveness of the Treasury in securing reductions of staff and salaries without the willing acquiescence of the department was as evident in the Local Government Board as elsewhere. An abortive attempt to curtail the expansion of the establishment led Bergne, the Treasury Principal Officer, to remark that Treasury restraint was 'of very little value unless one knows the detail of the work', an echo of Lingen's frustration when confronted with Simon's technical arguments at the Medical Department. MacLeod's comment on this episode is illuminating: 'The Treasury could hinder, but not stop this expansion; Bergne could not successfully refute seemingly justifiable departmental claims.'[36]

Treasury control, 1854-1890: some general propositions

The two main aims of Treasury control were: first, to ensure the legitimacy of departmental expenditure—the 'Registrar' function referred to by Welby; and, secondly, to restrain the level of that expenditure—Welby's 'Controller' function. The latter

---

[35] MacLeod, p. 18, n. 40.   [36] *Ibid.*, p. 36.

had a general and a particular aspect: to ensure that all money was wisely and necessarily spent, and to implement particular policies of financial economy.

The scope and effectiveness of the Treasury's control of a department's expenditure was a function of a number of different factors. Most obviously, as Henry Roseveare has shown, it was affected by the prevailing political and economic climate, and the predisposition of individual Treasury ministers.[37] It was also influenced by the type of expenditure and the degree of public, parliamentary and Cabinet support for it. Adopting the classification used by the Ridley Commission, it is possible to make very broad distinctions between different types of expenditure according to their relation to 'policy', to 'professional/technical' subjects, and to establishments. In theory, the less technical, less policy-oriented an item of expenditure, the better the Treasury's claim to control it, and the more effective it was likely to be as 'Controller'. Conversely, a department which had parliamentary and public support for a particular policy, and/or which was backed by the Cabinet, was in a better position to avoid or resist control.

The evidence, such as it is, suggests that in practice the Treasury did find it much more difficult to control 'policy-oriented' expenditure. To the theoretical difficulties noted above can be added two others found in practice: a failure on the part of ministers to define control and to instruct the departmental Treasury where they wanted the Treasury to intervene and how. Also, because 'policy-oriented' expenditure was *ipso facto* more political and hence more sensitive, review by the Treasury was regarded as less appropriate. Although the Treasury subscribed to the latter view in theory, it could not avoid impinging on policy when it demanded 'prima facie good grounds' for an increase of expenditure. The contradiction, and the uncertainty caused by the lack of political guidance, probably added to the difficulties.

The Treasury found it equally difficult to control 'professional/technical' expenditure. Here it was on even less sure ground because a department could argue with some justification that the Treasury could not make informed judgments on subjects about which it knew very little. This applied with

[37] *The Treasury*, ch. 7.

particular force to the expenditure of the Admiralty and War Office, and, as we have seen, to others like the Medical Department or the Education Department where, but for Lingen's special knowledge and interest, it seems unlikely that the Treasury could have had such an influence on education policy in the seventies and eighties.

On the face of it, establishments' expenditure ought to have been easier for the Treasury to control than other types of expenditure, but the evidence strongly suggests that its control as a restraint on the level of expenditure was very ineffective up to the nineties.

The third determinant of Treasury control was the degree of autonomy and respect enjoyed by a department, which was, in turn, a function of hierarchy. It was much more difficult to control, and in any case control was felt to be less appropriate, the 'first-class' departments: Foreign Office,[38] Home Office, Colonial Office and India Office, the older, traditional departments whose Ministers were usually senior members of the government. The superior status of these departments, on a par with the Treasury itself, was recognized and acknowledged in the greater deference accorded to them than to departments of the 'second-class', like the Board of Trade, the Local Government Board or the Education Department. Somewhere between the second and first class came the Admiralty and War Office which were generally dealt with in relation to each other, but separately from all other departments. Slightly below the 'second-class' departments in the hierarchy came the Revenue Departments, then the Irish Offices, and finally those departments subordinate to the Treasury, over which the Treasury exercised a much greater, but steadily declining, degree of control.[39]

The fourth factor was the status, seniority, experience and political weight of a minister, partly but not wholly a function of departmental status. This and the last factor, together, made it easier for the Treasury to control lowly placed departments without a minister, or those with an inexperienced or politically

[38] For the special position of the F.O., see Zara S. Steiner, *The Foreign Office and Foreign Policy, 1898–1914* (London, 1969), pp. 2–3; and Wright, *op. cit.*, pp. 96, 129–31.
[39] See Wright, *op. cit.*, p. xxiv, and notes 1 and 2.

light-weight minister, than those in the 'first class', in the hands
of a very able or senior member of the government. Allied to
this was the personality of the minister himself, and his interest
and sympathy for particular policies, for the organization and
management of his department, and so on. On these often
depended his willingness to do personal battle with the departmental Treasury and his ministerial colleagues there and in
Cabinet.

Perhaps the most critical factor of all was the extent and
strength of a reliable network of personal relationships available
to a minister or his permanent secretary, and the skill with
which it could be exploited to break down, or overcome,
Treasury resistance. Far from resenting this, the Treasury frequently preferred to deal with a department on the informal
network before either side had committed itself irrevocably.
Departments were often encouraged to see the Chancellor, the
financial secretary, or a senior official, when contemplating a
major change in establishments, 'and to avoid writing until the
subject was nearly matured'.

A further factor affected by and affecting those mentioned
above was the attitude of the Treasury towards its controlling
function—what may be called its 'style'. What follows is
derived largely from a study of the period from 1854 to 1874,
but it seems likely on the basis of Ridley to be valid also for the
next ten or fifteen years.

The Treasury conceived its function to be more than that of
a mere 'Registrar'. As 'Controller' it required departments to
explain and justify their demands on the grounds of necessity,
expediency and urgency. These 'criteria' were defined and
interpreted for the most part subjectively by the departmental
Treasury, whose political chiefs generally fought shy of providing
them with general instructions how they wished the control
exercised. It is frequently alleged that that interpretation
deservedly earned the Treasury a reputation for an inflexible
and parsimonious control. The evidence, at least for establishments' expenditure and some aspects of the supply expenditure
of some departments, points to a contrary conclusion. Treasury
ministers and officials were rarely unbending or concerned to
apply principles and precedents rigidly; in practice they were
intensely pragmatic, preferring usually to decide each case on

its merits, even to the point of contradiction with those principles and precedents. Decisions were made *ad hoc*.

A consequence of this was the Treasury's failure to anticipate and provide adequate staff for fast-growing departments like the Board of Trade, the Education Department or the Local Government Board.[40] This was less the result of deliberate policy than inherent in the nature of the Treasury's functions and its *modus operandi*. *Ad hoc*, short-term decisions were a reflection of the concern with the limitation of current rather than consequential or future expenditure; short-term economies were infinitely preferable to putative long-term benefits. The Treasury was not always to blame, however. Sometimes, like the Colonial Office in 1898, the department itself adopted a piecemeal approach 'without due regard to the prospective increase of work'.[41]

To a large extent the flexible and pragmatic system of decision-making was enjoined upon the Treasury by the operation of those factors described earlier. But the practical limitations to its power to control notwithstanding, the Treasury's style was essentially conciliatory, concerned with the avoidance of collision and conflict with the departments. Of course the Treasury niggled, as Welby freely confessed to Goschen, but this was part of the tactics of a larger strategy of bluff and deterrence. The Treasury well understood that in the last resort it could not deny a minister an increase in staff or pay, or the finance for a policy supported by parliament or public opinion, but it could oblige him to justify that expenditure; it could make it difficult for him to get approval; and it could try to deter him from future expenditure. The first tactical move, in what was often a protracted war of attrition, was the adoption by the Treasury of an apparently inflexible and hostile attitude to a proposal submitted to it for an increase of expenditure. This was the 'demur'.[42] What usually followed next was the re-submission of the application for the Treasury's reconsideration, with or without the information called for by the

[40] For an example, see Johnson, *op. cit.*, pp. 507–8.
[41] See R. C. Snelling, 'The Colonial Office 1870–1914' (unpublished working paper). I am grateful to Mr Snelling for permission to quote from this.
[42] See Wright, *op. cit.*, pp. 150–5.

Treasury. The Treasury might demur a second or third time, seeking specific assurances on particular points, or merely repeating its unwillingness to sanction the expenditure. This elaborate posturing in the official despatches, a ritual which made it impossible for the Treasury to give up lightly a position adopted officially, 'at least not without the conventional honours of war expressed by a further skirmish', could be transcended by recourse to one of several ways of exerting semi-official and private pressure upon the Departmental Treasury or its ministers through the network of personal relationships, and occasionally, by dogged persistence, even through the official channels of communication.

In many respects negotiations between a department and the Treasury resembled a very formal and elaborate game, the rules of which were well known to both contestants but never openly discussed between them.[43] It was 'like a formal ballet danced by exactly foreseeable rules: the man at the centre *must* yield after a certain number of formal motions to and fro'.[44] The game had four strategic aims. First, it provided the Treasury with a full written record of the department's reasons or lack of reasons for demanding an increase, together with the arguments deployed by itself in attempting to resist such expenditure. All this could be produced subsequently if the expenditure became the subject of inquiry. At the same time, it enabled the Treasury on future occasions to see how and why a particular increase had been approved or rejected if quoted by the same or another department as a precedent to be followed. Secondly, by insisting upon the requirement of 'prima facie good grounds' the Treasury demonstrated to the departments that increases were not to be had lightly; even if it remained unsatisfied with the explanation, it had caused the department to re-submit its application. When the Treasury demurred, an increase was never obtained easily, even if it was almost always obtained in the end. Departments were obliged to fight for their increases; that they did so was

---

[43] Henry Roseveare, *op. cit.*, p. 203, describes it thus: 'At best it was a kind of indoor sport with recognized rules and minimum stress. At worst it was a rather bitter conflict with political repercussions, and the severest friction tended to arise in areas where the Treasury was unsupported.'

[44] Professor W. J. M. Mackenzie in a letter to the writer.

taken to be some indication of the necessity for them. Thirdly, and there seems little doubt about this, the intention was to delay and hold up an increase as much as possible. This tactic was probably the cause of more bitter complaint about Treasury control than anything else. Procrastination was a very clumsy weapon, but often the only one in the Treasury armoury. Fourthly, an important object of the game was to deter departments from wanting to play it too often—hence the elaborate and formal 'rules' and the protracted and wearisome proceedings.

There is evidence that several Treasury and ex-Treasury ministers and officials believed that the threat of Treasury control was more important, perhaps more effective, than direct control. The Treasury's insistence upon 'prima facie good grounds' meant that departments were obliged initially, or after the Treasury had demurred, to present a reasonably strong case. Because of this all departments had to be selective to some extent in what they put up to the Treasury. In his Minute to Welby in 1887, Goschen had written:

> The first object of the Treasury must be to throw the departments on their defence, and to compel them to give strong reasons for any increased expenditure, and to explain how they have come to have to demand it. This control alone contributes to make the departments careful in what they put forward.

Earlier, Childers, Secretary of State for War, had written to Gladstone that he did all he could 'to curtail expenditure, and to enforce sound financial principles, and of the proposals for expenditure which come forward I think I may safely say that not one of a hundred reaches the Treasury'.[45] In the late 1880s the threat of Treasury control probably acted as a brake on the Education Department,[46] while its indirect influence as a potential check was probably more effective than anything else in limiting imperial expenditure between 1868 and 1880.[47]

That the threat of Treasury control, coupled with the prospect of a protracted and energy-consuming negotiation, may

[45] 5 December 1880, Gladstone Papers, B.M. Add. MSS. 44129, ff. 109–11.
[46] Sutherland, *op. cit.*, p. 680.   [47] Burton, *op. cit.*, p. 192.

have deterred departments from putting up certain proposals, or caused them to modify others, is significant; still more so if the Treasury lacked the means to enforce that threat. Gladstone argued that the Treasury had no direct power to regulate and control expenditure. 'We are only one department side by side with others, with very limited powers; it is more after all by moral suasion and pointing out things that our influence is exercised, than by any large power we have.'[48] In his and Hamilton's view the Treasury's control was an indirect or 'moral control'. Certainly the Treasury's most effective and complete control of establishments' expenditure was achieved not through the exercise of any direct power, but by virtue of the co-operation, understanding and mutual respect which characterized the working of the *ad hoc* Treasury committees of inquiry.[49] By their concern for greater efficiency, these committees were indirectly more successful in limiting expenditure than the day-to-day control where the Treasury relied upon the requirement of prior approval.

Until more is known in detail about the development of the organization and policy of Whitehall departments subsequent to the publication of the Ridley reports, no comparable analysis to that undertaken for the earlier period is possible. However, the general pattern is clear enough. During the twenty-five years prior to the outbreak of the First World War the manner in which the Treasury controlled other departments, and the effectiveness with which it did so, was changing. So much is certain from the available contemporary accounts, in particular the evidence given by the Treasury and other departments to the MacDonnell Commission between 1912 and 1914.[50] As the Treasury began to arm itself with the authority of Orders in Council mandatory on the departments, and to make greater use of general minutes and circulars to introduce a greater measure of uniformity into the organization and administration

[48] *Select Committee on Civil Services Expenditure*, P.P. 1873, VII, p. 699.
[49] See Wright, *op. cit.*, ch. 8.
[50] *Royal Commission on the Civil Service*, 1912–14, 1st and 2nd Reports, P.P. 1912–13, XV; 3rd Report, P.P. 1913, XVIII; 4th Report, P.P. 1914, XVI.

of the different departments, its control became a more effective restraint upon the levels of departmental expenditure. At the same time, the departments themselves were becoming more susceptible to Treasury example and suggestion, and more willing to acknowledge its role as a co-ordinating department and to seek its advice. These developments were a reflection of the Treasury's greater willingness to assume the initiative and to make general regulations. But the threat to invoke the powers of an Order in Council was probably more important than their actual use, in circumstances in which the Treasury relied even more than it had in the past on the example of its own department and those immediately subordinate to it.

The permanent secretary to the Treasury, Sir Robert Chalmers, struck a much more confident note before the Mac-Donnell Commission than Welby had before Ridley. His confidence was the more impressive, given the continuance of the belief that 'Departments are to a great extent autonomous, and the Treasury is certainly not in a position to dictate to them to the extent to which, I believe, public opinion generally believes'. But whereas Welby had gone on to emphasize the weakness of the Treasury's position, Chalmers was now able to claim that when the Treasury or its subordinate departments, such as the Customs or Inland Revenue, introduced a new regulation on pay or leave, and the Treasury issued a new general circular to departments for information, 'as a rule, the departments are very anxious to fall in with the principle vindicated by the department with whom it rests to formulate general views'. What is new here is the greater willingness of the Treasury to circularize departments generally, instead of dealing with each of them separately as each case arose, which was the common practice between 1854 and 1874, and which, to a large extent, persisted for another decade or so. Secondly, if it was true, a willingness on the part of the departments to acknowledge that the Treasury had responsibility for formulating general views and to accept that uniform regulations applied to individual departments—in short, the service had become more uniform, and departments were disposed to acquiesce in the consequences of that change.

The power of suggestion and example was, according to Chalmers, very effective, and departments usually complied.

But there was 'always this safeguard, that should departments resist (as they do not) a line of action which a Treasury Minister really requires, the Treasury can always turn its minutes, hitherto hortatory, into mandatory Orders in Council, if it has the executive Government behind it'. Thus by minutes and circulars the Treasury exercised both 'control and suggestion to a very considerable extent'. Chalmers also made it clear that departments approached the Treasury for advice and suggestion. Since he had returned to the Treasury, after four years at the Inland Revenue, he found that a good deal of his day was 'taken up by notes and remarks from other departments, saying, what shall we do in this case, what shall we do in that'. This had impressed on him that the Treasury was a coordinating department. In the light of his evidence, it is not difficult to understand why, unlike Welby, he thought the Treasury's present powers 'quite adequate'.

The MacDonnell Commission were less sanguine, however, and reiterated the concern expressed earlier by the Playfair and Ridley Commissions about the effectiveness of the Treasury's control of the establishments and organization of the different departments. Despite the power conferred by the 1910 Order in Council to inquire at least once every five years into the pay and numbers of any department, the MacDonnell Commission reported that 'whatever may be its indirect influence, the Treasury does not, in practice, exercise a sufficiently effective control over the organisation of departments unless a question of finance is involved'. Their recommendation of a special Treasury section to supervise and control the civil service generally was not implemented until 1919. By this time such action had become imperative and inevitable with the proliferation of new departments during the war, the powerlessness of the Treasury to control contracts and capital expenditure in the War Office and the Ministry of Munitions revealed in the reports of the Select Committee on National Expenditure, and the prompting of the Haldane Committee on the Machinery of Government, itself set up partly as a result of growing Treasury unease. In the reconstruction of the Treasury which followed there emerged an Establishments Department comprising five separate divisions covering a whole range of functions related to the pay, complementing and organization of the civil service.

Llewellyn Smith, the Labour Department and government growth 1886–1909

An outstanding feature of the growth of social administration in Britain before 1914 was the degree to which the Board of Trade monopolized the formulation, initiation and execution of labour policy. The inception of social security, through the Trade Boards and Labour Exchanges Acts of 1909, and the Unemployment Insurance Act of 1911, was dominated by the extraordinary expansion of this department. In terms of expenditure, while the civil service as a whole increased its outlay by 124 per cent from 1900 to 1914, the comparable figure for the Board of Trade was 595 per cent.[1] Its increase in establishment between the same years of 821 per cent was equally abnormal,[2] and appears doubly so to those historians who view the labour functions to which this staff was put as a marked *discontinuity* in the history of the department. Thus J. A. M. Caldwell has remarked, that seen from the standpoint of 1906 or thereabout, an intelligent observer might have drawn the boundaries of labour administration as follows:[3]

> The Home Office having responsibility for securing the compliance of employers with certain standards of wellbeing laid down by the Government for their workers; the Board of Trade having responsibility for securing to industry the best possible conditions for industrial progress; and the Local Government Board having res-

[1] J. A. M. Caldwell, 'Social Policy and Public Administration 1909–1911, Ph.D., Nottingham, 1956, Appendices, p. xxvii.
[2] *Ibid.*, Appendices, p. xxxvii.   [3] *Ibid.*, pp. 370–1.

ponsibility for persons who had dropped out of industry through some cause or another . . . In accordance with this division of functions, it would have been reasonable for trade boards to be found in the hands of the Home Office, and labour exchanges and unemployment insurance to be found in the control of the Local Government Board.

Why then, in the allocation of responsibility for this social legislation, did the Board of Trade receive all? The traditional explanation views political personality as the major determinant. It argues that had Winston Churchill been at the Home Office or Local Government Board, the division of powers would have been very different. Instead, given the indecisiveness of Herbert Gladstone and the sheer ineptitude of John Burns, the Board of Trade had at the crucial period the political initiative to secure the lion's share of the Liberal programme.[4] This interpretation is, however, both incomplete and misleading. Its over-emphasis upon the immediate interplay of political personality has led to a neglect of secular administrative factors, working, as this study is intended to demonstrate, in the same direction. Its denial of continuity has devalued the role of the parent stem of this expansion in the labour functions of the Board of Trade—the pre-existing Labour Department; which is either ignored as a formative influence, or treated as an appendix to the main theme—a passive agent of political decision. Finally, it seriously underrates the importance of Sir Hubert Llewellyn Smith, a brilliant and constructive civil servant, who as the first Commissioner for Labour presided over the foundation of the Labour Department in 1893, and as permanent secretary of the Board of Trade from 1907, played a leading part in the initiation of social legislation.

In terms of the debate over the explanation of Victorian administrative growth, the origins of the Labour Department

[4] J. A. M. Caldwell, 'The Genesis of the Ministry of Labour', *Public Administration* XXXVII (1959), pp. 371–82. See also B. B. Gilbert, 'Winston Churchill versus the Webbs: The origins of British Unemployment Insurance', *American Historical Review* LXXI (1966), pp. 846–62.

present an interesting case study. They had no clear relationship with any coherent body of thought or doctrine. The isolated efforts of individualist reformers, the collectivism of radical and socialist ideologies, the persistence of national and international statistical pressure groups, the incentives of foreign example and competition, of domestic economic insecurity and industrial unrest, the caprice of electoral tactics and political ambition, and the nature of administrative response; all combined to determine the character of the new Department. Yet, underlying this fusion, a number of broadly chronological phases of development can be detected, the first of which was the growth of demand for the establishment of a bureau of labour statistics.

Before 1886 the only official statistical sources available for an objective appraisal of the condition of labour in Britain were deficient, chaotic and unmanageable.[5] They largely lay in the evidence before Royal Commissions and Select Committees, the annual reports of departmental inspectorates and the mass of publications issued relating to trade. To disentangle significant data that were both continuous and comparable was virtually impossible. Royal Commissions were ideal media for the exposé of specific social evils, but they were unsuited to the demands of monitoring the overall welfare of the working classes. As the 'Labour Problem' came to the forefront of late-Victorian public debate, these statistical deficiencies became increasingly intolerable. They were particularly anathema to two groups of reformers: to a knot of middle-class, trade-union sympathizers who saw in the educative effects of the provision of adequate labour statistics the means of working-class self-improvement, and to social and administrative statisticians concerned to measure the degree and cost of social wastage.

The first recorded representations to the government for the provision of labour statistics were those of George Howell in 1869 as a member of the T.U.C. Parliamentary Committee.[6] His initial efforts brought no response, the more so as the labour representatives sitting in parliament after 1874 proved

---

[5] *Official Statistics Committee*, Mins of Ev., Appendix A: Memorandum by R. Giffen on 'The Compilation and Printing of the Statistics of the United Kingdom', P.P. 1881 (39) XXX, pp. 117–38.

[6] *Journal of the Royal Statistical Society* LVI (1893), p. 65.

apathetic to the issue.[7] Howell was therefore forced to renew
the attack in a forceful article in the *Beehive* in 1876:[8]

> The vast and daily increasing importance of all move-
> ments connected with labour, and especially the legisla-
> tive tendency of very many of these movements, point
> conclusively to the necessity of a Bureau of Statistics
> of Labour, where the statesman, philanthropist, author,
> journalist, or citizen, can at all times obtain authentic
> information and reliable statistics when attempting to
> deal with some of the many problems connected therewith.

However, individual effort was soon swallowed up in broader,
institutional offensives, and the question of labour statistics
became part of the wider issue of the improvement of administrative statistics in general. Two forceful memoranda from the
Board of Trade led the Treasury to appoint an Official Statistics
Committee in 1879,[9] but although its report stressed that the
major blame for statistical chaos lay in 'the sacrifice of the
requirements of the public and of Parliament to those of the
departments',[10] its recommendations for structural reform
were tentative and ineffectual. The Royal Statistical Society,
backed by officials of the Board of Trade with which it had
traditional affiliations,[11] therefore took the offensive in its
Jubilee Year of 1885. Sir Rawson Rawson set the tone in his
opening address to the Jubilee Conference, when he suggested
that the occasion should be used to press the government to
authorize the co-ordination of United Kingdom data, pointedly
listing European countries that had already adopted similar
measures.[12] Indeed, the touchstone of foreign example was a
recurrent theme in the arguments of reformers, and the Royal
Statistical Society made certain of maintaining this pressure
when, again at the Jubilee Session, the International Statistical
Institute was inaugurated 'to call attention of governments by

[7] C. Bradlaugh, 'Labour Statistics: their utility to employers and
employed', in *Our Corner* (ed. Annie Besant) VII (1886), p. 130.
[8] 12 February 1876.
[9] P.P. 1881 (39) XXX, p. 5.
[10] *Ibid.* p. 16.
[11] F. J. Mouat, 'The History of the Statistical Society of London',
Journal of the Royal Statistical Society, Jubilee Volume (1885), p. 49.
[12] *Ibid.* pp. 10–11.

means of *vœux* to matters capable of solution by statistical observation'.[13] With the Royal Commission on the Depression of Trade and Industry groping vainly through its task in the background, J. S. Jeans, the economist, summed up the mood of the time when he remarked:[14]

> It has now come to this, that a high degree of civilization, and a high and adequate standard of efficiency in regard to the collection of statistical data respecting matters of public concern, may almost be regarded as convertible terms.

Meanwhile, earlier in the year, the Statistical Society had organized the Industrial Remuneration Conference. It was a major landmark in the development of the Labour Department. Four of its leading participants were later to preside over the Department's inception at the Board of Trade. More immediately, its proceedings, riddled with ineffectual debate, were a telling picture of the sheer lack of statistical basis for objective discussion. This defect was consciously aired in many of the papers, but constructive suggestions were generally unforthcoming. Charles Bradlaugh, however, demanded something more concrete.[15] Accordingly, when on 2 March 1886, following the Liberal electoral victory, he proposed to the Commons that 'immediate steps should be taken to ensure in this country the full and accurate collection of labour statistics',[16] the Industrial Remuneration Conference had done much to prepare a receptive audience. In the subsequent debate, his resolution was adopted on behalf of the Board of Trade, and what had been a struggle for official recognition became one for administrative viability.

It should be explained why the responsibility for a Labour Bureau was given to the Board of Trade as opposed to other departments possessing extensive administrative commitments to labour, such as the Local Government Board and the Home Office. Prior to 1886, the Board of Trade had no direct concern

[13] J. W. Nixon, *A History of the International Statistical Institute 1885–1960* (The Hague, 1960), pp. 150–1.
[14] *Journal of the Royal Statistical Society*, Jubilee Volume (1885), p. 146.
[15] Industrial Remuneration Conference, *Report* (1885), p. 171.
[16] *Hansard*, 3rd series, vol. 302, col. 1769.

with conditions of employment, trade unions, industrial remuneration, or allied questions.[17] It was not, however, administrative functions that the early advocates of a labour bureau
envisaged. They viewed its duties as purely statistical, and it
was in statistics that the Board of Trade was paramount.
Historically, as the adviser on trade and industry, it had accumulated a mass of data. *De facto*, it represented the Central
Statistical Department of the country,[18] and, indeed, the
Treasury had been urged to formalize this position. Moreover,
in the compilation of 'public' as opposed to 'working administrative statistics', the Board of Trade possessed unique experience that was vital to the implementation of Bradlaugh's
motion. As Robert Giffen, the distinguished head of the Commercial Department, observed in 1889, the Board of Trade 'is
conspicuous as a department which publishes statistics for
statistical purposes alone, the statistics not being required for
daily administration'.[19]

The history of the Labour Statistical Bureau at the Board of
Trade from 1886 to 1891 is one dominated by the triumph of
economy. When Giffen reported on its progress in December
1888, he virtually ignored the bounds of official propriety in
exposing the crippling effects of Treasury control, itemizing
in his preamble the totally inadequate increase in personnel.[20]
With the exception of John Burnett, the Labour Correspondent, no addition had been made to the number of superior
officers of the Board. Even with his appointment, the Treasury
proved singularly obstructive, intimating that the duties involved could quite adequately have been performed by an
assistant clerk, and proposing that Burnett might 'be paid so
much per day as required'.[21] Given the public and departmental
expectations of the scope of the new work, Giffen was under-
standably enraged, and threatened to resign.[22] In the event, he

[17] H. Llewellyn Smith, *The Board of Trade* (London, 1928), p. 180.
[18] P.R.O. BT/12/27. Memorandum by R. Giffen on 'The Statistical
Functions of English Departments of State', 18 July 1889.
[19] *Ibid.*
[20] P.P. 1888 (433) CVII, pp. 122–3.
[21] P.R.O. BT/14 IND. 20472, Treasury to R. Giffen 28 April, 11 June
1886.
[22] Mundella Papers, University Library, Sheffield, Folio 3, Robert
Giffen to A. J. Mundella, 7 May 1886.

remained to do further battle to obtain adequate provision and remuneration of senior statistical officers; but to no avail. By late 1892 there were still only thirteen clerks devoted to labour statistics, only four of whom were under the immediate orders of Burnett, and even these were entirely unversed in the technicalities of working-class industrial and political organization.[23]

The effect of this economy was to cripple the scope and quality of the work. There was a notorious delay in the publication of reports that rendered them near-useless to labour. Original research was minimal, most of the output being merely a collation of pre-existing data. The *Census of Wages* and the *Report on the Relation of Wages to Costs of Production*, both potentially of immense importance to contemporary economic discussion, were seriously marred by a lack of staff to examine the schedules received.[24] The result was a defective system of inquiry that gravely impaired the ability of the Bureau to effect Giffen's preliminary objectives.[25]

In contrast, the years from 1891 to 1893 saw the transformation of a stunted Labour Bureau into a separate Labour Department. The transition was dominated by the interminable proceedings of the Royal Commission on Labour,[26] and

[23] D. F. Schloss, 'The Reorganization of our Labour Department', *Journal of the Royal Statistical Society* LVI (1893), p. 45. *Board of Trade Staff Lists*, Series 9070, pp. 481–5.
[24] D. F. Schloss, *op. cit.*, pp. 46–7.
[25] For Giffen's original memorandum of intent, see P.P. 1886 (48) LXXI, pp. 206–7.
[26] The Board of Trade and the Labour Commission were to pursue a long and intricate love-hate relationship. The Board provided the Commission with data and evidence, and with help in defining the scope of enquiry. John Burnett was seconded as its Joint-Secretary. For its part, the Commission provided an ideal platform for argument in favour of an adequate Labour Department and, in its recommendations, mapped out for it a future programme. Yet, equally, there were elements of conflict. As its Final Report only emerged in 1894, whatever the Labour Department, established in January 1893, had owed to its proceedings remained unacknowledged. In its statistical ineptitude, the Commission became publicly identified as the archetype of the very deficiencies that the Labour Department had been created to remedy. Finally, the Home Office had not only to sustain criticism as the Department with overall responsibility for the

the political manœuvres surrounding the General Election of 1892. In the process, the issue of labour statistics became confused with the general question of the co-ordination of all labour administration. Already, in 1890, suggestions for its centralization had proved receptible to the Lords' Committee on Sweating,[27] and by 1891 the degree of industrial unrest was giving further prominence to the issue.[28] The efforts of both parties to bid for working-class support also resulted in a number of similar proposals. In the case of the Liberals, this was the more so as a 'popular front' of advanced radical groups temporarily united to fill the vacuum in party ideology left by the 'Home Rule' split.[29] A leading article in the *Workmen's Times* underlined the prevailing discontent with the inadequacy and confusion of existing machinery, in which it affirmed:[30]

> Labour gets wedged in here and pigeon-holed there, and
> inspected somewhere else. Its health is kept in one
> length of red tape, its statistics are kept, or supposed to
> be kept in another, whilst the Minister round the
> corner has a department in the cellar which will see that
> the Factory and Mining Laws are duly observed. Labour
> candidate or no Labour candidate, whoever stands will
> have to pledge himself to a Ministry of Labour if he wants
> the workman's vote.

Accordingly, in May 1892, Dalziel gave notice of a resolution in the Commons 'to call attention to the necessity for the establishment of a department of labour, with a Minister responsible to Parliament'.[31] In anticipation of its discussion, both the Home Office and the Board of Trade prepared highly revealing memoranda. At the Home Office, Edward Troup re-

---

investigation, but also held strong objections to the administrative outcome of events.

[27] *Hansard*, 3rd series, vol. 345, cols 483–4.

[28] *Hansard*, 3rd series, vol. 350, col. 1896; *Review of Reviews* III (1891), p. 367.

[29] L. A. Clarke, 'The Liberal Party and Collectivism, 1886–1906', M. Litt., Cambridge, 1957, pp. 33–7.

[30] 7 May 1892.

[31] P.R.O. HO/45 10122/B 12457/1, G. Legge to C. E. Troup, 3 May 1892.

corded his opinion that the Factory and Mines Inspectorate should clearly constitute the nucleus of any such department.[32] Meanwhile, Giffen was revealing his ideas to Hicks-Beach at the Board of Trade. His memorandum was less devoted to pre-empting any future administrative growth than to exposing the weakness of the resolution as such: 'The talk is vague, many people evidently confusing the idea of a department of labour and a Ministry of Labour, and I have seen no statement anywhere of how such a Ministry should be constituted and what it would be expected to do.' He suspected that many of its advocates contemplated socialistic functions such as the provision of work—proposals which Giffen would have never entertained. Significantly, his major objection was that 'It would raise again the old question as to a Central Statistical department which *de facto* exists at the Board of Trade but which would be *pro tanto* impaired to the public inconvenience by the transference of labour statistics to another department.'[33]

If Giffen's concern over labour administration remained unambitious compared with that of the Home Office, A. J. Mundella, who as Liberal President of the Board of Trade had initiated the Labour Bureau in 1886, had no such inhibitions, writing to Gladstone in June that it should be extended, and concluding on a firm note of departmental rivalry:[34]

Factories, Workshops, Mines, etc., are all inspected by the Home Office, and by common consent very inefficiently and insufficiently inspected. I expect you will hear of a great appointment of Tory workmen to inspectorships in a few days. I would suggest that all this work should be put in the Labour Department and under the President of the Board of Trade.

[32] *Ibid.*, C. E. Troup to Sir Godfrey Lushington, 3 May 1892.
[33] Hicks-Beach Papers, County Record Office, Gloucester, PC/PP/60, Memorandum on 'A Minister of Labour' by Robert Giffen, 30 April 1892.
[34] W. E. Gladstone Papers, B.M. Add. MSS. 44258, ff. 274-7, A. J. Mundella to W. E. Gladstone, 9 June 1892.
Mundella, A. J. (1825–97). Manufacturer. Formed permanent conciliation board, Nottingham hosiery trade, 1866. Liberal MP 1868–95. Vice-President of Education Department, 1880–5. President of Board of Trade 1886, 1892–4.

The Liberal progressives, however, after their party's victory at the elections, pressed instead for a separate Ministry of Labour and Technical Education under Arthur Acland,[35] who protested 'rather warmly' at Mundella being in charge of labour affairs.[36] But Gladstone, with his avowed hatred for radical ideas, refused to accept their terms. In an attempt to forestall deadlock, Richard Haldane, sensitive to the need to secure 'the confidence of the nascent body of opinion in the constituencies' which cared 'little for an Irish policy' and concentrated 'itself on social questions', urged that Acland, who possessed the confidence of labour, be given a new post of Vice-President of the Board of Trade in charge of a proper Labour Department.[37] On the morning of 13 August, Acland was cheerfully contemplating the thought of such congenial work accompanied by Llewellyn Smith.[38] By the evening of the same day, the situation had changed entirely. As he recorded in his diary: 'I went to see Harcourt, who told me I should be offered the Presidentship of the Board of Trade and must accept it . . . I went home simply miserable, feeling the Board of Trade would simply crush me.'[39] On 14 August he opted instead for the Education Department, Mundella accepting the Board of Trade. Subsequently, Thomas Burt was offered the Parliamentary Secretaryship on the assurance that: 'the development of the labour bureau and the prosecution of the interests connected with it (would) engage the attention of the Government and open a long and broad perspective'.[40]

[35] Acland, A. H. D. (1847-1926). Politician and educational reformer. Educated Rugby and Christ Church. Tutor at Keble, 1871-5. Steward at Christ Church, 1880. Liberal MP for Rotherham, 1885-99. Promoted Welsh Intermediate Education Act and State grant to technical education. Vice-President of Education Department, 1892-5.

[36] Acland Diary, entries for 21 and 22 July 1892.

[37] D. Sommer, *Haldane of Cloan: His Life and Times 1856-1928* (London, 1960), p. 88.

[38] Acland Diary, entry for 13 August 1892.

[39] *Ibid.*, entry of 16 August 1892. Very probably, political tactics had determined that Acland should have a seat in the Cabinet, Haldane's proposal being rendered thereby impracticable (Sir Algernon West, *Private Diaries*, p. 49).

[40] W. E. Gladstone Papers, B.M. Add. MSS. 44515, f. 221, W. E. Gladstone to T. Burt, 19 August 1892.

Between 14 August 1892 and the formation of the Labour Department in January 1893, the future of the administration of labour remained in the melting pot of public debate. Before the Royal Commission on Labour, witnesses submitted a formidable array of functions that they considered a Labour Department should fulfil; that it should provide frequent and comprehensive labour statistics, act as a central labour exchange, administer the laws relating to mines and factories, and arbitrate in trade disputes.[41] Meanwhile, the Webbs wrote a memorandum for Asquith, the Home Secretary, on the transformation of the Factory Department into a Ministry of Labour,[42] whilst at the Royal Statistical Society, the proofs of a paper by D. F. Schloss on the reorganization of the labour statistical section of the Board of Trade were widely circulated.[43]

Thus, ostensibly, when in late 1892 Mundella and Burt came to consider what measures they should adopt, they were faced with a vast range of options. However, political and administrative considerations effectively closed most of them. Politically, the paucity of the parliamentary majority, the continued preoccupation with Home Rule, and the policy of evasion to social reform of the 'old gang', meant that any new departure had to be purely departmental in character.[44] Any possibility of a Ministry of Labour was therefore ruled out. Likewise, the acquisition of new responsibilities requiring legislative sanction, whether relating to industrial conciliation or unemployment, was impracticable. Administratively, the Home Office had no intention of allowing fresh powers over labour questions to be pre-empted by its junior department.[45] Moreover, even within the Board of Trade, there were personal factors working against the implementation of more than a minimal programme.

Burt, T. (1837–1922). Miner. General Secretary of Northumberland Miners' Association 1865–1913. MP 1874–1918. President of T.U. Congress, 1891. Parliamentary Secretary to Board of Trade, 1892–5.

[41] P.P. 1894 (C. 7421) XXXV, p. 631.

[42] Herbert Gladstone Papers, B.M. Add. MSS. 45989, f. 3, H. H. Asquith to H. Gladstone, 3 October 1892.

[43] Passfield Papers, British Library of Political and Economic Science, II, 3, i, S. Webb to B. Potter, 13 May 1892.

[44] *The Times*, 13 January 1893.

[45] The permanent officials were clearly incensed at the subsequent creation of the Labour Department. The Home Secretary was

Thomas Burt, appointed specifically to further the administrative interests of labour, was essentially anti-collectivist, upholding still the trade-unionist philosophy of the 1860s and 1870s, an ardent believer in self-help and orthodox classical economics, and an opponent of the Labour Party and 'New Unionism'.[46] As important was the conservative influence of Robert Giffen, who clearly indicated before the Labour Commission that, in his view, statistical functions were the only legitimate responsibility of the Board towards labour.[47]

Accordingly, when on 20 January 1893 the formation of a Labour Department was given the formal approval of the Treasury, it appeared a restricted enterprise.[48] Special staff were to be appointed at the central office and local correspondents throughout the country. Provision was to be made for the regular publication of a *Labour Gazette*, but as specified, the duties of the department were to remain those of a statistical bureau alone. Yet appearances were deceptive. As Mundella reflected: 'My Labour Department is a big thing—larger and more important than the Government itself apprehends. It will do great work in the future.'[49]

In the history of labour administration, the years leading up to 1893 were a decisive turning-point. They witnessed the first real appraisal of the distribution of departmental responsibilities towards labour; the first serious consideration of that panacea of social scientists and reformers—a Ministry of Labour. It was then and not later that the 'Cuckoo's Egg' of labour functions was laid in the nest of the Board of Trade, that was to hatch the fledgling destined to dominate the Board's activities.

As *The Times* editorial remarked on 25 January 1893, the future of the Labour Department would largely depend upon 'the

---

eventually forced to issue a special minute in an attempt to obviate interdepartmental friction over the issue. See PRO. HO 45/10122/B 12457/5/6.
[46] G. Best, *Bishop Westcott and the Miners*, Westcott Memorial Lecture, (Cambridge, 1966), pp. 13–14, 19.
[47] P.P. 1893–4 (C. 7063–I), XXXIX, pt. I, q. 7068.
[48] P.R.O. T9/28 19623, Treasury to Board of Trade, 20 January 1893.
[49] Leader Papers, University Library, Sheffield, A. J. Mundella to J. D. Leader, 29 January 1893.

conception that the first Labour Commissioner might form of his duties and the success with which he might impress his ideas upon the plastic organization'. The precedent would be set by Hubert Llewellyn Smith.

Born in Bristol in 1864, of middle-class Quaker extraction,[50] he had worked his way to college by academic distinction, and in 1883 went up to Oxford to an intellectual ferment of immense significance to administrative history. For it was from the Oxford of the 1880s, that emerged a new generation of public servants who, in the pursuit of constructive administration, were to combat the prevailing negative attitude to domestic policy within the civil service. Their careers set an administrative pattern as educationally distinctive as the earlier products of Jowett's Balliol, but whereas their predecessors had lacked any very deep commitment to social action and were recruited largely for their academic ability,[51] men such as Llewellyn Smith developed at Oxford lasting involvements that led on to specialized activities and the acquisition of expertise, prior to their integration within the civil service.

Llewellyn Smith arrived at Corpus amidst what came to be regarded as the 'new Oxford Movement'; an unprecedented outburst of concern over the condition of the working classes. The teachings of Jowett and T. H. Green, with their stress on obligation, the arrival of a more socially relevant, empirical school of economics, and the advent of the new historiography of Arnold Toynbee, provided the necessary preamble, while the immediate cause was the appearance of a series of sensational exposés of urban squalor, of which *The Bitter Cry of Outcast London* was the most prominent. In November 1883, Canon Barnett launched his project for University Settlement that was to become that hot-house of leading administrators, Llewellyn Smith included—Toynbee Hall; and drawing upon the same spirit of constructive zeal, another prolific field of apprenticeship for future office, the Oxford University Extension Movement, was making spectacular headway.

---

[50] Llewellyn Smith Papers, notes for an autobiography.
[51] J. R. B. Johnson, 'The Education Department 1839–64: A Study in Social Policy and the Growth of Government', Ph.D., Cambridge, 1968, pp. 316 ff.

In Llewellyn Smith the emotional and intellectual challenge of the times found a ready response. He was founder-member of the Adam Smith Society, a study group on economic problems.[52] In 1886, with Sidney Ball, he established a Social Science Club, devoted significantly to the pursuance of facts rather than propagandism.[53] However, his most vital attachment was to the 'Inner Ring', a highly seminal group presided over by Arthur Acland for those who shared his concern with social, political and economic questions.[54] His growing connection with Acland was a critical factor in the shaping of his subsequent career, and it is noteworthy that it was to the 'Inner Ring' that John Burnett came in 1886 as the newly appointed Labour Correspondent of the Board of Trade, whose visit, as Llewellyn Smith later recorded, 'gave a great impetus to the intelligent interest of young Oxford in organized labour'.[55] He also participated in the University Settlement Movement, playing host to parties of working men from Bethnal Green.[56]

Academically, his record was equally impressive, constituting a double First in mathematics. More significantly, in 1886, he won the Cobden Prize for an essay on the 'Economic Aspects of State Socialism', which gives an invaluable insight into his views as a political economist and towards state intervention in particular. Deeply influenced by the works of Stanley Jevons, Llewellyn Smith condemned the 'Manchester School' whose doctrinaire rigidity had led to cruel administrative complacency.[57] Government intervention, he stressed, must be judged on purely pragmatic grounds, according to social priorities.[58] He was, however, just as critical of the lack of empiricism within prevailing socialistic doctrines.[59] Self-reliance was still to Llewellyn Smith the basis of social amelioration, to be at

[52] *Pelican Record* X (1910), p. 104.
[53] *Oxford Magazine* V (1887), p. 101. Graham Wallas Papers, Box I, Sidney Ball to Graham Wallas, 18 September 1887.
[54] Acland Diary, entries of 10 June 1883; 4 January, 16 June 1884.
[55] Wallas Papers, British Library of Political and Economic Science, Box VIII, H. Llewellyn Smith to G. Wallas, 25 June 1929.
[56] Llewellyn Smith Papers, H. Llewellyn Smith to Miss L. Smith, 17 May 1885.
[57] H. Llewellyn Smith, *Economic Aspects of State Socialism* (Oxford, 1887), p. 2.
[58] *Ibid.*, p. 9.   [59] *Ibid.*, p. 54.

most supplemented by the state, and its circumvention would merely lead, as in the existing Poor Law, to further pauperization.[60] His thesis was entirely consistent with the 'refined collectivist' that he was later to become as a leading labour administrator.[61]

He came close to entering the civil service direct from Oxford, by open competitive examination. In 1886 he was placed second, but was offered a position in the War Office, and through his connection with the Quakers, he declined the post.[62] For the future social administration of the country, it was a fortunate accident that turned his gifts in a direction in which they were most needed, and enabled him to enter the civil service as a specialist at a later date, to a position tailor-made for a man of his ability and inclinations.

The years between university and office were for Llewellyn Smith ones of hectic and protean activity. In late 1887, his Oxford contemporary, L. T. Hobhouse, remarked that all Llewellyn Smith lacked was confidence 'to make him a first-rate force in the world'.[63] By 1893 he had fully acquired it. In the interim, immersed in the kaleidoscopic world of late-Victorian progressivism, he had built up an array of social, political and academic contacts. Integrated early on into the aristocratic, radical milieu of the Carlisles at Castle Howard, he had progressed to that 'mecca of social reformers' and of future Labour Department personnel—the East End of London, where at Toynbee Hall and later at Beaumont Square, where he founded a sub-colony called the 'Swarm',[64] he had participated in the University Settlement Movement. Meanwhile, in the Booth inquiry, at the British Association, the Royal Statistical and Economic Societies, at the Denison Club, and in his travels as an Extension Lecturer, he had made contact with the élite of social scientists and the leading statisticians of the day—both academic and governmental. Additionally, his espousal of the

---

[60] *Ibid.*, pp. 43, 54, 77, 117.
[61] A. G. Austin ed., *The Webbs' Australian Diary: 1898* (Melbourne, 1965), p. 27.
[62] *Journal of the Royal Statistical Society*, new series, CVIII (1945), pp. 483–4.
[63] Llewellyn Smith Papers, L. T. Hobhouse to Mrs S. W. Smith, 25 October 1887.
[64] *Ibid.*, H. Llewellyn Smith to Mrs S. W. Smith, 28 May 1889.

cause of the 'New Unionism' and his participation in London politics had made him the confidant of the Labour leaders. Above all, his political and educational activities had soldered him to the radical wing of the Liberal Party, while at the same time introducing him to the elder statesmen of labour reform, especially A. J. Mundella.

As a social statistician, his most prominent contribution was to the Booth inquiry, in which his analysis of the influx of rural and alien population into London attracted widespread attention.[65] The effect on Llewellyn Smith as a sociologist and statistician in working for Booth was immense. He shared in the initiation of a new empirical sociology that was to revolutionize the basis of social policy by the creation of a statistical framework—significantly not a theory—in which an accumulation of facts might be received, and from which social legislation might be evolved.[66] The inquiry constituted also a rigorous apprenticeship in the use of statistics, from which Llewellyn Smith emerged with an immense talent both for painstaking field-work and the original and imaginative use of hypotheses, that was to prove vital in the overseer of a national bureau of information.

Meanwhile, through their mutual interest in social data, the earliest contact had been established between Llewellyn Smith and the Webbs.[67] Indeed, until her engagement to Sidney Webb, Beatrice Potter conceived of Llewellyn Smith as her working partner, though it must be admitted that in her eyes his true value lay 'as an executant rather than originator'.[68] However, he was not one to be 'used' or 'permeated', and as Beatrice moved into the Fabian fold, Llewellyn Smith became increasingly distant, and in October 1891 challenged the very

[65] *Life and Labour of the People of London*, ed. C. Booth, vol. I (1889), pp. 501–64; vol. II (1891), pp. 444–77. He demonstrated that contrary to popular assumption, rural immigrants were the cream of the urban labour force and that there was no evidence that alien immigrants displaced domestic workers from employment.
[66] T. S. and M. B. Simey, *Charles Booth – Social Scientist* (Oxford, 1960), p. 4.
[67] Beatrice Webb Diary, British Library of Political and Economic Science, 16 December 1888.
[68] *Ibid.*, 22 January 1891. She pointedly added: 'Such ways he suits me.'

basis of the Webbs' statistical method by questioning whether their work was 'for science or propaganda'![69] Such a revealing outburst from so normally reticent a man gives the clue to that studied avoidance of the Webbs that he later displayed in his official career.

Llewellyn Smith also entered other leading centres of statistical activity. At the Royal Statistical Society he met the leading personalities of the Board of Trade and joined the movement for the reform of administrative statistics.[70] In November 1890 he participated in the formation of the Economic Society, dedicated to the restoration of a constructive, socially meaningful, economics, whose first meetings were convened in Giffen's rooms at the Board of Trade.[71] Moreover, Llewellyn Smith's statistical talents were used by the government itself, when in March 1889 the Local Government Board asked for the use of his material as ammunition to counter a motion in the Commons on the highly emotive question of alien immigration.[72] Indeed, by December 1890, his reputation was such that on the advice of Alfred Marshall he stood for the Chair of Economics at Oxford.[73]

In the light of his appointment as Labour Commissioner in 1893, perhaps the most arresting feature of his earlier life in East London was his exploits in the field of union agitation. The 'education of association' was to him a leading motive force in social change. In 1888, along with other members of Toynbee Hall, he mobilized public opinion against the employers in the celebrated Bryant and May's match-girls' strike.[74] In 1889, with Vaughan Nash, he provided invaluable publicity for Ben Tillett in the Great Dock Strike.[75] The

[69] Passfield Papers, II, 3, i, S. Webb to B. Potter, 24 October 1891.
[70] He signed a Memorandum on the improvement of industrial statistics, submitted to the Select Committee on the Census, P.P. 1890 (C. 6071), LVIII, pp. 118–20.
[71] Royal Economic Society Minutes, 24 November 1890.
[72] Llewellyn Smith Papers, H. Llewellyn Smith to Miss L. Smith, 28 March 1889.
[73] Clara Collet Papers, Henry Higgs to H. S. Foxwell, 13 December 1890.
[74] Llewellyn Smith Papers, H. Llewellyn Smith to Miss L. Smith, 9 July 1888.
[75] Ben Tillett, *Memories and Reflections* (London, 1931), pp. 136–7.

following year he attempted to promote union branches amongst the rural labourers of Oxfordshire,[76] while in the London omnibus strike of 1891 he co-ordinated strike action for John Burns in East London, organizing picket lines and deploying sympathetic commuters to disrupt remaining services.[77] It may be questioned why these escapades did not compromise Llewellyn Smith's eligibility for public office. The answer is that his espousal of trade unionism was that of a sympathetic radical, not of a doctrinaire extremist, and by late 1892, apart from his many other qualifications for the post, his contacts with labour were regarded by the Liberal government as a positive political asset to be capitalized upon in his appointment as Labour Commissioner.[78]

If Llewellyn Smith can be said to have had a political philosophy, it was essentially an operational one; a set of practical alternatives and proposals. The 'Swarm' was notorious for its antipathy to socialist propaganda.[79] Yet, under the umbrella of London Progressivism, he was able to participate with Sidney Webb in London labour politics of the early 1890s to modify Liberal orthodoxies and promote social reform, especially in technical education.[80] More importantly, as Acland's protégé, he was introduced to the inner counsels of the radical wing of the national Liberal Party. He followed him on to the Liberal Publications Committee which they strove to revitalize on more radical lines, and throughout the summer months of 1892, Llewellyn Smith collaborated with Acland in his manœuvres to establish a Minister for Labour.[81] His affiliations with the Liberal progressives were almost certainly a strong determinant

[76] J. A. Hobson and M. Ginsberg, *L. T. Hobhouse: His Life and Work* (London, 1931), p. 29.
[77] A. P. Laurie, *Pictures and Politics* (London, 1934), pp. 87–8.
[78] Mundella Papers, folio I, T. Burt to A. J. Mundella, 21 December 1892.
[79] Passfield Papers, Graham Wallas to B. Potter, 25 June 1892.
[80] Between 1888 and 1893, as Assistant Secretary to the National Association for the Promotion of Technical Education, Llewellyn Smith collaborated in turn with Acland and Sidney Webb to effect major structural reforms in the system of national and metropolitan technical education.
[81] Acland Diary, entries of 22 February, 25 October 1891; 7 February, 13 August 1892.

in his subsequent appointment as Labour Commissioner. Regrettably, no documents survive to provide a conclusive answer. All one can say is that the man and the office were ideally suited; both had emerged from the very same mélange of late-Victorian movements—social, political and scientific.

Administrative historians have increasingly recognized the importance of the ability and initiative of official personnel to the realization of government growth.[82] In the case of the Labour Department of the Board of Trade, this was particularly so. It exemplified the dynamic effects of a positive and valid application of Section four of the 1859 Superannuation Act, by which staff might be appointed at an age exceeding that at which public service ordinarily began, if they possessed professional or peculiar qualifications necessary for the efficient discharge of the office.[83] In consequence, Llewellyn Smith had at his disposal, as Labour Correspondents and Investigators, specialists with reputations as economists and statisticians who were recognizedly influential in labour circles before their appointment.

They included John Burnett, former Chairman of the Nine Hours League, member of the Parliamentary Committee of the T.U.C., and for eleven years General Secretary of the Amalgamated Society of Engineers; C. J. Drummond, previously a member of the Royal Commission on Trade and Industry and the Conservative Secretary of the exclusive London Society of Compositors until ejected in 1892 by the pressures of 'New Unionism'; C. J. Dent, a leading figure in the world of working men's clubs and the productive side of the Co-operative Movement; Clara Collet, a prominent social worker and expert on the industrial condition of women, former investigator for Charles Booth and Assistant Commissioner to the Royal Commission on Labour; and David Frederick Schloss, a barrister and prolific writer on all aspects of the 'Labour Problem', a specialist on industrial remuneration, sweating, co-operation and profit-sharing, a member of the Booth inquiry and

[82] See, for example, D. Roberts, *The Victorian Origins of the Welfare State* (New Haven, 1961), p. ix.
[83] 22 Vict., c. 26, s. 4.

founder-member of the Economic Society. A measure of his drive can be seen in a letter to Sidney Webb in July 1892:[84]

> The official liberals having got their majority will try and get off cheap as to social legislation. The thing to do is to form a Fourth Party who will push the social side; this Fourth Party to have a following outside the House, which following can be led by you and by the Daily Chronicle. Fourth Party to include a few men with money— swells who don't get the plums they expect in the sharing of the spoils. Some organs will be wanted. Buy the Star cheap, acquire the dull Speaker or kill it by starting a bright weekly—the Democrat perhaps. The National Liberal Club, to say nothing of the Fabians, against the old crusted Reform Club and Devonshire. The young blood will win in the end.

Finally, there was Arthur Wilson Fox, eldest son of the Physician in Ordinary to Queen Victoria. A barrister, educated at Marlborough and Cambridge, he was from its inception a vigorous adherent of the Primrose League and primarily recognized as an expert on agricultural labour.

Moreover, these personnel were favoured with an administrative environment in which their initiative had full play. The official files[85] reveal that they all had an opportunity to participate in the formulation of policy decisions. They benefited also from the fact that the Labour Department was part of the Commercial, Labour and Statistical Branch, separated off from the Board of Trade proper like the Patent Office.[86] It therefore avoided much of the formalization that overtook the Board, while retaining the benefit of the statistical expertise and data for long accumulated within the Commercial Department.[87] There were other features conducive to administrative vitality. Robert Giffen, who had overall supervision of the Branch as Comptroller-General, retired in 1897. This meant that the

[84] Passfield Papers II, 2, Item 40, D. F. Schloss to S. Webb, 3 July 1892.
[85] P.R.O. Lab. 2 Series.
[86] P.R.O. T9/28 19623, Treasury to Board of Trade, 20 January 1893.
[87] P.R.O. BT/13/134, Note on the Organization of the Commercial, Labour, and Statistical Department, by G. J. Stanley, 30 March 1909.

Labour Department reaped the benefit of his unparalleled statistical talent in its formative years, but was not burdened by his antipathy to state intervention for long enough to stunt its growth. His successor, Alfred Bateman, though also a confirmed individualist, was more concerned with commercial policy and the preservation of Free Trade, leaving Llewellyn Smith in almost complete control of questions relating to labour.

Finally, the permanent secretaries who held office from 1893 to 1906 were such as to encourage initiative. Ironically, it was Thomas Farrer, who as permanent secretary from 1865 to 1886 had done most to preserve the tradition of laissez-faire within the Board,[88] who was mainly responsible for its upset. Both in 1886 and 1893 he strongly opposed the appointment of Robert Giffen as head of the Board of Trade as being 'a very poor administrator' and 'lacking the tone and temper of absolute loyalty to the service which makes the best men proud of belonging to it'.[89] Instead, Courtenay Boyle, an altogether more progressive personality, was appointed; a departmental head who fully appreciated the value of specialists. As he later observed of the routine of the Board of Trade: 'There are some experts who are as resourceful in administration as they are full of wisdom in their own line. Those men are rare treasures, and may be given an all but absolute free hand.'[90] His successor, Sir Francis Hopwood, was an even greater contrast to Farrer. As Lloyd George remarked to his brother on taking office in 1906; 'of one thing I am glad. I have got a first-rate chief of the permanent staff—a very able man and an excellent radical.'[91]

Bearing in mind the rigorous exposé by Lucy Brown of the campaign by Board of Trade officials in the early nineteenth

---

[88] W. H. G. Armytage, *A. J. Mundella 1825–97. The Liberal Background to the Labour Movement* (London, 1951), p. 367.
[89] Mundella Papers, Folio 3, T. Farrer to A. J. Mundella, 18 May 1886; W. E. Gladstone Papers, B.M. Add. MSS. 44517, ff. 144–5, T. Farrer to Sir Algernon West, 7 May 1893.
[90] Courtenay Boyle, *Hints on the Conduct of Business. Public and Private* (London, 1900), p. 124.
[91] William George, *My Brother and I* (London, 1958), p. 206.

century for the adoption of *laissez-faire*,[92] it would not be over-
fanciful to suggest that within the late-Victorian Labour Department a similarly progressive effort was made to accelerate
the break-up of those assumptions in so far as they determined
social policy. Inevitably, the administrative terrain would have
changed and more subtle tactics have been required; but it is
conceivable that by slanted memoranda and investigations,
biased evidence to Select Committees, and the manipulation of
statistical returns, collectivist legislation could have been deliberately fostered under the supervision of Llewellyn Smith.

Instead, the evidence points to the fact that the Labour Department strictly conformed to the inaugural intentions of
A. J. Mundella that it should not 'disseminate any set of opinions
or maintain or prove any thesis'.[93] Though it evaded the worst
repercussions of the 'triumph of law' and precedent within the
civil service, by the 1890s the limits of official propriety were
narrower and more clearly defined. Moreover, the staff of the
Labour Department were far from being doctrinaire 'zealots'
hell-bent on social collectivism. Even Schloss felt compelled to
uphold the 'scientific analysis' of the 'moderate investigator'
against what he alleged to be the 'utopian optimism' and 'propagandist methodology' of the Webbs.[94] The political environment was equally restrictive. From its inception, largely through
the appointment of trade unionists as local Labour Correspondents, the Labour Department was widely condemned as a
'machine for radical jobbery'.[95] To survive as an accredited
Office of State, it had to be seen to be impartial. Any show of
statistical bias would have spelt its doom under the subsequent
Conservative administrations. Finally, the message of American
experience was unequivocal. As Elgin R. Gould, a statistical
expert of the United States Labour Department, had testified
before the Labour Commission, to be effective, labour bureaux
must be 'considered as organs of enlightenment, not in any
respect as agencies of propaganda or reproof'.[96]

[92] L. Brown, *The Board of Trade and the Free Trade Movement
1830–42* (Oxford, 1958).
[93] *The Times*, 24 January 1893.
[94] Passfield Papers, II, 3, i, S. Webb to B. Potter, 19 January 1891.
[95] *Hansard*, 4th series, vol. 9, cols 1707–8, 1835–6.
[96] P.P. 1893–4 (C. 7063–I), XXXIX, pt. I, q. 6550a. For the effect of

However, the high standard of statistical objectivity already displayed by Llewellyn Smith prior to his taking office rendered such restraints superfluous. The output of the Labour Department bore the hall-mark of a man who had early learnt the vital need to differentiate 'science' from 'propaganda'. Typical was his editorship of the *Labour Gazette*. A monthly publication, it represented a potential medium through which a series of radical proposals might have been disseminated. Instead, it contained entirely neutral summarizations of available data. As Llewellyn Smith stressed in his introduction to the first issue: 'With mere questions of opinion, the Labour Gazette will not be concerned. The aim of the department . . . is to provide a sound basis for the formation of opinions and not to supply opinions.'[97] Beatrice Webb remarked in 1898 that the use made by the editor of the New Zealand *Journal of Labour* for the promulgation of socialism would have made 'Llewellyn Smith's hair stand on end',[98] and when in 1912 an eager first division clerk took on the writing of reviews and articles for the *Labour Gazette* under the impression that it was akin to the *Economic Journal*, his disillusionment was complete.[99]

The reports, abstracts and returns prepared by the Labour Department were equally free of bias. For the most part, the statistics were left to speak for themselves. Where commentary was attached, it was either to elucidate points of methodology, or designed to aid mental digestion by isolating major trends, rather than to spotlight legislative requirements. At most, the special investigations clarified the issues and options open for public discussion and decision. Similarly, an analysis of the evidence of the Department before Select Committees and Royal Commissions reveals no organized campaign, no collectivist

---

American developments on British measures, see E. H. Phelps Brown and M. H. Browne, 'Carroll D. Wright and the Development of British Labour Statistics', *Economica*, new series, XXX (1963), pp. 277–86. An excellent comparative study is provided by J. Leiby, *Carroll Wright and Labor Reform: The Origin of Labor Statistics*, Harvard Historical Monographs XLVI (Harvard, 1960).

[97] *Labour Gazette*, vol. I, no. I (May 1893), p. I.
[98] Beatrice Webb Diary, 24 August 1908.
[99] C. K. Munro, *The Fountains in Trafalgar Square* (London, 1952), p. 194.

plot, to manipulate public opinion. With the multiplicity of public inquiries relating to labour, there was constant demand upon the expertise of its personnel, but rarely did they hazard definite opinions as to legislation. Before the Select Committee on Distress from Want of Employment in 1895, Llewellyn Smith resolutely refused to be drawn on questions of policy,[100] and Sir George Askwith, the foremost industrial negotiator deployed by Llewellyn Smith under the Conciliation Act, testified to the Royal Commission on Trade Disputes that the Board of Trade 'took no view' and wished to 'hold an impartial attitude'.[101] The one exception was the evidence of Clara Collet in 1907 before the Select Committee on Home Work, when as a collaborator of Ramsay MacDonald[102] she vehemently rejected Trade Boards as a possible solution to the problem of sweating.[103]

Yet, if there was an absence of indoctrination in the labour statistical activities of the late-Victorian Board of Trade, they still possessed an inherent, almost irresistible, collectivist momentum. In a very real sense, the Labour Department had been established to measure and interpret the 'Labour Problem', and however impartial official statisticians might strive to be, their efforts were inevitably identified with the concept of reform. It was this ambivalence of statistical quantification that was to have such profound administrative repercussions. O. R. McGregor, drawing heavily upon the earlier reflections of H. L. Beales,[104] has indicated the importance to government growth of the urge to quantify 'the economic costs of the social wastage inherent in unregulated industrialism'.[105] He sees in the transference of the treatment of affairs from a polemical to a statistical basis the necessary pre-condition for defining new areas of public concern and obligation, and stresses that the strategic role of civil servants and administrative agencies in

[100] P.P. 1895 (365), IX, qq. 4874, 5003.
[101] P.P. 1906 (Cd. 2826) LVI, qq. 4–5.
[102] Clara Collet Diary, entry 23 February 1908.
[103] P.P. 1907 (290), VI, qq. 776, 822.
[104] H. L. Beales, *The Making of Social Policy*, Hobhouse Memorial Lecture, 1945.
[105] O. R. McGregor, 'Social Research and Social Policy in the Nineteenth Century', *British Journal of Sociology* VIII (1957), pp. 146–57.

this respect has been neglected. A major area of this neglect has been the late-Victorian Labour Department which possessed unique potential for the quantification of vital social data.

For the greater part of the nineteenth century, industrial relations were the recognized responsibility of the Home Office. It was only after 1886 that the Board of Trade took any direct part in regulating the social conditions under which industries were carried on.[106] Labour statistics were to provide the entrée. When the 'Labour Problem' emerged to the forefront of public debate, the Home Office was severely hampered by the lack of an intelligence division. The amount of time and money that it spent in the preparation of statistics for administrative guidance was dangerously little. In 1889 its Industrial Department possessed no statisticians at the central office,[107] and apart from formalized annual reports, the Factory Inspectorate were either unable or unwilling to collate the mass of available data arising from their field-work. Indeed, this deficiency was a leading feature of the subsequent debate over the co-ordination of labour administration, and the proposal to integrate the labour statistical section of the Board of Trade and the Factory and Mines Department of the Home Office was specifically designed to remedy it.[108]

In the absence of any such reorganization, the Home Office, clearly nettled at the creation of the Labour Department, instituted in late 1893 an internal investigation into the whole question of factory and workshop statistics. The existing 'system of collecting and tabulating information', it was argued, left the Office 'very much in the dark'.[109] As a result, a statistical branch was created within the Industrial Department. However, this reform was rendered largely abortive by the

---

[106] H. Llewellyn Smith, *The Board of Trade*, pp. 180–1.
[107] P.R.O. BT/12/27, memorandum by Robert Giffen on 'The Statistical functions of English Departments of State', 18 July 1889.
[108] See the evidence of Sidney Webb before the Royal Commission on Labour, P.P. 1893–4 (C. 7063—I), XXXIX, pt. I, q. 4402.
[109] Herbert Gladstone Papers. B.M. Add. MSS. 45989, ff. 9–10, 'Memorandum on the proposed reorganisation of Home Office Statistics' by Herbert Gladstone, 18 July 1893.

attitude of the inspectorate whose objective was 'not so much . . . the production of improved statistical tables, as . . . relief from over-pressure of work'.[110] Moreover, the permanent officials were deliberately obstructive towards the efforts of the Labour Department to accumulate and disseminate meaningful social data and were positively elated at a vicious public attack on Llewellyn Smith's statistical ability by Geoffrey Drage, the Joint Secretary of the Labour Commission.[111] They attempted to confine the scope of the *Labour Gazette* to those sections of labour over which the Board of Trade exercised administrative control,[112] and persisted in calling for returns rendered valueless by their own inept draftsmanship.[113]

Appropriately, in 1896 the Conciliation Act was passed under the aegis of the Board of Trade, and industrial relations became primarily the responsibility of the Labour Department. Undoubtedly, the 'judicial smack' of the Home Office went a long way to rendering it unsuited for the administration of voluntary conciliation and arbitration, but the decisive factor was the ability of the Labour Department to supply the relevant data upon which negotiation might proceed and settlement be reached.[114] The need was for the clarification and popularization of the issues involved to dispel the militancy of ignorance and mobilize the moral suasion of enlightened public

[110] P.R.O. HO 45/9877/B15358, H. Gladstone to H. H. Asquith, 24 November 1893.
[111] P.R.O. HO 45/B10296a/9837, C. E. Troup to E.L. Pemberton, 26 July 1894.
[112] P.R.O. Lab.2/1597 C.2031, Sir Godfrey Lushington to Courtenay Boyle, 27 April 1894.
[113] P.R.O. Lab.2/1481 L.117, H. Llewellyn Smith to R. Giffen, 23 January 1896.
[114] The importance of labour statistics for the furtherance of industrial conciliation had been a central argument of those who had campaigned for the creation of the Labour Department (see, for example, D. F. Schloss, *op. cit.*, pp. 51–2; A. J. Mundella, *Help* III (April 1891), p. 49; C. Bradlaugh, *The New Review* III (1890), p. 441). It had also figured prominently in the proceedings and recommendations of the Royal Commission on Labour. Already, in August 1894, Giffen had remarked upon the unofficial intervention of the Labour Department in trade disputes as duties having 'been put upon it by . . . the fact of its being an "Intelligence Department" '. P.P. 1894 (C.7565), LXXX, p. 407.

opinion. As the recognized information bureau on all that pertained to industrial conflicts with its statistics of strikes and lock-outs, trade combinations, employment and wage rates, and with easy access to more general economic data, the Labour Department was uniquely qualified to satisfy such a need.

By 1906 the Home Office had fallen even further behind in its ability to provide its administrative machine with statistical guidance. The debilitating effect was such that even officials of the calibre of Sir Edward Troup were incapable of initiating a legislative programme.[115] Its most serious sins of statistical omission related to sweating. Though technically responsible for the supervision of wages under the Truck Acts and Particulars Section of the 1901 Factory Act, the Home Office possessed next to no information on the implementation of the home work provisions of existing legislation. The evidence of Delevingne, the Principal Clerk of the Industrial Department, before the Select Committee on Home Work in June 1907 was a blatant avowal of ignorance. Despite the importance of the issue in public debate, he admitted that the Home Office statistics on home work were in a 'very primitive state' and 'of no real value',[116] Consequently, when the Committee later recommended the statutory provision of Trade Boards under the Home Office,[117] the Department was impotent to respond.

The necessary data and expertise lay instead with the Labour Department. Many of its leading personnel had undertaken investigations into the sweating problem in the course of the Booth inquiry. John Burnett's report on Sweating in East London had been the immediate cause of the Lords' Committee of 1889–90.[118] Moreover, between 1893 and 1906 the Labour Department, in the course of its inquiries, in collating material for the *Labour Gazette*, and in administering the Conciliation Act, became thoroughly conversant with every aspect of the question, from the effects of alien immigration to the complexities of defining a minimum wage. It had a detailed appreciation of colonial experimentation long before Ernest Aves was

---

[115] Llewellyn Smith Papers, Sir Edward Troup to Sir H. Llewellyn Smith, 21 December 1907.
[116] *Select Committee on Home Work*, Mins of Ev., P.P. 1907 (290), VI, qq. 49–57, 190, 124.   [117] P.P. 1908 (246), VIII, p. 15.
[118] *Hansard*, 3rd series, vol. 322, cols 1598–603.

despatched by the Home Office to report on the Wages Boards of Australia and New Zealand.[119] Therefore, when in 1909 the Trade Boards Act was introduced by the Board of Trade, the long-term effect upon administrative initiative of statistical proficiency was clearly a major consideration.

The Local Government Board, like the Home Office, 'had no technique of objective tests in its work of supervision and no precise measurement of the results of particular policies'.[120] Although in 1889 it nominally employed seventeen staff for the processing of data, they were mere counters, and in no sense true statisticians.[121] In 1892, reflecting upon the impetus of a paper by Charles Booth, Sidney Webb remarked: 'He will have done what I have tried for years to do, viz. get the Local Government Board to improve its statistics. If I were at that office I would have revolutionized its statistical department by this time.'[122] No reform followed, however, and it continued to be overburdened by 'introspective' data unrelated to the social issues of contemporary debate and merely designed to keep a routine check upon the Inspectorate.[123] In 1893 it remained totally apathetic to the investigations of the Labour Department into measures adopted by local authorities for the relief of unemployment. Indeed, the permanent officials of the Local Government Board did everything to dissociate their activities from the concept of 'labour' as such, in a desperate attempt to avoid responsibility for returns.[124] Predictably, the Committee appointed in 1897 to report on the staffing of the Department was particularly critical of its statistical deficiencies.[125]

[119] *Labour Gazette*, vol. VI (1898), p. 318; vol. VII (1899), p. 262; vol. XI (1903), p. 97.
[120] K. B. Smellie, *A History of Local Government* (London, 1946), p. 101.
[121] P.R.O. BT/12/27, Memorandum by R. Giffen on 'The Statistical functions of English Departments of State', 18 July 1889.
[122] Passfield Papers, II, 3, i, S. Webb to B. Potter, 4 January 1892.
[123] R. M. MacLeod, *Treasury Control and Social Administration: A Study of Establishment Growth at the Local Government Board 1871–1905*, Occasional Papers on Social Administration (London, 1968), p. 31.
[124] P.R.O. IND 21454, Board of Trade to Local Government Board, 29 April, 1 October, 9 November 1896.
[125] R. M. MacLeod, *op. cit.*, p. 35.

As the problem of unemployment became a leading political issue, this inadequacy grew into a serious embarrassment to both the Conservative and Liberal administrations. In 1905 Charles Hobhouse wrote of its lack of statistical direction to Walter Runciman on his appointment as parliamentary secretary: 'I know how much waking up that Department requires—and if you can galvanize its officials—not into activity—but into common sense—you will have cleared an Augean stable.'[126] Yet, as Runciman left for the Treasury in 1907, his chief inspector was still lamenting 'the deplorable state of the Gazette and the statistics'.[127]

Meanwhile, such returns as the Local Government Board did produce on unemployment and pauperism were 'universally regarded as useless'[128] and considered as a dilution of the real situation 'to alienate sympathy from the unemployed and avert executive action'.[129] Significantly, the figures contained in the *Labour Gazette* were frequently quoted against the Department. By July 1906 a vociferous group in parliament was calling for a more systematic provision of information, and the Board's inability to quantify the social wastage which it was supposed in part to administer came under increasing attack. As late as October 1908, despite the seriousness of the situation, it had still not seen fit to call for the necessary returns from local authorities.[130] The 'cloven hoof' of the Local Government Board was not therefore so much its inheritance of a 'Poor Law mentality' as its perpetuation of statistical ineptitude, for without the necessary data it was impotent to innovate policy.

In contrast, under Llewellyn Smith's supervision, a whole series of investigations into the causes, effects and possible remedies for unemployment had been undertaken at the Board of Trade. His own *Report on Agencies and Methods for Dealing with the Unemployed*,[131] and his evidence before the Select

[126] Runciman Papers, Charles Hobhouse to Walter Runciman, 21 December 1905.
[127] *Ibid.*, J. S. Davy to W. Runciman, 30 January 1907.
[128] R. Giffen, *Statistics—Written about the Years 1898–1900* (ed. H. Higgs), (London, 1913), p. 7.
[129] *Hansard*, 4th series, vol. 152, cols 877–8.
[130] *Ibid.*, 4th series, vol. 195, col. 494.
[131] P.P. 1893–4 (C.7182), LXXXII.

Committee of 1895,[132] by breaking down the volume of recorded unemployment into seasonal and cyclical variations, pioneered modern unemployment analysis. He indicated the need to differentiate 'types' of unemployment, isolated the necessary safeguards for effective labour bureaux, and firmly established the close correlation between employment and the trade cycle. Meanwhile, the *Labour Gazette* gave as its leading article a national and regional summary of major employment trends. In addition, as unemployment became an important electoral issue, the Labour Department was called upon by successive Governments to refute the figures of opposition spokesmen,[133] a demand greatly intensified by the 'fiscal controversy'.

However, Llewellyn Smith was not prepared to compromise the quality of statistical investigation in pandering to the whim of political debate. In 1903 he rejected the suggestion that the Labour Department should undertake an analysis of a forecast by Campbell-Bannerman that with the advent of protectionism a large proportion of the working population would be 'submerged'. 'It is a waste of time,' he minuted, 'to apply illusory tests to illusory guesses of this kind.'[134] Instead, he directed his subordinates to more tangible investigations. D. F. Schloss was delegated to report upon foreign agencies and methods for dealing with the unemployed 'designed to give public authorities in the United Kingdom a practical lead'.[135] Regular reports on the state of employment were submitted to the Cabinet, their objectivity standing in marked contrast to those of the Local Government Board which often consisted of reactionary diatribes against the unemployed. Llewellyn Smith also took to engaging, informally, leading experts to supplement the information already in the possession of the Board of Trade. Thus in 1905 he asked William Harbutt Dawson, an authority on German social legislation, to inquire into the methods of labour

[132] P.P. 1895 (365), IX, qq. 4526–5019.
[133] See, for example, P.R.O. Cab 37/38/2, 'Memorandum on a recent estimate of the number of the unemployed' (made by Keir Hardie), by H. Llewellyn Smith, 8 January 1895.
[134] P.R.O. Lab. 2/1555 L.1099, H. Llewellyn Smith to A. E. Bateman, 18 July 1903.
[135] P.P. 1905 (Cd. 2304), LXXIII, p. 471.

registries in Germany, emphasizing that 'the more quietly such enquiries are made the better—and it would not be desirable in any case that they should be made as coming from the Board of Trade'.[136] William Beveridge was subsequently employed to the same ends.

Indeed, the campaign for a national system of labour exchanges clearly indicated that they were seen as complementary to the publication of labour statistics and therefore as a logical extension of the functions of the Board of Trade.[137] At the instigation of John Burnett, E. T. Scammell, Secretary to the Exeter Chamber of Commerce, had recommended to the Labour Commission that labour bureaux be established under the Board's supervision and the Commission itself had proposed that the Department should assist in the promotion of local and voluntary registries as a part of its labour statistical duties.[138] Though the Labour Bureaux (London) Act of 1902 was passed under the aegis of the Local Government Board, its officials were clearly of the opinion that the measure belonged within the purview of the Board of Trade, and it was almost entirely accidental that the latter should have failed to become the first central department empowered to establish a national system of labour exchanges.[139]

Faced in 1908 with an urgent political demand for reform, the Local Government Board, despite its administration of the 1905 Unemployed Workmen Act, lacked the necessary data for legislative initiative. In contrast, the Board of Trade was well equipped. Just as its comparative studies had broadly indicated the pre-conditions for an effective network of labour registries, so its statistical investigations into the nature of fluctuations in certain trades had provided a crude actuarial basis upon which unemployment insurance might be built. Its influential

[136] P.R.O. Lab.2/1564 L745, H. Llewellyn Smith to W. H. Dawson, 7 May 1905.
[137] J. F. Chambers, 'The Problem of Unemployment in English Social Policy 1886–1914', Ph.D., Cambridge, 1907, p. 396.
[138] P.P. 1894 (C. 7421), XXXV, p. 97.
[139] J. F. Chambers, *op. cit.*, p. 397. As the central aim of the Unemployed Workmen Act was to rationalize existing forms of relief, the creation of labour exchanges was automatically included among the powers conferred by the Act upon the L.G.B. despite its lack of contact with both sides of industry.

memoranda for the Poor Law Commission were but the continuation of years of constructive inquiry. Viewed in this
context, the stress placed by John Burns in 1909 upon the
superior capacity of the Board of Trade 'for all forms of information and communication with regard to labour'[140] when
justifying the transference of responsibility for unemployment
from the Local Government Board, cannot merely be dis-
counted as an excuse for his personal inability to compete with
the political dynamism of Winston Churchill.[141]

In the meantime, in conjunction with the Royal Statistical
Society, the Board of Trade had continued to campaign for the
reform of late-Victorian government statistics. Before the
Official Statistics Committee, Giffen laboured to expose the
myopic attitude of other departments towards the issue,[142] but
while acknowledging that the Board could unquestionably
'claim to have made great and steady progress towards supplying the want of a Central Statistical Department', the Committee regarded it as having 'reached the utmost development
possible for an office affiliated to one branch of the public
service'.[143] They rejected an alternative scheme urged by
Farrer and Giffen that in conjunction with the Treasury, the
Chief Statistical Officer of the Board of Trade should do a
'Northcote–Trevelyan' upon all other departments.[144]

In turn, Alfred Bateman as a leading member of the International Statistical Institute, and Llewellyn Smith as Comptroller-General and later permanent secretary of the Board of
Trade, took up the cause. Llewellyn Smith was a firm believer
in the need for the centralization and reform of official data.[145]
He carried with him into office a frustrated ambition for the
reorganization of the National Census—the essential basis
for all social investigation—which he vainly sought to realize
by inter-departmental negotiation.[146] In 1906 he collaborated

[140] *Hansard*, 5th series, vol. 2, cols 464–6.
[141] Such is the interpretation of J. A. M. Caldwell, 'The Genesis of the
Ministry of Labour', *Public Administration* XXXVII (1959), pp. 380–1.
[142] P.P. 1881 (39), XXX, pp. 90–102.
[143] *Ibid.*, pp. 24–5.   [144] *Ibid.*, pp. 33–4.
[145] H. Llewellyn Smith, *The Board of Trade*, p. 217.
[146] P.R.O. BT 13/23/E 11499, H. Llewellyn Smith to Courtenay
Boyle, 8 January 1895.

with Charles Dilke to introduce the general question of co-ordination before the Committee inquiring into Official Publications,[147] but its recommendations were designed to effect financial economy rather than statistical efficiency. In 1907 the Board of Trade again collaborated in the preparation of Dilke's presidential address to the Royal Statistical Society. Writing to Dilke, Bateman revealed the enduring obstacles to reform:[148]

> The statistical department of the Board should be strengthened but there would be departmental jealousies and difficulties if they took Census work from the L.G.B. I think . . . that a Central Commission such as exists in most European countries would help towards the solution. The Treasury would oppose probably as they did the scheme of 30 years ago of strengthening the Board of Trade.

Accordingly, the subsequent address highlighted the need for the centralization of administrative data and pointedly referred to the fear of the Treasury for the 'men of science, regarded in the light of sturdy beggars'.[149] In May 1908, mindful of Asquith's promise of a further inquiry into official publications, Wilson Fox encouraged Dilke to press the Treasury to use the occasion for a further reappraisal of the need for a Central Statistical Department.[150] Their reply was predictably unsympathetic.[151] None the less, before the Select Committee on Publications and Debates of 1909, the Board of Trade again endeavoured to resubmit its case.[152] Again, the effort was to no avail.

The result was that on the eve of a period of massive social

[147] Dilke Papers, B.M. Add. MSS. 43919, f. 68, C. Dilke to H. Llewellyn Smith, 15 May 1906.

[148] *Ibid.*, ff. 228–9, A. E. Bateman to C. Dilke, 2 June 1907, Clara Collet Diary, 30 June 1907.

[149] *Journal of the Royal Statistical Society* LXX (1907), p. 557.

[150] Dilke Papers, B.M. Add. MSS. 43920, ff. 108–9, A. Wilson Fox to C. Dilke, 13 May 1908.

[151] *Ibid.*, f. 110, Sir George Murray to C. Dilke, 16 May 1908.

[152] P.P. 1909 (285), VIII, qq. 499–545. Their advocate was R. H. Rew, Secretary of the Royal Statistical Society.

legislation, the Board of Trade alone possessed the statistical data and expertise that could provide the basis for informed debate and the formulation of policy. The failure of other departments to initiate structural reforms in their statistics not only reduced the efficiency with which they performed their administrative functions, but rendered them incapable of creative response to the growing demand for social reform. Moreover, whereas administrators, dulled by routine, were unable to undertake statistical functions, statisticians of the calibre recruited by the Board of Trade were well equipped to tackle the responsibilities of administration, and none more so than those of the Labour Department.

Given that the ability to quantify was so fundamental to the growing hegemony of the Board of Trade in labour matters, the question remains as to how labour statistics were instrumental in the formulation of social policy. Inevitably, no sure historical answer can be advanced. Any mechanical analogy which would interpret the statistics of the Labour Department as the input into a machine whose final product was neatly packeted decisions, is a false one. Nevertheless, in a very simplified and partial respect, the historian may identify certain functions that statistical investigation performed in relation to policy.

Firstly, in summarizing in a popularly digestible form the extent of social and industrial dislocation, it helped activate public opinion, faced with which governments were compelled to legislate. In this respect, the role of the Labour Department was identical to that of a Royal Commission. Thus, its early reports on strikes and lock-outs revealed the intolerability of industrial anarchy, while those on unemployment indicated the irrelevance of a doctrine of self-help to the victims of cyclical fluctuation.

Secondly, on the assumption that late-Victorian administrators, confronted with the complexities of the 'Labour Problem', employed simplified mental pictures or models, then statistical investigations, in summarizing past experience both at home and abroad, helped establish probabilities for the future and thereby limited the range of such models, excluding certain policies from practical consideration, and discriminating between those that remained. This was acknowledged by Llewellyn Smith when, in his study of alien immigration, he concluded:[153]

> It is not within the functions of this report to express any opinion on the merits of this controversy, or even to sum up the arguments on each side. It may, however, fulfil a useful purpose to indicate how far the facts set forth have a bearing on various aspects of the problem, *and serve to some extent to define and narrow the issue.*

Similarly, the reports on strikes and lock-outs underlined the uselessness of conciliation machinery that incorporated judicial sanctions. The investigations into profit-sharing and co-operation showed them to be ineligible as alternative paths along which industrial relations might be directed, and the comparative studies of foreign and colonial provisions for old age and unemployment were clearly dedicated to presenting practicable alternatives for domestic application.

Finally, a decision having been implemented in the form of social legislation, labour statistics could monitor its results and provide a feed-back for future decisions. Thus, the reports of proceedings under the Conciliation Act provided data upon which further legislation on industrial relations was formulated, and were vital in revealing the feasibility of a Trade Boards Act.

It was by these means, as a data-bank for late-Victorian government, and not by propagandism, that the Labour Department brought its influence to bear upon labour policy. While therefore the importance of political initiative as displayed by A. J. Mundella and Winston Churchill is undeniable, it remains necessary to modify the traditional explanation of the allocation of responsibility for Liberal labour legislation with its neglect of secular departmental trends and its denial of continuity between the new functions of the Board of Trade towards labour and its previous administrative role. The measures it adopted after 1909 can readily be reconciled with the preceding history of the Department if only the administrative repercussions of statistical investigation and the ability to quantify are fully

153 P.P. 1894 (C.7406), LXVIII, p. 482.

recognized.[154] In the absence of a Ministry of Labour, it is arguable that it was this ability, judiciously guided by Llewellyn Smith, that did most to enable the Board of Trade to dominate the inception of a massive programme of social reform.

[154] These repercussions also characterized the commercial activities of the Department. Under Llewellyn Smith, the development in the machinery for commercial intelligence soon gave the Board of Trade the major role in the negotiation of Commercial Treaties. Just as the initiative in labour policy was slowly taken from the Home Office and Local Government Board, so in commercial policy, control largely passed from the Foreign Office to the Board of Trade. The same magnetism was also displayed in the years 1914–16, when the statistical superiority of the Board, as transplanted by Llewellyn Smith into the Ministry of Munitions, wrested the control of manpower policy from the War Office.

Administrators in education after 1870: patronage, professionalism and expertise

The Education Department continued to recruit its inspectors and examiners through patronage until 1914.[1] In various ways, its appointments appeared to confirm the flexibility of patronage as a mode of recruitment. Most of the entrants stood up respectably to comparison with entrants to other departments recruited by open competition. Yet this flexibility could be a source of weakness in periods of rapid expansion. Given the need to find a number of men in a hurry, the tendency was not so much to hand-pick as to grab those already known to be available; and accusations of jobbery were made both in the years immediately after 1870 and those following the reorganization of 1899–1902.

The determination to retain patronage also entangled the Department with far more serious problems of defining professionalism and expertise. For its representatives chose to defend patronage as the best method of recruiting the 'experts' which they maintained the work regularly required. Yet precisely because it was so easy to compare recruits to the Department with the products of open competition, it was the more difficult to describe them as experts. At times it looked as if

[1] In 1900 the Education Department and the Science and Art Department were amalgamated to form the Board of Education. But the personnel and style of the old Education Department dominated the new Board; thus it is convenient and not unduly anachronistic to treat the Board primarily as a continuation of the Education Department and to talk of 'the Education Department' throughout the period.

the Education Department was arguing that the qualities and training which made a man eligible for entry by open competition—a potential professional—in the case of the Education Department made him an expert. More important, by invoking the concept of expertise the Department raised the whole question of its definition in education.

The experience of the Education Department thus illuminates some limitations of the concept of the professional civil servant formulated by Northcote and Trevelyan.[2] It was essentially a negative concept. The peculiar professionalism of the permanent civil servant lay in *not* being expert in the familiar sense; in *not* being committed in advance to any particular framework of approach or doctrine; yet being of sufficient ability and judgment to advise the transient politician and where necessary mediate between him and the expert. The difficulties involved in interpreting the one to the other may be relatively obvious and clear-cut when scientific, medical or technological questions are at issue. They are less clear but much more intractable when questions of social policy are at issue. Then even the identification of expertise may involve a number of fundamental value judgments; and the categories of 'expert' and 'professional' may not mean very much.

The flexibility of patronage had, as Richard Johnson has shown,[3] enabled the Education Department to begin recruiting young men of the middle and upper classes with good, if not distinguished academic records, before the ideal type of a first division civil servant was fully elaborated in the Northcote–Trevelyan Report, or generally accepted. By 1870 the only relic of the days when the distribution of patronage had resembled a spoils system was the examiner Walter Severn, son of Sir Joseph Severn, one-time British consul in Rome, who had been found a place in the old Privy Council Office at the age of eighteen. A noted water-colour artist, he appeared to have little interest in or aptitude for administrative work; and efforts were made to have him pensioned off early. The Treasury,

[2] e.g. *Report on the Organisation of the Permanent Civil Service*, P.P. 1854, XXVII, p. 3.
[3] See above 'Administrators in education before 1870: patronage, social position and role'.

however, was adamant; and Cumin, the permanent secretary was reduced to trying to find him some work less demanding at the Science and Art Department at South Kensington, 'such as examining drawings or some thing of the sort'.[4]

Severn apart, the standards set by the Balliol recruits at the end of the 1840s were maintained. Examiners and inspectors continued to be graduates and, indeed, to include a number of men of academic and intellectual distinction. Nearly three-quarters of those examiners appointed between 1870 and 1900, and nearly half those appointed between 1900 and 1912, had first-class degrees.[5] At one time or another the examiners included Henry Babington Smith, Eton, Trinity, Chancellor's Medallist at Cambridge 1886, private secretary to the Chancellor of the Exchequer by 1892, and the leading government adviser on international finance from 1916 on; A. J. Butler, the Dante scholar; J. W. Mackail, son-in-law of Burne-Jones and biographer of William Morris; E. K. Chambers, the Shakespearean scholar; C. L. Kingsford, the medieval historian; and Sir Lewis Amherst Selby-Bigge, editor of still-standard texts of Hume and the *British Moralists*. Mackail was also Professor of Poetry at Oxford; and beside Matthew Arnold, HMI, the Education Department provided two more holders of that Chair, in W. J. Courthope, biographer and editor of Pope, and F. T. Palgrave, the devoted friend of Tennyson, compiler of the *Golden Treasury* and poet of sorts in his own right.

Before 1870 the members of the inspectorate had, if anything, been more distinguished than the examiners. After 1870

[4] Cranbrook Papers, Ipswich and East Suffolk County Record Office, HA 43/o: T 501/101, Craik to Cranbrook, 9 December 1885, and Cumin to Cranbrook, 2 October 1885.
[5] Biographical data on examiners and inspectors 1870–1900 is drawn from the *Dictionary of National Biography, Who was Who* and university *Calendars*, unless otherwise indicated. Data on examiners and inspectors 1900–12 are summarized in Appendix XII, I and II to *First and Second Reports and Minutes of Evidence of the Royal Commission on the Civil Service* (henceforward cited as MacDonnell Minutes), P.P. 1912–13, XV, ff. 768–91. A much fuller discussion of the departmental establishment 1870–95 than is possible here is contained in chs 2 and 3 and pp. 597–604, 664–72 of my unpublished Oxford D.Phil. thesis, 'Some Aspects of the Making of Policy in Elementary Education in England and Wales 1870–1895', henceforward cited as 'Policy-Making in Education 1870–95'.

the positions were reversed. The HMIs too had their literary and cultural pundits. Matthew Arnold did not retire until 1886. F. W. H. Myers, the friend of Sidgwick and Jackson and a leading figure in the Society for Psychical Research, inspected elementary schools; as did the Egyptologist Peter le Page Renouf and A. P. Graves, notable not only as Robert Graves's father but also as an active participant in the Celtic revival. While a much more important figure in the Celtic literary world, O. M. Edwards, Stanhope prizewinner, Lothian prizewinner, Fellow of Lincoln College, Oxford, became Chief Inspector of Secondary Schools for Wales in 1907. But on the whole, the inspectorate after 1870 was not academically distinguished. First-class degrees were the exception rather than the rule; and the majority of the inspectors' reports convey a uniform mediocrity.

The principal reason for this dilution seems to have been the rapid expansion necessitated by the legislation of 1870 and 1902. Between 1870 and 1880 the number of HMIs doubled, increasing from sixty-two to 131.[6] The need to find so substantial a number in so short a time must have curtailed the searching scrutiny to which Lord Presidents and their successors, the Presidents of the Board of Education, claimed they subjected all potential recruits.[7] W. V. Harcourt jocularly told Arthur Helps, Clerk to the Privy Council, in 1873 that 'he had heard that there were no appointments that had been jobbed more than those of school inspectors'. Helps denied it vigorously.[8] But successful recruits of this period had no doubt that their political connections had been of the greatest help. A. J. Swinburne secured appointment in 1875 'through the patronage of the Duke of Richmond which was procured for me by Lady Wynford, a friend of my aunt Mrs Vicars'.[9] E. M. Sneyd-Kynnersley enlisted the help of two of his father's friends in the ministry of the day. One of them was in the Cabinet and in 1871 managed to swap an appointment for a protégé of the Lord President's for an inspectorship for Sneyd-Kynnersley.[10]

[6] 'Policy-Making in Education 1870–95', Appendix II, Table 1.
[7] MacDonnell Minutes, P.P. 1912–13, XV, qq. 8,699–8,713.
[8] Ripon Papers, B.M. Add. MSS. 43,540, ff. 197–8, Helps to Ripon, 4 January 1873.
[9] A. J. Swinburne, *Memoirs of a School Inspector* (London, 1912), p. 27.
[10] E. M. Sneyd-Kynnersley, *HMI. Passages in the Life of an Inspector of Schools* (London, 1908), pp. 78–9.

Such allegations were not heard again after 1902, although between 1900 and 1912 over a hundred new inspectors were appointed.[11] By that time, as we shall see, the composition of the inspectorate was under a much more fundamental attack. But accusations of crude jobbery were levelled against appointments to examinerships. Between 1907 and 1910 a series of very pointed questions about criteria for appointments was asked in the Commons.[12] As a member of the MacDonnell Commission on the Civil Service in 1912, Philip Snowden did his best to make something of the fact that a considerable number of examiners, especially those securing early promotion, were Wykehamists, as the permanent secretary who had just resigned had been.[13] He did not get very far with Selby-Bigge, the new permanent secretary. Although Selby-Bigge did admit to the Commission that among the current examiners were two whose fathers had held appointments in the Department (C. T. Sykes and M. G. Holmes): for a short time the Inspectorate had included the son-in-law of a Cabinet Minister: while the stepson of a former President of the Board of Education (A. B. S. Tennyson) had, during his step-father's period of office, been transferred from a clerkship in the House of Lords to an examinership, although he had resigned within the year.[14]

But although none of the people on this faintly ridiculous little list was markedly distinguished on appointment, none, except for the ex-House of Lords clerk, was markedly incompetent either. Maurice Holmes, indeed, was to become permanent secretary. Again it seems more plausible to interpret such appointments not as a return to corruption but as a hazard of recruitment by patronage in a period of extraordinary expansion. For it was only between 1900 and 1912 that the central office underwent an expansion comparable with that experienced by the inspectorate after 1870. Although the examiner

[11] MacDonnell Minutes, Appendix XII, II. P.P. 1912–13, XV, ff. 782–91.
[12] *Hansard*, 4th series, CLXXX, col. 1304, CLXXXI, cols 467–8; *Hansard*, 5th series, VI, col. 674, VII, col. 2370, XIX, col. 2671 and XVIII, col 341.
[13] MacDonnell Minutes, P.P. 1912–13, XV, qq. 9,220–53.
[14] *Ibid.*, qq. 9,234–7, 9,247, 9,251–3.

class had nearly trebled between 1870 and 1880 the absolute numbers involved were small—from thirteen to thirty.[15] But between 1900 and 1912 no less than seventy-nine new examiners were appointed.[16]

Nevertheless, as A. H. D. Acland pointed out:[17]

> You will always find in every public office everywhere, in any given group of men, a certain number who have not quite come off, whose colleagues are doing their best to prop them up and help them—most worthy people. I do not think there is a larger number among that body than anywhere else.

And with such insignificant skeletons in the cupboard, Selby-Bigge felt justified in arguing strongly to the MacDonnell Commission—as his predecessors had argued to other inquiries before—that the *average* Education Department recruit was at least as good as the *average* product of open competition; therefore patronage should be retained.[18]

Such arguments had sufficed in the days when open competition was the exception rather than the rule. But they were no longer good enough: as the Majority Report was to make clear, most of the members of the Commission thought patronage was only defensible if it produced *better* people than open competition.[19] Under their persistent questioning, Selby-Bigge was forced to rely more and more on the Education Department's second line of defence, also well worn, namely that only patronage gave the flexibility necessary to seek out the men of special experience which the work required. Since 1859 examiners and inspectors had been classified under section four of the Superannuation Act as men of whom 'professional or other peculiar qualifications not to be acquired in the public service are required'. 'Professional or other peculiar qualifications' are and were usually taken to mean one or a combination

---

[15] 'Policy Making in Education 1870–95', Appendix I, Table 1.
[16] MacDonnell Minutes, Appendix XII, I, P.P. 1912–13, XV, f. 768.
[17] *Ibid.*, q. 4,338.
[18] *Ibid.*, qq. 8,703–40. Cf. also P.P. 1854, XXVII, f. 234, and P.P. 1875, XXIII (Playfair Commission), qq. 5,367–5, 456.
[19] MacDonnell Commission, 4th Report, ch. ix, para. 28, P.P. 1914, XVI, f. 74.

of three elements: a skill or technical qualification, for example in French or engineering, experience of work within the system the civil servant would have to administer, or simply varied and extensive experience in a number of different occupations. The Education Department interpreted these in a manner all its own. Selby-Bigge told the Commission:[20]

> for our particular work, which is extraordinarily controversial, which runs up against religious, social and political controversies at every turn, which has, as a matter of fact, been complicated by legislation, changes in legislation and attempted legislation to a very great extent, it is particularly important to recruit the office with men of rather greater age than ordinarily enter the civil service and of rather more varied experience and character.

The same qualities were required of inspectors; although he conceded that in certain cases technical skills could be important and experience of work in education desirable.[21]

But in making this appeal to 'specialism' the Education Department exposed its vulnerability to criticisms far more serious than any prompted by a comparison with departments recruited by open competition or gossip about jobbery. For it was simply not true that the Department had consistently recruited men of varied and extensive experience, whether in education or any other field, and/or men with particular technical skills. By 1914 both examiners and inspectors included some such men; but they were a token minority. The majority can be more easily described negatively than positively. They were neither particularly old, nor particularly experienced, nor had special qualifications. As the very ease of the comparison with recruits by open competition suggests, they were amiable young gentlemen who had achieved a reasonable degree of academic success. To describe such men as experts obviously entailed a number of assumptions about social and educational values which became increasingly controversial. By 1914 the

[20] MacDonnell Minutes, P.P. 1912–13, XV, q. 8,731; also qq. 8,726–7 and the references to the Northcote–Trevelyan Report and the Playfair Commission cited above, n. 18.
[21] MacDonnell Minutes, P.P. 1912–13, XV, qq. 8,739–40 and 8,822.

composition of the Department directly reflected all the tensions, disagreements and uncertainties of the time about the relationship of the educational system to the society which formed its matrix.

Two main phases can be distinguished in recruitment during the period from 1870 to 1914, the dividing line being around 1888–92. There was a consistency about the appointments 1870–90 which appointments later lacked, but it was emphatically not a consistency of experience or maturity. The average age of examiners on appointment was only a little higher than the maximum age of entry into the civil service by open competition—twenty-six as opposed to twenty-three. The average inspector was older—twenty-eight: but as most candidates had spent at least a year waiting for appointment after their names had been put forward, the difference was not great. Nor had any of these young men done anything particularly out of the ordinary between graduation and appointment. Over half the examiners had held college fellowships for a brief period and/or made efforts, of varying degrees of seriousness, to read for the Bar, perhaps after the fashion of Kekewich: 'I was driven, as hundreds of other unemployed products of the Universities have been to the legal profession, which appeared to be the only one except the Church for which I was not absolutely unfit.'[22] Three of them had spent some time as inspectors before moving into the central office; and two had spent a year teaching, one as an assistant master at Marlborough, the other at Winchester. The inspectorate, too, had its share of briefless barristers; and only ten of the ninety-seven appointed had done any teaching, none of it in public elementary schools of the type they were to inspect.

It is worth noting that virtually all the men of distinction appointed in this period, for example, Henry Babington Smith Butler, Mackail, Kingsford, Myers, Graves, made their reputations *after* appointment, not before. In fact appointment to the Education Department looks less the culmination of a career of literary or intellectual distinction than a convenient means to achieve such a career. For, 'unless he had very special

22 Sir G. W. Kekewich, *The Education Department and After* (London, 1920), p. 5. Kekewich served as an examiner in the Education Department 1869–90 and then as permanent secretary 1890–1902.

talents or interests, the choice of a career for a young man of good family in the mid-nineteenth century was appallingly limited'.[23] And if the young man did not have much in the way of private resources on which to fall back, he might find it very difficult to earn a steady income from writing. The work in the central office was not demanding,[24] and an examinership might therefore provide a respectable occupation for a gentleman, while leaving him free—and secure—to indulge his literary pretensions if he desired. The friend who delivered the address at the funeral service of the former examiner F. C. Hodgson, summed up such considerations most delicately:[25]

> I remember being a little surprised at the time at his seeking and accepting a position under the Education Department of the Privy Council. . . . I had thought of him much more as gaining influence in the realms of scholarship and literature, but it is impossible to deny the magnitude and importance of the task of regulating the education carried on in the primary schools of the country and to have a share in that is an honour to every man. Yet I must not omit to add what has only lately come to my knowledge, that a motive of profound unselfishness, saintly in its degree, was what most influenced him in his choice of profession: this was the wish to support his nearest and dearest relatives in real comfort. To their wish he made all his ambitions subordinate. His profession did not prevent literary occupation in him also.

A number of the inspectors, too, like Edmond Holmes, 'looked about me for a calling which, without being too exacting or absorbing, would provide me with the means of subsistence'.[26] A. P. Graves wanted a post, any post, in the civil service because he wanted to live in London, or at least in England (he came from Dublin) and write free-lance; and he ended up with

[23] Phyllis Grosskurth, *John Addington Symonds* (London, 1964), p. 99.
[24] 'Policy Making in Education 1870–95', pp. 60–9. Although the work was to change somewhat and the pressures increase after 1900 the excessive centralization of the Department remained legendary well into the twentieth century.
[25] J. R. Mozley in *In Memoriam F. C. Hodgson*, ed. J. R. Leeson (Oxford, 1921), p. 4.
[26] Edmond Holmes, *In Quest of an Ideal* (London, 1920), pp. 16–17.

an inspectorship because he could not get anything else.[27] The work of inspecting could be demanding.[28] But if the inspector were ruthless and exacted the maximum from his assistants and his sub-inspector, he could, like Almeric Fitzroy, manage three days' hunting a fortnight.[29]

Literary—or sporting—ambitions can hardly be described as expertise. To call such men experts or specialists amounts to saying that the education appropriate to a gentleman is the essential qualification for administering and inspecting the schools of the labouring poor. It was, in fact, put as baldly as this in evidence to the Cross Commission 1886–8. Patric Cumin, then the permanent secretary of the Department, declared:[30]

> If there is any virtue in education at all, it seems to the Department to be reasonable that you should get the best-educated men you can to occupy very responsible positions. Inasmuch as the persons who have been at the Universities are generally considered to be persons who have received the best education; these Inspectors have been selected from University men . . .

Chief HMI the Rev. D. J. Stewart stressed the social dimension of this view. He quoted approvingly the statement of the New-castle Commission in 1861 that

> it is absolutely necessary that the inspectors be fitted by previous training and social position to communicate and associate on terms of equality with the managers of schools and the clergy of different denominations. It is one of the alleged grievances of school-masters that these persons do not recognize them as social equals; and that state of things, with which no public authority can interfere is in itself conclusive against the suggestion that they should be made inspectors . . .

and he added:[31]

> I think that decision is sound. One or two teachers on whose judgment I place great reliance, have agreed . . .

[27] A. P. Graves, *To Return to All That* (London, 1930), pp. 149–71.
[28] 'Policy-Making in Education 1870–95', pp. 101–25.
[29] Almeric Fitzroy, *Memoirs*, 2 vols (London, 1925), I, pp. x–xiv.
[30] Cross Minutes, P.P. 1886, XXV qq. 2,124–5.
[31] *Ibid.*, qq. 2,290 and 2,292.

and they have pointed out that the education of teachers is so limited to purely professional ends as to be a hindrance to the cultivation of those wider views of national education which ought to regulate the management of schools.

But such a view assumed a degree of vertical integration in the educational system and in society remote from reality. Until 1902 the only schools supported by the state, and thus the only schools with which examiners and inspectors were officially concerned, were the public elementary schools. Yet examiners and inspectors not only did not teach in such schools they did not attend them either. Nor would they have dreamt of sending their children to them. Elementary education was not 'first-stage' or primary education, it was education for the children of the labouring poor, separate and different from education for the children of the middle and upper classes. It was a programme of basic literacy for children who were, by the age of twelve, or at the very latest fourteen, expected to be earning their own living. For the most part, it was taught by men and women of working-class or lower-middle-class backgrounds who as adolescents had been apprenticed as 'pupil-teachers' to existing teachers. Only a small minority of them had scraped their way with scholarships and savings to a 'Normal School' or training college.[32]

Examiners' and inspectors' social and academic superiority was thus officially intended to be a leaven, a stimulus to intellectual ambition, a source of enlightenment to such schools and such teachers. But there was little evidence that in practice this was so. The very quality of the examiners' literary pursuits and intellectual concerns seems to have bred detachment from, boredom with, the life and work of elementary schools. Kekewich was perhaps providing something of a caricature when he wrote[33] that

The staff of distinguished and aristocratic scholars from the Universities treated elementary education and ele-

[32] For fuller discussion of the nature of elementary education, see my pamphlet *Elementary Education in the Nineteenth Century* (London, Historical Association, 1971) and Richard Johnson, 'Educational Policy and Social Control in Early Victorian England', *Past & Present* no. 49 (November 1970), pp. 96–119.   [33] Kekewich, *op. cit.*, p. 10.

mentary teachers with contempt. Their cherished creed
was that no education mattered or was of any real value
except Classics and Mathematics. . . . They had no use
for village Hampdens, nor any idea that a child from the
'lower' classes might, after all, possess a modicum of
brains. A ploughman's son was destined to be a ploughman as his father was.

But the detachment was also recognized by the examiner
H. W. Hoare in his contribution to a *Memoir of A. J. Butler*:[34]

in 1870 we were both given a post in the Education
Office under Sir F. Sandford and Mr Forster. Much of the
work at the time was mechanical and deadly dull. This
part of it was largely regulated by carefully recorded
'precedents' which, in the administration of the 'Annual
Grant' to elementary schools, were our Bible. But 'precedents' had no terrors for Butler, nor did he burn incense
to them. On the contrary he challenged them right and
left and picked great holes in them at every conceivable
opportunity. But here his interest was apt to end. Vital
points of administrative detail, such as the sufficiency of
wash-hand basins or of pupil teachers, offered no attraction
to him whatever. He preferred Dante and other wholly
unofficial seers. The result was, that as an administrator
Butler fell short of success. None the less for that, many
of his colleagues delighted in breaking a literary lance
with him. Among such were F. T. Palgrave, W. J. Courthope, and our deeply lamented Sidney Joyce, the Charles
Lamb of the Office.

The inspectors, at least, were in daily contact with teachers
and children. But the attitudes with which they approached the
work often provided an insulation; and equally often this was
reinforced by the system under which they worked, payment
by results. Under this system, the bulk of the government
grant, roughly half a school's income, depended upon the performance of each child, each year in examinations conducted
by the inspector. Edmond Holmes, looking back in 1920 on

[34] Sir Arthur Quiller Couch, *Memoir of A. J. Butler* (London, 1917),
p. 89.

his early years as an inspector, in the late 1870s, early 1880s, wrote:[35]

> For me they were so many examinees and as they all belonged to the 'lower orders', and as (according to the belief in which I had been allowed to grow up) the lower orders were congenitally inferior to the 'upper classes' I took little or no interest in my examinees either as individuals or as human beings, and never tried to explore their hidden depths. Indeed, the idea of their having hidden depths was foreign to my way of thinking, and had it ever presented itself to my mind I should probably have dismissed it with a disdainful smile.

The sheer arrogance of such attitudes invited opposition: and the growth of a national organization of elementary school-teachers after 1870 brought mounting criticism. The teachers combined an attack upon the system of payment by results, which invited the inspector to sit in judgment upon them, with an attack upon the convention that no elementary schoolteacher could be appointed an examiner or an inspector; and they made a powerful case to the Cross Commission 1886–8. Their arguments gained further point and impact from the fact that, although HMI actually signed the forms and took responsibility, a great deal of the actual, detailed work of examining children was done by assistants and sub-inspectors, recruited entirely from experienced teachers. Thomas Healing, who had worked for a long time as Matthew Arnold's sub-inspector, stated, 'I had entire charge of the work, for all the schools that were handed over to me', including writing the reports for HMI to sign. 'One inspector told me he never altered them.'[36]

Yet although in practice the official's exploitation of his social authority dominated his relationship with the teacher, the question of cultural authority remained a real one. When Cumin remarked to the Cross Commission, 'If there is any virtue at all in education, it seems to the Department to be reasonable

---

[35] Holmes, *op. cit.*, p. 64.
[36] Cross Minutes, P.P. 1887, XXX, qq. 56,126–32. For a survey of their position and a summary of their case, see 'Policy-Making in Education 1870–95', pp. 125–34.

that you should get the best-educated men you can . . .', he was making a statement as much about cultural values as about social authority; and many teachers acknowledged these same values, at least to the extent that they opposed no alternative ideal of enlightenment to that of the examiners and inspectors. Much of the energy of those ex-teachers, the inspector's assistants and sub-inspectors, went into showing themselves more HMI-like than HMI, working for external degrees, administering rules to the letter, zealous in support of payment by results. F. H. Spencer provided a pupil-teacher's eye view of their work:[37]

> In technique the assistants were nearly always the
> superiors of the HMI's. They were skilled practitioners
> and as a rule tried to make the best of the class and its
> poor little bits of knowledge; frequently they succeeded.
> Occasionally there was a severe or a crusty assistant, or
> a mean one. But my recollection is that the large majority
> of them were nothing of the kind. What we disliked was
> the competence with which they exposed weak-spots,
> for they were poachers turned game-keepers. They knew
> the game. The great man their master might offend us
> by his incompetence in a technique of which he had no
> knowledge, which indeed he not infrequently despised. It
> was the competence of his assistants which we at once
> dreaded and admired.

Canon Warburton, first appointed HMI in 1850, condemned the practice whereby a new and wholly inexperienced HMI was let loose straightaway on elementary schools, with no sort of apprenticeship.[38] But he felt very unhappy at the idea of assistants becoming full inspectors, because 'they often approach their work in a narrow technical spirit, which is very undesirable; and instead of being as one could expect, as a rule, too sympathetic with the teachers, I do not think they are sympathetic enough, which is a rather unexpected result'.[39]

Thus the recruitment of experienced teachers to the in-

[37] F. H. Spencer, *An Inspector's Testament* (London, 1938), p. 95.
[38] Cross Minutes, P.P. 1886, XXV qq. 7,414 and 8,165.
[39] *Ibid.*, q. 7,789. Cf. also Rev. W. Aston in Cross Minutes, P.P. 1887, XXX q. 45,592.

spectorate need not, of itself, be a liberalizing factor. And the narrowly mechanistic fact-grubbing of some elementary school-teachers could be just as stultifying as the lofty disdain of HMI. Beside the aspirations of Hardy's *Jude the Obscure* must be set the crudity of Dickens's Bradley Headstone. He was a cruel caricature but he was not a fantasy. A teacher's enthusiasm and idealism could all too easily be blunted and deadened by the weight of the workload, particularly under payment by results, and the struggle for recognition, as the bitter, some-times savage stories of James Runciman show.[40]

But the cultural poverty of some teachers was no real de-fence of the Education Department's attitude—and the patro-nizing arrogance of the official could itself help to breed and foster such poverty. The Cross Commission therefore hazarded a few tentative steps to improve the position of the teacher. They recommended the recruitment of some teachers as full inspectors and a substantial modification of payment by results.[41]

Thus by 1890 the Education Department's retention of patronage and their interpretation of expertise had been sub-ject to considerable public criticism. In the nineties, too, serious plans for more extensive state involvement in education were beginning to be made. In its recruitment 1890–1914 the Education Department began to respond to these develop-ments, but intermittently and unevenly. Patronage enabled a quicker response than a more formal or institutionalized method of selection would have done; but its very flexibility allowed the continuing play of idiosyncrasy and meant that the response was less than complete. There was no sustained attempt to interpret expertise more rigorously along the lines sketched by Selby-Bigge to the MacDonnell Commission. The appointment from time to time of men with particular qualifications, varied

[40] Runciman had been a practising teacher, who contributed short stories regularly to *The Teacher*. These contributions were so successful that he took up writing full time. He published at least two collections of short stories about school life, savagely ironic in a sub-Gissing style—see *School Board Idylls* (London, 1885) and *Schools and Scholars* (London, 1887).

[41] There were in fact two Minority Reports as well as a Majority Report. These were, however, points on which there was fairly general agreement, see 'Policy-Making in Education 1870–95', pp. 511–14.

and extensive experience, or practical teaching experience resembled rather a series of placatory gestures, owing much to the particular commitments of individual politicians and officials.

One exceptional group must, however, be noted. The women inspectors appointed from 1905 onwards all possessed a battery of qualifications in their particular specialisms and/or extensive experience of teaching and educational administration. The average age on appointment of the thirty-four women employed in 1912 was thirty-six; only four of them had in fact been under thirty on appointment and in each case the professional and academic record shows there were good reasons for the appointment.[42] But the credit is probably not all due to the Education Department. The quality of the female inspectorate was almost certainly primarily a function of the scarcity of good jobs for able, educated women. Here, too, however, personalities played a part. The decision to recruit women inspectors on a regular basis from 1905 was in line with a general civil service trend.[43] But its rapid implementation and the maintenance of interest and concern seem to have owed something to the fact that Sir Robert Morant, permanent secretary 1903–11, was sympathetic to feminist aspirations.[44]

The women apart, the inspectors and examiners appointed during the period were a very mixed bunch. A first gesture was made towards the teachers in 1892 by the Tory Lord President Cranbrook, who appointed inspector's assistant F. S. Marvin, HMI. It was hardly a whole-hearted gesture. For Marvin, born into a middle-class, although not affluent family, had taken Firsts in Mods and Greats and a Second in History at St John's College, Oxford, and had been appointed to a vacant inspec-

[42] MacDonnell Minutes, P.P. 1912–13, XV, ff. 785–6, Appendix XII, II, viii.
[43] See Hilda Martindale, *Women Servants of the State 1870–1938* (London, 1938), ch. I, esp. pp. 36–45. The Department had in fact employed specialist consultants on needlework, etc., since 1883 and women sub-inspectors since 1895.
[44] *Ibid.* See also Marvin Papers, Bodleian Library, Oxford, letters from Morant to Edith Mary Deverell Marvin 1904–14. Edith Deverell was one of the first women inspectors. She resigned on her marriage to another HMI, F. S. Marvin (for whom see below), but Morant continued to seek her advice informally.

tor's assistantship in 1889 largely through the influence of his great friend and mentor the Positivist Frederic Harrison, who was also an old friend of Cumin's. The appointment was duly condemned by the NUT.[45] Nevertheless it was not a complete fraud. Marvin was passionately committed to education, and on leaving St John's in 1887 he had gone to teach in an Oxford board school, moving after a year to a London board school in Bow. Although he taught for only two-and-a-half years, after he left he maintained for some time a correspondence with former colleagues and pupils which makes it clear he entered fully into the life of the school.[46] Throughout his career, too, he remained in touch with the small, socially committed group of men centred round Sidney Ball, who linked Oxford in so many important ways with Toynbee Hall and East End social work.

A much more serious and substantial gesture was made by A. H. D. Acland, Liberal Vice-President of the Committee of Council 1892–5. Acland had a seat in the Cabinet, thus replacing the Lord President as the effective political head of the department: he was also one of the most committed reformers ever to hold office.[47] In 1892 he wrote to his old friend Michael Sadler, 'How I wish it were possible to stir into it [the Department] with a great spoon some of the newer hopes and the fresher spirit,'[48] and in his three short years he did his best. Of his eight new HMIs all but one, indeed, had been to either Oxford, Cambridge, or Trinity College, Dublin. But five had gone up as mature students. Nobody's father or father-in-law appeared to be anyone in particular; and all eight had genuine and varied experience of work in elementary schools.[49] By the end of 1894 Acland had also secured Treasury approval for the creation of a research unit within the central office, taking the Labour

[45] *The Schoolmaster*, 23 April 1892, pp. 724, 738–9; 30 April 1892, p. 770 and 14 May 1892, 'The Inspectorate' by James Scotson. For the full background to Marvin's appointment, see 'Policy-Making in Education 1870–95', pp. 601–4.
[46] Marvin Papers, letters to F. S. Marvin 1889–95, especially those from W. H. Pullinger, Harry Cox and S. Meyrick.
[47] 'Policy-Making in Education 1870–95', ch. 9.
[48] Sadler Papers, Bodleian Library, Oxford, Acland to Sadler, 8 October 1892.
[49] *The Schoolmaster*, 11 May 1895.

Department of the Board of Trade as his model.[50] The first
Director of Special Inquiries was his friend Michael Sadler, who,
after Firsts in Mods and Greats, had succeeded him as Steward
of Christ Church, Oxford, and as Secretary of the Standing
Committee of the Delegacy for Local Examinations, which dealt
with all the University Extension work. He was also the active
and influential secretary to the Bryce Commission on Secondary
Education 1893–5.[51] Morant, who was recruited by Sadler as
his assistant, just as the Liberal government fell in the summer
of 1895, had taken a First in Theology at New College, Oxford,
then worked in a prep. school for a year, in the Far East as
tutor to the Crown Princes of Siam 1886–94, and at Toynbee
Hall 1894–5. It was through the Toynbee Hall connection that
he was first brought to Acland's and Sadler's attention.[52] Both,
thus, looked rather more like 'experts' than the other members
of the Department which they joined.

After Acland's flurry of activity there was a lull. But the
waves of new appointments generated by the reorganization
of the Education Department and Science and Art Department
into the Board of Education and the legislation of 1902 went
in two different, almost contradictory directions. There were
some more experts, of various sorts; but there was also a substantial number of bright young gentlemen on the old pattern.

The Science and Art Department had always been much
more conventionally specialist;[53] and its staff brought into the
Board of Education both a nucleus and a model for the development of specialist branches, particularly in the inspectorate.
The creation of a small new inspectorate to inspect those
secondary schools now receiving state aid obviously also required a greater concern with expertise. A Senior Wrangler,
however distinguished, could not be guaranteed to acquit himself well in examining the teaching of French. The twenty-two
inspectors at work in secondary schools in 1912 had a res-

[50] 'Policy-Making in Education 1870–95', pp. 668–71.
[51] Michael Sadleir, *Michael Ernest Sadler. A memoir by his son*
(London, 1949); Lynda Grier, *Achievement in Education. The Work of
Michael Ernest Sadler 1885–1935* (London, 1952).
[52] B. M. Allen, *Sir Robert Morant* (London, 1934).
[53] See Michael Argles, *South Kensington to Robbins: An Account of
English Technical and Scientific Education since 1851* (London, 1964),
chs 2 and 3.

pectable array of qualifications and teaching experience in a suitable variety of subjects. Only one was under thirty (twenty-nine) on appointment and the average age on appointment was thirty-six.[54]

But in the central office the old pattern remained dominant. The Department of Special Inquiries was soon drawn into the bitter controversy over schemes for secondary education; and with Morant's elevation to the permanent secretaryship in 1902 and Sadler's resignation in 1903 it lost what potential it might have had for generating new ideas. Henceforward it investigated only what it was told to.[55] Apart from the one or two political dependants already mentioned, the seventy-nine new examiners appointed between 1900 and 1912 resembled their predecessors closely. They were a little less academically distinguished; fewer were briefless barristers and more had had some experience of educational work. Eighteen had actually taught, although only two in public elementary schools; six more had worked in the offices of local education authorities; and one had been tutor to the children of the Duke of Connaught, assistant master at Clifton and then assistant secretary to the Girls Public Day School Company. But as the average age on appointment was still only twenty-eight, few of them could boast experience even as varied and extensive as that.[56] As Philip Snowden virtually forced Selby-Bigge to admit to the MacDonnell Commission, to classify such men under section four of the Superannuation Act 1859 was to declare that, for Education Department purposes, a university degree was a 'peculiar qualification'.[57]

Snowden included in his attack recruits to the elementary education inspectorate since 1900. For in that year a new category of inspector had been created, the junior inspector,

[54] MacDonnell Minutes, P.P. 1912–13, XV, ff. 789–90, Appendix XII, II ss. x, xi and xii and III s. i.
[55] This is a long and tangled story: see *Papers Relating to the Resignation of the Director of the Department of Special Inquiries*, P.P. 1903, LII, ff. 763–832 and D. N. Chester, 'Robert Morant and Michael Sadler', *Public Administration* XXVIII (1950), pp. 106–16, and 'Morant and Sadler—Further Evidence', *ibid.* XXXI (1953), pp. 49–54.
[56] MacDonnell Minutes, P.P. 1912–13, XV, ff. 768–9, Appendix XII, I.
[57] *Ibid.*, qq. 9,141–9.

and recruitment to the old classes of assistants and sub-inspectors was stopped. Appointment direct to a full inspectorship also virtually ceased.[58] In one way this was an improvement, since the junior inspector was more obviously an apprentice and initially he was assigned to work with an established inspector.[59] But in other, more important ways, it represented a return to the old pattern. For the majority of the 106 junior inspectors appointed between 1900 and 1912 were yet more bright young gentlemen. Average age on appointment was twenty-nine; and by no means all had had real teaching experience. Of the forty-three junior inspectors serving in 1912, seventeen had no experience of teaching in public elementary schools at all and only ten of the twenty-six who had taught there had done so for longer than a year.[60] As Snowden badgered Selby-Bigge into admitting, a number of them had taught in public elementary schools for a few token months simply to be able to say they had done so.[61]

The effect of the creation of this class appeared to be the reduction of the ordinary teacher's chances to reach the inspectorate. In the 1890s the establishment of an unbroken line of promotion from assistant through sub-inspector to full inspector had seemed a strong possibility. Now there was not even an established mode of entry for the teacher into the lower ranks of the inspectorate. From 1912 on the Department was proposing to amalgamate junior inspectors and the remaining sub-inspectors into yet another new category of 'assistant inspector' and recruit to this primarily from those with teaching experience.[62] But teaching experience need not be acquired in the schools of the state system and it was clear that the Department did not expect such schools to supply many of its new recruits.[63] Even before the MacDonnell Commission met, the continuing gulf between education for the working class and all other education in the society had become painfully clear through the affair of the Holmes Circular.

Since 1870 some local authorities had employed their own

---

[58] Only three were appointed during the period—*ibid.*, f. 790, Appendix XII, III (i) (b).   [59] *Ibid.*, qq. 8,742–5, 9,049–50, 9,290–1.
[60] *Ibid.*, ff. 788–91, Appendix XII, II ix; III (i) (a); V.
[61] *Ibid.*, q. 9,268.   [62] *Ibid.*, qq. 8,746–53.
[63] See, e.g., *ibid.*, qq. 8,753–8,775, 9,289.

inspectors to supplement the periodic inspection and examination conducted by HMIs and the practice continued and spread after 1902. Obviously it was in everyone's interest if local and national inspectors' activities complemented each other; and in 1908 the Chief HMI, Edmond Holmes, sent out a circular of inquiry about local inspectorates to his staff. On the basis of the replies he circulated a Memorandum to the government inspectorate on 6 January 1910 as follows:

> No fewer than 104 out of the 123 (local inspectors) are ex-elementary teachers, and of the remaining nineteen not more than two or three have the antecedents which were usually looked for in candidates for junior inspectorships, namely that they had been educated first at a public school and then at Oxford and Cambridge.
>
> The difference in respect to efficiency between ex-elementary teacher inspectors and those who have had a more liberal education is very great. Very few of our inspectors have a good word to say for local inspectors of the former type, whereas those of the latter type are, with three exceptions, well spoken of. . . .
>
> . . . elementary teachers are as a rule uncultured and imperfectly educated, and . . . many, if not most of them are creatures of tradition and routine . . .
>
> . . . local inspection as at present conducted in the large towns is on the whole a hindrance rather than an aid to educational progress and we can only hope that the local chief inspectors, who are the fountainhead of a vicious officialdom, will be gradually pensioned off, and if local inspection is to be continued in their areas their places will be filled by men of real culture and enlightenment.
>
> As compared with the ex-elementary teacher usually engaged in the hopeless task of surveying, or trying to survey a wide field of action from the bottom of a well-worn groove, the inspector of public schools of the varsity type has the advantage of being able to look at elementary education from a point of view of complete detachment, and therefore to handle its problems with freshness and originality.

Holmes' Memorandum was emphatically not for publication. But someone—perhaps one of those token ex-elementary schoolteachers in the government inspectorate—leaked it, and to force full publication the MP H. W. Hoare read it into the record during the Estimates Debate on 21 March 1911.[64] Walter Runciman, then President of the Board of Education, repudiated all responsibility for its circulation, but refused to commit himself on its content.[65] And a former minister, Sir William Anson, added fuel to the flames by remarking that 'on the whole the principle on which the statements in the circular were based commend themselves to anyone who is earnestly desirous of seeing the education of the country properly conducted'.[66] The NUT was in uproar. The ex-teachers in the House battered away at Runciman, inevitably broadening the attack into a denunciation of the inspectorate and Department as a whole. Resolutions of protest poured in.[67] In the end they succeeded in forcing the resignation of Morant, the permanent secretary—although constitutionally it was Runciman who should have gone.

By the time the row broke, Holmes himself had in fact retired. Even so, it is significant that at no point did attack focus on him personally, It seemed agreed all round that he himself was a generous, humane and enlightened man, scrupulous in his dealings with teachers and lacking anything that could be construed as patronizing in his manner.[68] He it was, after all, who had diagnosed how received attitudes and the system of payment by results interacted to insulate the middle-class inspector from the idea that working-class pupils and teachers could share any of his ideals and aspirations.[69] The gradual

[64] *Hansard*, 5th series, XXIII, cols 277–8.
[65] *Ibid.*, XXIII, cols 267–310.
[66] *Ibid.*, XXIII, col 685.
[67] By 3 August 1911, 140 had been received—*ibid.*, XXIX, col 572. For the attacks during 1911, see *ibid.*, XXIII, cols 684–9, 878–81, 1,326–7, 2,155–7, 2,211–13; XXIV, cols 1,966–7; XXVI, col 1,670; XXVIII, cols 511–77, 601–24 and 1,281. Skirmishings also continued well into 1912. See also A. Tropp, *The School Teachers: the Growth of the Teaching Profession in England and Wales from 1800 to the Present Day* (London, 1957), pp. 199–203.
[68] *Ibid.*, p. 201, and *Hansard*, 5th series, XXIII, col 296.
[69] See above, p. 275.

dismantling of the system of payment by results in the 1890s had helped him to break through these attitudes and he spent the rest of his career campaigning both in schools and among his colleagues for the destruction of the rigid, mechanistic, mindless habits which payment by results left behind.[70]

Once again, the conflict raised questions of cultural as well as social authority. Altogether, it is difficult to explore the dilemma of the Education Department at the end of the nineteenth century adequately through the categories of 'professional' and 'expert'. Graham Wallas put it better when he asked the representatives of the Department appearing before the MacDonnell Commission to consider[71]

> whether, if it were true . . . that the whole directing force consisted of men closely assimilated to one social type, even if that social type were the most excellent of all social types, it might to a certain extent limit their sympathy with various social types in the country and limit the unreserved trust in their impartiality which ought to be given by the public?

[70] Edmond Holmes, *What Is and What Might Be* (London, 1914).
[71] MacDonnell Minutes, P.P. 1912–13, XV, q. 4,541.

Index of proper names